IMPLEMENTING for Results

Your Strategic Plan in Action

SANDRA NELSON

for the

PUBLIC LIBRARY ASSOCIATION

AMERICAN LIBRARY ASSOCIATION

Chicago   2009

Sandra Nelson is a consultant, speaker, trainer, and writer specializing in public library planning and management issues. She has presented hundreds of training programs in forty-eight states during the past three decades. During her career, Nelson has worked in both large and small public libraries and in state library agencies. She is the author of *Strategic Planning for Results* (2008) and *The New Planning for Results: A Streamlined Approach* (2001) and is coauthor of *Creating Policies for Results: From Chaos to Clarity* (2003), *Managing for Results: Effective Resource Allocation for Public Libraries* (2000), and *Wired for the Future: Developing Your Library Technology Plan* (1999), all published by the ALA. She is the senior editor of the PLA Results series. Her awards include Arizona Librarian of the Year (1987), the Professional Achievement Award from the Association of Specialized and Cooperative Library Agencies (1996), Outstanding Alumna Award, University of North Texas, School of Information Science (1999), and the ALA's Melvil Dewey Medal (2008).

While extensive effort has gone into ensuring the reliability of information appearing in this book, the publisher makes no warranty, express or implied, on the accuracy or reliability of the information, and does not assume and hereby disclaims any liability to any person for any loss or damage caused by errors or omissions in this publication.

The paper used in this publication meets the minimum requirements of American National Standard for Information Sciences—Permanence of Paper for Printed Library Materials, ANSI Z39.48-1992. ∞

Library of Congress Cataloging-in-Publication Data

Nelson, Sandra S.
  Implementing for results : your strategic plan in action / Sandra Nelson for the Public Library Association.
    p. cm. — (PLA results series)
  Companion volume to Strategic planning for results.
  Includes bibliographical references and index.
  ISBN 978-0-8389-3579-8 (alk. paper)
  1. Public libraries—Planning. 2. Public libraries—United States—Planning. 3. Public libraries—Administration. 4. Public libraries—United States—Administration. 5. Strategic planning. 6. Organizational change. 7. Organizational effectiveness. I. Public Library Association. II. Title.
  Z678.N447 2009
  025.1'974—dc22   2008048232

ISBN-13: 978-0-8389-3579-8

Printed in the United States of America

13 12 11 10 09   5 4 3 2 1

Contents

Figures

Acknowledgments

Writing is often a solitary process—one person and one computer. That may work well for people who write fiction or those who write about ideas and theories. However, it can be a problem for people who write how-to books like those in the Results series. It is far too easy for a single person to fall into the trap of assuming that she knows the one right way to do everything. Thankfully, I didn't have to write this book by myself. June Garcia was always there to serve as a sounding board, to offer suggestions when I got stuck, and to help field-test ideas and concepts. This book, like *Strategic Planning for Results,* is very much a collaborative effort. I literally could not have done it without June.

The work to develop the concepts, processes, and workforms in this book has been going on for years, and the managers and staff in many libraries have contributed to the final product. However, the managers and staff in the Mid-Columbia Public Library (Kennewick, WA) and the Calcasieu Parish Public Library (Lake Charles, LA) deserve special recognition for the assistance they provided. June and I worked with the staff members in both of these libraries as they completed the full *Implementing for Results* process—and we all learned a lot during the journey. The managers and staff in both libraries were flexible and adaptable when things didn't work as planned, and offered excellent suggestions to make the things that did work even more effective. The two project managers, Kyle Cox (Mid-Columbia Public Library) and Loretta Gharst (Calcasieu Parish Public Library), were creative and hard-working, and several of their innovative ideas have been included in the final version of *Implementing for Results.*

Other people have provided assistance and support as well. Sara Dallas, Wayne Piper, and Loretta Gharst spent hours reviewing the final manuscript and made excellent suggestions for revisions and additions. Paul Mendelson has been copyediting the Results books for several years, and he worked on both *Strategic Planning for Results* and this book. He is an excellent copyeditor who adds the many commas I omit and corrects my often shaky spelling. More important, he provides the final check for continuity and is always able to identify things that are ambiguous and suggest ways to clarify them.

Finally, I want to thank my husband, Charles. I have been writing and editing Results books for fifteen years, and Charles has been wonderfully supportive for all of those years. He helps me maintain my sense of humor and balance when the writing gets hard—and writing is almost always hard.

Introduction

Just do it!—Nike slogan

Implementing for Results (IFR) has been written as a companion volume to *Strategic Planning for Results* (SPFR). As you can see in figure 1, the planning book ended with the approval and dissemination of the library's goals, objectives, organizational competencies, and strategic initiatives. The very short last chapter of *SPFR* began with these two paragraphs:

> This is the point in previous public library planning books when the focus shifted from planning to implementing—briefly. The average length of the four previous PLA planning books was about 250 pages, of which an average of thirteen pages was dedicated to implementation issues. In other words, about 95 percent of the content in the previous planning books addressed the process of planning, and about 5 percent of the content focused on translating the plan from ideas to action. Sadly, these percentages were probably similar to the number of libraries that used the planning books to develop plans and the number of libraries that fully implemented the plans they developed.
>
> The truth, of course, is that planning should—and does—take only about 5 percent of your time and energy. Most of your time should be spent on implementation. Planning is simply the process you go through to be sure that your implementation efforts are both effective and efficient. The issues that you will need to resolve to translate the goals and objectives in your strategic plan into reality are more complex than the issues you faced during the planning process. To be able to manage your implementation issues, you will need more help than you can get in a few pages at the end of this book. You will need a manual that picks up where this book ends and describes the tasks and steps that will help you identify, evaluate, and select activities and then allocate the resources needed to implement the activities you selected. You will need workforms and examples to help you and your colleagues make the hard decisions that will be required to actually make the changes needed in your library.

Implementing for Results is the manual you will need to transform your strategic plan from dream to reality, and the tasks and steps in this book begin where the tasks and steps in *SPFR* ended.

FIGURE 1

Strategic Planning for Results Tasks and Steps

Task 1: Design the Planning Process

    Step 1.1: Identify the reasons for planning
    Step 1.2: Define planning responsibilities
    Step 1.3: Prepare planning schedule and budget
    Step 1.4: Develop a communication plan
    Step 1.5: Design and present a staff orientation

Task 2: Start the Planning Process

    Step 2.1: Obtain board approval
    Step 2.2: Select community planning committee members
    Step 2.3: Invite committee members
    Step 2.4: Prepare and distribute community and library information packets

Task 3: Identify Community Needs

    Step 3.1: Present an orientation for the members of the planning committee
    Step 3.2: Develop community vision statements
    Step 3.3: Define current conditions in the community
    Step 3.4: Decide what needs to be done to reach community vision

Task 4: Select Service Responses

    Step 4.1: Present an overview of the library to committee members
    Step 4.2: Select preliminary service responses
    Step 4.3: Describe the effect of preliminary service responses on current library services
    Step 4.4: Select final service responses

Task 5: Prepare for Change

    Step 5.1: Assess the library's readiness for change
    Step 5.2: Plan to create a positive environment for change
    Step 5.3: Review and revise communication plans
    Step 5.4: Train supervisors and managers

Task 6: Consider Library Values and Mission

    Step 6.1: Define values
    Step 6.2: Consider the library mission

Task 7: Write Goals and Objectives

    Step 7.1: Write system goals
    Step 7.2: Write system objectives
    Step 7.3: Determine the priority of goals and measures of progress for each unit

Task 8: Identify Organizational Competencies

    Step 8.1: Understand organizational competencies and initiatives
    Step 8.2: Identify organizational issues
    Step 8.3: Write organizational competencies and initiatives

Task 9: Write the Strategic Plan and Obtain Approval

    Step 9.1: Write and review the strategic plan
    Step 9.2: Submit the strategic plan for approval

Task 10: Communicate the Results of the Planning Process

    Step 10.1: Define the target audiences
    Step 10.2: Develop a communication plan
    Step 10.3: Develop and field test communications to target audiences

What If You Have Not Developed a Plan Using *SPFR*?

Implementing for Results is based on the premise that a library's public service priorities should provide the framework and context for all resource allocation decisions and that there has to be some way to measure the effectiveness of the resource allocation decisions that are made. It is certainly possible to use the tools in this book without a formal strategic plan, but to do so you will need a clear understanding of the public service priorities in your library and clearly defined ways to measure your progress toward reaching those priorities.

In the *SPFR* process, goals describe the library's service priorities, and the measures of progress are incorporated into the objectives for each goal. If your strategic plan was developed using another planning process or if your library doesn't have a formal strategic plan, you will have to do some preliminary work before beginning the tasks and steps in *IFR*. First, you will have to identify your library's service priorities. This is relatively easy to do using *Public Library Service Responses*.[1] The service responses "are designed to describe the most common clusters of services and programs that libraries provide."[2] In other words, service responses describe the services the public receives. They do not address internal library issues such as marketing, resources, staff training, governance, and so on. In *SPFR,* issues of that type are addressed in the organizational competencies, which describe "the institutional capacity or efficiency that is necessary to enable the library to achieve the goals and objectives in its plan."[3]

The eighteen service responses in the most recently revised version of *SPFR* are listed in figure 2. As you review them, you will see that virtually every library offers at least minimal services or materials that support all eighteen of the service responses. If your library does not have a strategic plan, the quickest way to identify service priorities is to review the service responses and identify those that seem to most accurately reflect your library's current, if unwritten, service priorities. Your selections may be more valid if you involve staff from different units and different classifications in the process. However, there is no real substitute for involving community leaders when identifying the library's priorities, and you might want to consider doing a community-based needs-assessment process at some later date.

If you work in a library with a plan that was developed using a process other than *SPFR,* you and your colleagues will want to review the service goals in the plan and identify the corresponding service responses. In some instances, there may not be a direct one-to-one link. A general goal of providing services to teens may encompass multiple service responses, depending on the types of activities that will be provided. In other instances, there may be no real link between the plan's goals and the service responses at all. If that is the case, you will have to identify the service responses that seem to most closely match the intent of the plan.

After you have identified your service priorities, you should next decide how you will measure your progress toward reaching those service goals. You can use a variety of data to do this, including the number of people you served, how satisfied those people were with the services they received, the number of units of service delivered, or the outcomes of the services you provided. For more information on measuring progress, see Step 7.2 in *SFPR*. When you have identified your service priorities and your measures, you will be ready to begin the *IFR* process.

FIGURE 2
Public Library Service Responses

Be an Informed Citizen: Local, National, and World Affairs Residents will have the information they need to support and promote democracy, to fulfill their civic responsibilities at the local, state, and national levels, and to fully participate in community decision making.

Build Successful Enterprises: Business and Nonprofit Support Business owners and nonprofit organization directors and their managers will have the tools they need to develop and maintain strong, viable organizations.

Celebrate Diversity: Cultural Awareness Residents will have programs and services that promote appreciation and understanding of their personal heritage and the heritage of others in the community.

Connect to the Online World: Public Internet Access Residents will have high-speed access to the digital world with no unnecessary restrictions or fees to ensure that everyone can take advantage of the ever-growing resources and services available through the Internet.

Create Young Readers: Early Literacy Children from birth to age five will have programs and services designed to ensure that they will enter school ready to learn to read, write, and listen.

Discover Your Roots: Genealogy and Local History Residents and visitors will have the resources they need to connect the past with the present through their family histories and to understand the history and traditions of the community.

Express Creativity: Create and Share Content Residents will have the services and support they need to express themselves by creating original print, video, audio, or visual content in a real-world or online environment.

Get Facts Fast: Ready Reference Residents will have someone to answer their questions on a wide array of topics of personal interest.

Know Your Community: Community Resources and Services Residents will have a central source for information about the wide variety of programs, services, and activities provided by community agencies and organizations.

Learn to Read and Write: Adult, Teen, and Family Literacy Adults and teens will have the support they need to improve their literacy skills in order to meet their personal goals and fulfill their responsibilities as parents, citizens, and workers.

Make Career Choices: Job and Career Development Adults and teens will have the skills and resources they need to identify career opportunities that suit their individual strengths and interests.

Make Informed Decisions: Health, Wealth, and Other Life Choices Residents will have the resources they need to identify and analyze risks, benefits, and alternatives before making decisions that affect their lives.

Satisfy Curiosity: Lifelong Learning Residents will have the resources they need to explore topics of personal interest and continue to learn throughout their lives.

Stimulate Imagination: Reading, Viewing, and Listening for Pleasure Residents who want materials to enhance their leisure time will find what they want when and where they want them and will have the help they need to make choices from among the options.

Succeed in School: Homework Help Students will have the resources they need to succeed in school.

Understand How to Find, Evaluate, and Use Information: Information Fluency Residents will know when they need information to resolve an issue or answer a question and will have the skills to search for, locate, evaluate, and effectively use information to meet their needs.

Visit a Comfortable Place: Physical and Virtual Spaces Residents will have safe and welcoming physical places to meet and interact with others or to sit quietly and read and will have open and accessible virtual spaces that support social networking.

Welcome to the United States: Services for New Immigrants New immigrants will have information on citizenship, English Language Learning (ELL), employment, public schooling, health and safety, available social services, and any other topics that they need to participate successfully in American life.

A Preview of the Process

This book has been divided into six chapters. Figure 3 lists all of the tasks and steps in the *IFR* process, and each chapter is briefly described below:

Get Ready for Change. In this chapter, the library's senior managers will prepare for the implementation process by creating a change-friendly environment and developing a comprehensive communication plan to ensure that all stakeholders remain informed and engaged throughout the process.

Explore the Possibilities. The actual implementation process begins in this chapter. Staff will identify their current activities that support each of the goals in the strategic plan and then develop a list of new or modified activities that could support the goals.

Identify Essential Activities. In this chapter, a team of staff will evaluate the effectiveness of current and proposed activities that support the library's goals. Then the library's senior managers will determine the priority of each of the current, new, or expanded activities that are considered to be the most effective.

Eliminate and Streamline. The preceding chapter focused on effective activities. In this chapter, staff will identify current activities that support service responses that are not library priorities and will consider ways to streamline policies, procedures, and practices. The senior managers will decide what activities to eliminate, reduce, or streamline.

Consider Time and Other Resources. This chapter focuses on resources. Unit managers will estimate how much time and other resources will be saved by eliminating, reducing, or streamlining ineffective or inefficient activities. They will then work with senior managers to determine the resources that will be needed to support the effective activities with the highest priority. Senior managers will select the final activities for the planning cycle and work with staff to develop plans to implement them.

Make It Work. In this chapter, managers will develop plans to monitor the implementation of the activities that were selected and make adjustments as needed. They will also begin to integrate the changes made during the implementation process into the library's infrastructure by modifying performance appraisal processes, revising collection development policies, and so on.

On first reading, this may seem like a complicated and cumbersome method to manage something you and your colleagues have been doing intuitively for some time. However, as you work through the tasks and steps you will discover that there are many benefits to working through a structured decision-making process, particularly when you are trying to implement significant changes in your library. This process ensures that all staff members have a chance to participate and share their expertise, which in turn will make them more likely to support the final changes. The process also provides a clear set of criteria for deciding which programs and services are effective and which are not. In the absence of a process like this, decisions can appear to be arbitrary and overly subjective; when decisions are made using these criteria, everyone understands the rationale.

As you can see in figure 4, you should be able to work through all fourteen of the tasks in approximately three months. If you were able to complete your planning process

FIGURE 3
Implementing for Results Tasks and Steps

Chapter 1: Get Ready to Change

Task 1: Set the Stage

Step 1.1: Commit to making changes
Step 1.2: Create the capacity to support change

Task 2: Communicate Effectively

Step 2.1: Review the library communication processes
Step 2.2: Develop and implement a communication plan

Chapter 2: Explore the Possibilities

Task 3: Identify Activities

Step 3.1: Review the library's goals and objectives
Step 3.2: Identify current activities
Step 3.3: Identify potential activities

Task 4: Organize Activities

Step 4.1: Consolidate and sort activities by goal and cluster
Step 4.2: Determine what is missing

Chapter 3: Identify Essential Activities

Task 5: Evaluate Activities

Step 5.1: Determine criteria for evaluation
Step 5.2: Evaluate current and potential activities

Task 6: Establish the Priority of Effective Activities

Step 6.1: Review the criteria for establishing priority
Step 6.2: Apply the criteria to the effective activities

Chapter 4: Eliminate and Streamline

Task 7: Identify Activities That Do Not Support the Library's Goals

Step 7.1: Identify service responses that were not selected as priorities
Step 7.2: Identify current activities that support service responses that are not priorities
Step 7.3: Organize the current activities that support service responses that are not priorities

Task 8: Identify Inefficient Activities and Steps

Step 8.1: Identify sacred cows
Step 8.2: Organize the sacred cows

Task 9: Decide How to Address Inefficient and Ineffective Activities

Step 9.1: Determine how to address the ineffective activities that support the library's goals
Step 9.2: Determine how to address activities that do not support priorities
Step 9.3: Determine how to address sacred cows

Chapter 5: Consider Time and Other Resources

Task 10: Identify Resources Available for Reallocation

Step 10.1: Identify resources available for reallocation in each unit
Step 10.2: Revise the materials budget to support the library's goals

Task 11: Identify Needed Resources

Step 11.1: Identify the resources needed for essential activities
Step 11:2: Summarize unit data

Chapter 6: Make It Work

Task 12: Select and Implement Activities

Step 12.1: Select final activities to implement and to eliminate, reduce, or streamline
Step 12.2: Implement your decisions

Task 13: Monitor Implementation

Step 13.1: Collect data and monitor progress monthly
Step 13.2: Adjust as needed

Task 14: Make Change the Norm

Step 14.1: Integrate changes into library operations
Step 14.2: Stay ahead of the curve

FIGURE 4

Implementing for Results Time Line

Task and Steps	Who	When
Task 1: Set the Stage	Library board, director, senior managers, unit managers, supervisors	Month 1 and ongoing
Task 2: Communicate Effectively	Library board, director, senior managers, unit managers, supervisors	Month 1 and ongoing
Task 3: Identify Activities	All staff	Month 1
Task 4: Organize Activities	Small review team appointed by director	Months 1–2
Task 5: Evaluate Activities	Director, senior managers	Month 2
Task 6: Establish the Priority of Effective Activities	Director, senior managers	Month 2
Task 7: Identify Activities That Do Not Support the Library's Goals	Cross-functional team appointed by director	Month 2
Task 8: Identify Inefficient Activities and Steps	Director, senior managers, unit managers, supervisors	Month 3
Task 9: Decide How to Address Inefficient and Ineffective Activities	Director, senior managers	Month 3
Task 10: Identify Resources Available for Reallocation	Director, senior managers, unit managers, supervisors	Month 3
Task 11: Identify Needed Resources	Director, senior managers, unit managers, supervisors	Month 3
Task 12: Select and Implement Activities	Director, senior managers, unit managers, supervisors, staff	Month 3 and ongoing
Task 13: Monitor Implementation	Library board, director, senior managers, unit managers, supervisors	Ongoing
Task 14: Make Change the Norm	All staff	Ongoing

> **CAUTION**
>
> Do not get bogged down in minutiae or sidetracked into exploring interesting but irrelevant issues.

in the three to four months recommended in *SPFR,* the combined time for both *SPFR* and *IFR* will be between six and seven months, which is considerably less than the nine to twelve months that some libraries spend on the planning process alone. This, of course, assumes that you stay focused on completing the tasks.

There are a number of points in the process when you might be tempted to gather too much data, spend too much time trying to reconcile differences of opinion that are probably irreconcilable, or get so focused on "what if" that you can't make a decision. Many of those points have been identified with the *caution* sign. You will want to be particularly careful about how you manage the process at those times.

Examples, Figures, and Workforms

Readers who are familiar with *SPFR* will recognize the Tree County Public Library. This fictitious library has been used to illustrate how staff from one library completed the tasks and steps in *SPFR* and a number of other Results titles. In *IFR,* you will meet some of the Tree County Public Library staff and see how staff in a typical library might respond to the changes that occur during the implementation of the strategic plan.

There are forty figures scattered throughout the six chapters of this book. Many of the figures illustrate how the Tree County Public Library staff completed each of the workforms. Others illustrate a point or provide supplemental information. Electronic versions of the workforms are available at http://e-learnlibraries.mrooms.net. You are strongly encouraged to use the electronic versions rather than the paper versions included in this book. The data on several of the workforms will need to be sorted into groups, which would be impossible with print forms but would be simple using the Excel spreadsheet embedded in the electronic workforms.

Some Basic Definitions

Before you start to use this book, it will be helpful if you understand how some basic terms have been used. These words mean different things in different libraries, but this is how the words are defined in this book.

Branch. A separate library facility.

Central library. The largest library facility, usually in a downtown area; referred to as the main library in some places.

Department. A unit within a single facility that is normally a central library.

Library. The entire organizational entity and its units.

Library board. The authority board that governs the library, and to which the library director reports; in some cases this may be a city or county government. An authority board hires the director, sets library policy, and has fiduciary responsibility. The library may have an advisory board if the director reports to a city or county government.

Library management team. The senior managers in a library; typically this team includes the director, assistant director, head of branches (if any), head of the central library, and any senior staff positions (personnel, marketing, finance, etc.). In very small libraries, the library administrative "team" is the director.

Manager. A generic term that refers to the staff member or staff members who are responsible for resource allocation in a particular area; in some libraries the "manager" is actually a team of staff members.

Team. A group of staff members brought together to work on a specific project or program; it may include members from different departments and with different job classifications.

Unit. A term used to refer to individual library departments and branches (if any).

Other Results Books

During the past ten years, the Public Library Association has provided support for the development of a family of nine management publications that are being used by library managers, staff, and boards around the country to manage the libraries in their communities more effectively. All of the Results books share the same vocabulary and are based on the same management principles. They are all based on the processes described in *Strategic Planning for Results* and *Implementing for Results*. The other seven titles are as follows:

Managing for Results: Effective Resource Allocation for Public Libraries[4]

Staffing for Results: A Guide to Working Smarter[5]

Creating Policies for Results: From Chaos to Clarity[6]

Technology for Results: Developing Service-Based Plans[7]

Demonstrating Results: Using Outcome Measurement in Your Library[8]

Managing Facilities for Results: Optimizing Space for Services[9]

Human Resources for Results: The Right Person for the Right Job[10]

How to Use This Book

This book was written to be used by staff in public libraries of all sizes and in all parts of the country and, as we all know, one size not only doesn't fit all, it rarely fits anyone exactly. Therefore, you may have to make modifications in one or more steps so that the process works for you and your staff. However, before you begin to make changes, read through the entire book. Some of the things that you may think you want to change early in the process may be critical elements in later steps or tasks. Once you understand the components of each of the fourteen tasks, you will be in a better position to judge how you will use these processes and tools in your library.

Notes

1. June Garcia and Sandra Nelson, *Public Library Service Responses* (Chicago: American Library Association, 2007).
2. Sandra Nelson, *Strategic Planning for Results* (Chicago: American Library Association, 2008), 144.
3. Ibid., 108.
4. Sandra Nelson, Ellen Altman, and Diane Mayo, *Managing for Results: Effective Resource Allocation for Public Libraries* (Chicago: American Library Association, 2000).
5. Diane Mayo and Jeanne Goodrich, *Staffing for Results: A Guide to Working Smarter* (Chicago: American Library Association, 2002).
6. Sandra Nelson and June Garcia, *Creating Policies for Results: From Chaos to Clarity* (Chicago: American Library Association, 2003).
7. Diane Mayo, *Technology for Results: Developing Service-Based Plans* (Chicago: American Library Association, 2005).
8. Rhea Rubin, *Demonstrating Results: Using Outcome Measurement in Your Library* (Chicago: American Library Association, 2006).
9. Cheryl Bryan, *Managing Facilities for Results: Optimizing Space for Services* (Chicago: American Library Association, 2007).
10. Jeanne Goodrich and Paula M. Singer, *Human Resources for Results: The Right Person for the Right Job* (Chicago: American Library Association, 2007).

Chapter 1

Get Ready for Change

For tomorrow belongs to the people who prepare for it today. . . . —African proverb

MILESTONES

By the time you finish this chapter you will be able to

- identify and address the issues in your library that may impede your ability to implement your strategic plan
- demonstrate your commitment to creating a library environment that supports change
- respond effectively to staff who are pessimistic about change and react negatively to the implementation process
- define the characteristics of an effective library director
- create a more risk-tolerant environment in your library
- assess the effectiveness of your library's communications processes and procedures

You have finished your strategic planning process, and you and your staff are feeling good. The planning process went well, the final strategic plan focuses on services that will meet the unique needs of your community, and the members of the library board have endorsed the plan with enthusiasm. Developing your strategic plan took a lot of work, but the results make it clear that all of your efforts were worth the time and energy you expended.

Suddenly it is six months later. The planning process is a fading memory. The strategic plan is sitting on a shelf in your office, but you haven't looked at it lately. There was a crisis right after you finished the plan that you had to resolve, and then all of the work that didn't get done while you were planning had to be addressed. Somehow you have never found the time or energy to fully implement the plan you worked so hard to develop. Sure, some things are being done, but the plan has not become the blueprint for decision making that it was intended to be.

If all of this sounds depressingly familiar, you can take comfort in the fact that you are not alone. Too few libraries fully integrate their strategic plans into their ongoing operations. In these libraries, the plan remains separate from the day-to-day resource allocation decisions that are made by staff throughout the library. As a result, the needed changes that everyone worked so hard to identify during the planning process never materialize.

Why does this happen? Given the amount of work it takes to complete a strategic plan and the complexity of today's library resource-allocation environment, it certainly seems reasonable to assume that once library managers and boards complete a planning process, they will use the resulting priorities as the framework for making resource allocation decisions. In fact, one might expect planning and doing to be two sides of the same coin. However, we all know that this has not always been the case. Why would so many people do so much work and then ignore the final product? The facile answer is the one described above—we were too busy doing other things and didn't have the time to implement the plan. This answer abdicates responsibility. It suggests that as managers we have no control over how we spend our time and how we make decisions, and we all know that isn't true. We do make our own choices, and we do have to live with the consequences of those choices.

The real question is why we allow other things to take priority over the work that is needed to implement the strategic plan. The answers to this question vary by library, but there are some common themes that are important to acknowledge and address if we are ever going to firmly link planning and doing.

Planning assumptions may be invalid. Staff and board members in some libraries enter into a planning process with the assumption that planning is about defining new services and that those new services will require new resources to be implemented. Implicit in this assumption is the belief that everything the library is doing now is both effective and efficient and that there is no need to change current services or practices. If new funds are not available for the services, however, they will not be implemented. In today's economy, new funds are rarely available in the quantities needed to fund significant new services, and so the plan goes on the shelf—unfunded and ignored.

Line-item budgets support the status quo. Most library strategic plans are organized by goals, with each goal having several objectives. Library staff then develop activities to support the goals and objectives in the plan. As noted above, activities tend to describe new or expanded services to be offered to meet the needs identified during the planning process. Even if library board members and managers are willing to make changes to support the services, they can find it difficult to work within the framework of the traditional library line-item budget.

Line-item budgets are organized by category of expenditure: personnel, library materials, telecommunications, equipment, supplies, and so on. Each major category is then broken down into subcategories. Personnel costs are tracked by salary and benefits. Library materials funds may be separated into children, young adult, and adult, and then further divided into print, nonprint, and so on. It can be difficult to determine the cost of a new or expanded program or service using a traditional line-item budget.

Program budgets provide a more effective way to identify the resources required to support an activity. Program budgets allocate resources to specific program areas. They focus first on the services to be delivered and then on the resources required to support the services. For example, children's services could be subdivided into multiple program budgets: preschool story time in the library; preschool programs in local day care centers; summer reading program; homework support; children's readers' advisory, and so on. Each program budget would then be further subdivided by personnel costs, materials, and so on. You will note that the program budgets are normally subdivided by the same categories found in the library's line-item budget. They just reflect the allocation for the specific program within each category.

Program budgets can be very helpful when reallocating resources, but they are time-consuming to prepare and often have to be translated back into one general line-item budget to be submitted to the library's governing authority. Few library staff members have the training needed to prepare effective program budgets or the time to develop and reconcile multiple program budgets for the library's main line-item budget.

Many library managers have little or no formal management training. Almost all directors of medium and large libraries have an MLS degree, and most of those libraries require the MLS degree for entry-level librarian positions. We expect professional librarians to have learned the fundamentals of our profession in a formal educational environment.

This is in contrast to our approach when hiring or promoting library managers. Generally, librarians with exemplary library skills are promoted to management positions. These librarians are not expected to have any formal management education, other than the one or two management overview courses offered by most library schools. The unspoken assumption is that they will "learn on the job," but this assumption is only valid if there is someone with management skills available to "teach on the job." This is too often not the case.

An MLS education teaches people the underlying principles of librarianship and provides the skills needed to find, evaluate, and use information. A management degree teaches people organizational principles and provides the skills needed to allocate resources and guide an organization through change. These are very different skill sets.

There are too few "how-to" books about library management. There are many "how-to" books for librarians that provide instructions for everything from presenting puppet programs to cataloging media to creating an interactive website to serving new immigrants. Missing from this list are how-to books about library management. Typical library management books explain why to do something, but do not provide step-by-step instructions on how to do it. Library managers who hope to be able to learn the management skills they need by pursuing a course of independent study may end up with a good understanding of theory but no idea of how to implement that theory in their own libraries.

Strategic plans can seem restrictive. Sometimes staff members think that operating within the framework of a strategic plan is too restrictive. These are often the staff members who enjoy the creative parts of their jobs and who normally focus on unit activities rather than organizational goals. They like to be able to implement the new programs or services that they hear about at conferences or read about in library literature—whether or not those programs or services support the priorities in the library's strategic plan. This can be a particular challenge in libraries that have traditionally allowed unit or branch staff to have considerable autonomy. In these libraries, strategic planning can be perceived as a process designed to stifle creativity and spontaneity and replace them with a lockstep adherence to what "they" want us to do, "they" being library administrators and the board.

Wishful thinking. Even the most pragmatic manager can succumb to the wishful thinking trap. We have all done it both at work and at home. We identify a goal or outcome ("I want to lose ten pounds by my class reunion") and then we hope that somehow we can achieve our desired result. The operative word in the preceding sentence is "hope." Hope is defined as *wanting* something to happen. It is not defined as *doing* something to make it happen.

A typical objective in a library strategic plan might be "The circulation of children's fiction will increase by 10 percent each year." Library managers who practice wishful thinking will hope that enough new kids come to the library to boost circulation and hope that monthly displays of new books will encourage kids to take out more fiction. Library managers who operate in a more pragmatic environment will add money to the budget for children's fiction and weed the collection—the only two things that we know for sure will lead to increases in circulation. An ongoing mantra in this book will be that "nothing happens unless someone does something to make it happen."

Change is hard. This is more than a cliché—it is very true, as any manager who has ever tried to change "the way we've always done this" can testify. Newton's law of inertia states that an object in motion will stay in motion and an object at rest will stay at rest unless acted on by an unbalanced force. (Newton's law refers to physical objects, but we have all observed similar behaviors in the work environment. Staff will continue to do what they have always done, the way they have always done it [stay in motion . . .], and resist doing anything they have not done before [stay at rest . . .] until they are forced to make changes [acted on by an unbalanced force . . .].) In the world of physics, an unbalanced force is a push or pull on an object that is not balanced by an equal push or pull. In the world of libraries, an unbalanced force might be considered any internal or external change that library managers mandate and monitor—and staff often react to these mandated changes as though the manager were in fact unbalanced.

Implementing for Results has been developed to help you and your colleagues deal with these issues in your library. As you work through the tasks in this process you will evaluate the effectiveness of your current activities, encourage staff to explore creative new programs and services, identify activities that do not support your priorities, acknowledge and resolve operational inefficiencies, reallocate the library's resources to support the goals in your strategic plan, and learn how to adapt quickly to an ever-changing environment.

Getting Started

Work on implementation typically begins after a relatively long period devoted to planning. *Strategic Planning for Results* recommends that the strategic planning process be completed in three or four months. Other planning processes can take up to a year. Typically, many nonsupervisory staff remain relatively disengaged during most of the strategic planning process. It is hard for them to get too interested in community visions and needs, mission statements, and goals and objectives, all of which can appear to be pretty theoretical. However, once you start talking about the specific things that the library will do to implement the plan, most of these staff start paying closer attention to what is going on. Staff know all too well that libraries don't do anything—it is the library staff who do the work. It will be clear to all staff that changes in the library's activities will have an effect on their day-to-day work. Therefore, your first task is to prepare for the changes that are coming.

TASK 1: SET THE STAGE

Task 1: Set the Stage
     Step 1.1: Commit to making changes
     Step 1.2: Create the capacity to support change
Task 2: Communicate Effectively
Task 3: Identify Activities
Task 4: Organize Activities
Task 5: Evaluate Activities
Task 6: Establish the Priority of Effective Activities
Task 7: Identify Activities That Do Not Support the Library's Goals
Task 8: Identify Inefficient Activities and Steps
Task 9: Decide How to Address Inefficient and Ineffective Activities
Task 10: Identify Resources Available for Reallocation
Task 11: Identify Needed Resources
Task 12: Select and Implement Activities
Task 13: Monitor Implementation
Task 14: Make Change the Norm

The two steps in Task 1 will help library managers create an environment that supports change, rather than one that resists change. This task will begin before the implementation process is initiated. The work you do and the decisions you make during this task will be integrated into the ongoing operations of the library and will involve all staff. Although change starts at the top of the organization, ultimately every staff member will share part of the responsibility of creating and sustaining a creative and dynamic organization.

Step 1.1
Commit to Making Changes

On one hand, this step should be so obvious that it is not needed here. On the other hand, this is probably the single most difficult—and important—thing that the members of the library's management team and board will do during the entire implementation process. A surprising number of library managers, staff, and board members enter into a strategic planning process with the unspoken but very real assumption that the planners (whoever they might be) will say that the library is doing a fantastic job and that only a few cosmetic changes are needed. Many strategic planning processes do validate the work the library is currently doing. But—and this is a big but—those same processes also almost always end up recommending some shifts in service priorities.

It would be very difficult to complete a strategic plan for any public library in today's rapidly changing technology environment that did not acknowledge the evolving nature of what users want and need from their public library. Inevitably, meeting these new user demands will mean new services and new programs to support new priorities—in other words, significant change. Thus, the message from the planning process is often twofold:

The library is great and we love and support it.

The library needs to change to continue to meet our needs.

As a result, managers and board members find themselves in a quandary. It is gratifying to hear that the library is doing a good job and tempting to only listen to the first half of the message. Certainly that is what many staff will do. (The phrase "if it ain't broke, don't fix it" is always popular in these situations.) The reality is that the first message—the library is great—is a reflection of the library's past performance. It is the second message—the library needs to change—that provides the direction for the library's future.

Why after All This Time Is Change Still So Hard?

Ask any employee who has worked in a library for more than five years about change and you are likely to hear a long litany of changes that occurred. Based on that, you would think that library managers and staff would be more comfortable operating in a fluid environment than many seem to be. One possible reason why some people still find dealing with change so difficult is that many of the big changes came about because of external forces, not internal choices.

- Grants from the Bill and Melinda Gates Foundation have made it possible for almost every public library in the United States to provide public access computers, but many of the smaller and midsized libraries that received those grants have made no provisions for replacement or repair. This suggests that without the grant funding, far fewer public libraries would be providing public access computers today.

- Many state library agencies provide access to an array of reference databases for the libraries in their states, and most libraries link to those databases. However, many local library staff members don't know how to use the databases and, therefore, cannot help library users access the information they contain. Furthermore, if given a choice, some of those staff members would choose to use the state money to purchase print reference resources instead of the electronic resources.

- There were 6,676,120,288 Internet searches in March 2008.[1] That is over 6.6 *billion* searches in one month. In 2005 there were 302,513,000 reference transactions in all of the public libraries in the United States.[2] There is literally no comparison between these two numbers. Library reference questions are less than 0.4 percent of the Internet questions. Only the most fanatical reference librarians can deny that reference use in libraries is decreasing as Internet use continues to grow each year. Yet staff in many libraries have made only minor modifications to their current reference collections, the number of staff who provide services from reference desks, or the amount of space that is allocated to reference services.

- Libraries that want to continue to buy videotapes (and, yes, in mid-2008 there are still libraries that want to do just that) are no longer able to find them and now spend time and money repairing the dwindling supply they own. This is another reminder of how difficult it is for some libraries to adapt to ever-changing media formats.

These are all examples of library managers and staff members responding *reactively* to change—either willingly or unwillingly. The public libraries that succeed in the future will be led by managers and boards who are willing and able to respond *proactively* to change. These leaders will understand the change process and be able to acknowledge that change does not mean repudiating the past. Every library starts today with an existing organizational culture and traditions and a collection of accumulated resources. The current status of each public library is the sum of all the decisions—good, bad, and indifferent—that have been made in the past. It is important for managers to understand the difference between acknowledging the past and being held hostage by it.

We can, for example, acknowledge the valuable role that bookmobiles played in the past by providing library services to people who had no other access to libraries. At the same time we can recognize that today, with many more libraries serving a much more mobile population, the role of bookmobiles has changed.

We know that in the past very few people had an array of current reference materials in their homes. Encyclopedias were expensive and became dated quickly. Families might have had a dictionary and an almanac, but typically that was all. In that environment, a public library reference collection and a public library staff with the skills to use that collection were critical resources for students, business people, researchers, people making life choices, and anyone else who needed an answer to a question. At the same time, we have to acknowledge that today the Internet has superseded most reference materials. People use Google and other search engines to find the answers they need, and the role of the reference librarian has changed. The role of the print reference collection is even more problematic at a time when even the firms that publish reference materials are moving away from print publications.

How Can Managers Express Their Commitment to Change?

Library managers who begin this process must truly believe that the library needs to change, but belief will not be enough to create the needed changes. The change message must be communicated to all staff again and again in spoken and written communications and in the actions of every manager in the library. The commitment to change must be demonstrated in every decision made throughout the process.

Many library staff members are pragmatists who have worked in the same environment for years. They know money is tight and they know change is hard. These staff may want to focus on past factors that have impeded change, rather than look at the infinite possibilities of the future. Library managers must be prepared to address their questions and concerns openly and positively. Nothing makes it more difficult to build a library-wide commitment to change than a pervasive pessimism about the future. There are a number of ways that managers and supervisors can demonstrate their commitment to creating an environment that supports change.

LISTEN

The most important—and most difficult—thing to do is to listen carefully to every staff member who has concerns. Communication requires at least two people to be actively engaged in an exchange of information. You cannot expect people to listen to you if you don't listen to them. You may think that you already know what Janice is going to say because you have heard her say it before (many times), but until you listen to her *this time* you can't be sure. This time she may say something different. Even if Janice's message is the same as it has always been, if you do her the courtesy of listening carefully to her, you create an expectation that she will give you the same courtesy.

While you are listening to Janice and others with concerns, try to identify what is really bothering them. Janice may be *saying* that there is no point in thinking about providing more downloadable digital content because it will only be used by a few technophiles and will take money away from the library's limited print and audiovisual budget. Janet may be *feeling* that her job will be in jeopardy if people download materials from home rather than coming to the library. If you respond to what Janice is saying, you will probably try to use logic and data to support the need for more digital services. If you respond to what Janice is feeling, you can talk to her about possible new roles for library staff and encourage her to think about ways in which she can use her skills to support the new service priorities.

USE THE ORGANIZATIONAL COMPETENCIES

One of the most common negative reactions to any new idea is "We can't do that because _____."

> We can't put vending machines in the teen area because we have a policy that people can't eat or drink in the library.
>
> We can't promise to transfer materials from one branch to another in forty-eight hours because the delivery service is too slow.
>
> We can't provide programs in day care centers because there is no way to get reimbursed for using our own cars to drive to the center.
>
> We can't provide video-editing equipment and software because no one on the staff knows how to use it.
>
> We can't cosponsor programs with the county extension service because the last time we did, they got all the credit and we did all of the work.

You can no doubt add dozens of other examples to the "we can't" list from your own library. These "we can't" items often accurately describe current conditions and constraints. Even when they are not an accurate reflection of reality, they are almost always an accurate reflection of staff perceptions of reality. In either case, managers and supervisors need to be prepared to address these "we can't" feelings. If the "we can't" is perceptual rather than actual, managers and supervisors should find out why staff have the perceptions they do and provide the information needed to clarify the situation.

If the "we can't" is accurate, managers and supervisors must find a way to resolve the problem. Fortunately, the *SPFR* process provides a method for these "we can't" issues through organizational competencies and initiatives. An *organizational competency* is defined as "the institutional capacity or efficiency that is necessary to enable the library to achieve the goals and objectives in its strategic plan." An *initiative* is defined as "a temporary endeavor with a defined scope designed to produce a clearly identified product that will develop an organizational competency within a specified time frame."[3] In other words, the organizational competency describes the conditions needed to deliver new and modified services, and the initiative describes how those conditions will be achieved.

If you used the *SPFR* process, you already have a list of organizational competencies and initiatives that were identified during the planning process. If you did not use *SPFR*, consider completing the three steps in Task 8, Identify Organizational Competencies, in *SPFR*. The organizational competencies can stand alone and do not have to be developed in conjunction with *SPFR* goals and objectives. No matter what planning process you used to identify goals and objectives, you will have to have the organizational capacity required to implement your plans.

FOCUS ON REALLOCATION

The most common negative reaction to a discussion of any new activity is some version of "We don't have time to do what we are supposed to do now and we absolutely cannot do anything new!" This statement, like many of the other "we can't" statements, is often absolutely true. Many staff are overwhelmed by their current responsibilities. Managers have been adding an activity here and an activity there to staff assignments for years but rarely removing any activities. Even when a staff member is told to stop doing some activity and do another instead, the staff member sometimes tries to retain the old while adding the new. The net result is that many staff members have 80 hours of assigned work to do in a 40-hour workweek. This is further complicated when one factors in vacations, holidays, sick leave, and break time. The average staff member is only available to work between 30 and 32 hours a week in a 40-hour workweek (or 75–80 percent of the time).

When a staff member has more assigned work than she can possibly accomplish, she has to decide which activities she will do. Some staff may make their selections based on the library's service priorities, but most will choose based on their own personal values and preferences. The only way to ensure that staff focus on activities that support the library's service priorities is to be sure that staff assignments are realistic and then to hold staff accountable for accomplishing their assignments. To ensure that staff assignments are realistic, you have to first decide what needs to be done to accomplish the library's goals, which you are beginning to do in this task and will complete in Tasks 3, 4, 5, and 6. You will also need to identify the activities that do not support any of the library's priorities and decide how to eliminate, reduce, or redesign those activities. You will do that in Tasks 7, 8, and 9.

When staff say "We don't have time to do anything new," managers should agree with them and then assure them that one of the most important reasons for going through this activity process is to be sure that every staff member has appropriate responsibilities and that all staff are working together to accomplish the goals and objectives in the new strategic plan. The process is designed to reallocate staff time from less important activities to more important activities. Staff who are given significant new responsibilities will have existing responsibilities reduced, reassigned to someone else, or eliminated.

Step 1.2
Create the Capacity to Support Change

It isn't enough to make a commitment to change. A library must have the capacity in place to support the change process. The public libraries that are thriving in today's rapidly changing environment share a number of characteristics. Most important, they have strong leaders and excellent library boards. They have management teams and library boards that understand the difference between effectiveness and efficiency. Decisions are made based on data and not emotion. These libraries are market-driven in the true sense of marketing; they develop products that the people they serve want, and they provide those products at the most convenient times and in the most convenient places. Libraries that manage change well are "early adapters." They experiment with new technologies and new service models before others. They create and support an environment that encourages taking risks, and they reward risk-takers. Finally, successful libraries have an effective group of managers and supervisors who have the skills needed to implement changes and the responsibility and authority to do so.

What Are the Characteristics of a Strong Library Director?

Change starts at the top. The library director is responsible for creating an environment that supports change. In "The Enduring Skills of Change Leaders," Rosabeth Moss Kanter writes:

> Change-adept organizations share three key attributes, each associated with a particular role for leaders.
>
> > *The imagination to innovate.* To encourage innovation, effective leaders help develop new concepts—the ideas, models, and applications of technology that set an organization apart.
> >
> > *The professionalism to perform.* Leaders provide personal and organizational competence, supported by workforce training and development, to execute flawlessly and deliver value to ever more demanding customers.
> >
> > *The openness to collaborate.* Leaders make connections with partners who can extend the organization's reach, enhance its offerings, or energize its practices.[4]

Library leaders who want to create an environment that supports change will need all three of these attributes. *Innovation* is the key to providing effective library services in the future. It has fallen to our generation of librarians to transform the public library from an institution developed to meet the needs of people in the later nineteenth and early twentieth centuries into an institution that will meet the needs of people in the twenty-first century and beyond. A quick look back at the changes in library services and programs over the past fifteen years is a reminder of how far we have come in a relatively brief period of time. The next fifteen years promise to be even more challenging as library leaders face rapidly evolving technologies, continually shifting community demographics, and stagnant or decreasing public funding. It will take creative, courageous, and innovative leaders to succeed in the coming years.

Innovative thinking is only part of the answer. It must be coupled with the *professionalism to perform.* It isn't enough to think big thoughts; you must be able to translate those thoughts into quality customer services and programs. Libraries that commit to change must also commit to making sure that every change is driven by a desire to provide a more positive experience for the customer—and not a more comfortable experience for the staff.

The third key attribute in Kanter's list is the *openness to collaborate.* This is supported by other leadership experts. In *When Complex Systems Fail: New Roles for Leaders,* Margaret J. Wheatley says that leaders will be required to do the following:

> Engage the whole system. Only participation can save you.
>
> Keep expanding the system. Ask "Who else should be involved?"
>
> Create more openness and ease of access in everything.

Create abundant information, and circulate it through dedicated channels (such as websites or intranets).

Develop simple reporting systems that generate information quickly and broadcast it easily.

Make relationship development a top priority. Trust is your greatest asset.

Resist competitive behaviors; support only collaboration.

Demolish boundaries and territories. Push for openness.[5]

The approaches to collaboration that Kanter and Wheatley recommend are not typically the way libraries operate today. Too many library staff think of the library in a proprietary way: "my library," "my books," "my program," "my patrons." "My library" is a library that is self-contained. In "my library" we have all of the services, programs, and materials we need to serve the public, and we know this because "my books" were selected by us and "my programs" were designed and delivered by us. "My patrons" are the people who make use of the library regularly for "real library work" (reading, reference, program attendance, etc.). When libraries began offering public access computers, a whole new group of users started coming to the library, and many staff made it clear to these new users that they were not considered to be "my patrons."

A lot of library staff members and managers still think that collaborative efforts are one-way streets—the wrong way: library staff do all of the work and the library's partners get all of the credit. These staff say that it costs more and takes more time to collaborate than it does to do it ourselves. Yet, in the face of these preconceived ideas and negative attitudes, some libraries are collaborating more than ever and finding that the benefits of collaboration far outweigh the drawbacks. Public monies are limited, and there is an increasing expectation among funders and the general public that publicly funded organizations that collaborate provide better value. It is tempting to think of the Department of Parks and Recreation as a competitor for a shrinking pool of tax dollars. It is smarter to join forces with staff from the Department of Parks and Recreation to plan cooperative programs that allow you to pool your resources to meet the needs of your shared users.

What Effect Do Data-Based Decisions Have on the Library?

Effective decision making is critical to creating an environment that is committed to making changes. Board members and managers often think that it is the big decisions that transform a library.

What automation system should we buy?

Do we need a new building?

Where should we build the new building?

Should we centralize the selection process?

Although these decisions are all important, they will not change the library's organizational culture. Library managers and staff members make hundreds of small decisions every day, and it is the aggregate of these small decisions that creates the library's culture. John, the reference librarian, reviews the standing orders and decides not to make changes because the reference staff feel strongly about the collection. Beth, the clerical supervisor, allows Hazel to continue to collect and tabulate data manually because Hazel doesn't like computers. Julia, the branch manager, allows children's staff members Maria and Lenore to spend one day each month creating a new bulletin board because they find the process rewarding. Marina, the collection development coordinator, bases her collection budget allocations on circulation data, except in the case of media, which has been allocated a fixed proportion of the budget for the past seven years.

The staff who make these decisions often are not fully aware of the fact that they are making decisions. They are reacting instinctively to situations based on past practice, emotion, and intuition, none of which will ever support a change-responsive environment. The status quo is remarkably powerful, and unless everyone makes a continual and concentrated effort to base every decision—large and small—on data, change is going to be difficult.

Data-based decision making will be an ongoing theme in this book. Every library in the country collects a plethora of data every day. How many people came to the library today? How many DVDs did we circulate? How many of those DVDs were from the children's collection? How many children attended preschool story time this morning? How many items were processed? How many holds were filled? How many security issues did we have? How many photocopies were made? How many Internet sessions were logged? How many hours was the library open? How many staff members worked during those hours? The list goes on and on and on and on and on and still doesn't tell us anything. The issue is not how much data you collect. It is what you do with that data.

If your library is like most, some of the data you collect are tabulated quarterly, semiannually, or annually and are submitted to your state library agency. Other data are collected automatically by your circulation system, and you may print reports showing monthly circulation figures and other data. Yet other data are collected by someone for some reason, but never tabulated. Far too little of the data you collect is used to identify and evaluate options prior to making decisions.

In the earlier example, John was so concerned about staff feelings that he didn't even look at data about the use of the reference collection. Beth was unwilling to face a potential conflict with Hazel and allowed her to continue to manually tabulate figures even though it was both inefficient and inaccurate. Julia wanted her staff to be happy, so she allowed them to spend a considerable amount of time on bulletin boards with no thought about the value of the bulletin boards—or the value of other things that Maria and Lenore might have been doing instead. Marina didn't use the available data to check the assumptions that led to the fixed allocation for media seven years ago.

In every case, the decisions made by the staff in these examples supported the status quo. And in every case, the staff had access to data that could have been used to make more effective decisions. Instead, feelings trumped facts. Library leaders who want to create climates that support change will ensure that all staff have the data they need to make decisions—and that all staff *use* those data. If the data needed to make effective decisions are not available, library leaders will make it clear that they expect the needed data to be collected and analyzed before decisions are made.

Why Are Libraries So Risk-Averse?

People who are adrenaline junkies rarely wake up one morning and decide to work at the library. Instead they become policemen or firemen or enter some other high-risk profession. People who are drawn to libraries tend to be orderly, structured, analytical, strongly supportive of books and learning, and risk-averse. Those were excellent characteristics for librarians throughout most of the twentieth century. They are less positive today.

In order to commit to making changes, library leaders will have to commit to creating a more risk-tolerant environment, which in turn means creating an environment that supports uncertainty. It is a tenet of the profession that every reference question has an answer which can be found and cited. This belief in "the one right answer" permeates library decision making. Sadly, there is almost never one right answer to a management question. There are usually multiple options, few of which are terrible and none of which are perfect. The "right" answer often starts with "It depends. . . ." This is difficult for library managers who are looking for absolutes before moving forward.

You won't be able to create a risk-tolerant environment in your library overnight. It will take thought, time, and consistent nurturing to change the library's culture. The process starts at the top with the library board, the library director, and the library management team, all of whom need to model the behavior they expect the staff to emulate. If these library leaders don't take risks, there will be little incentive for other staff members to do so. Why should supervisors or staff members go out on a limb and try something new or different if they never see the members of the library's management team take a chance? It is easier and safer to "just do what I'm told to do." In order to model behavior, the members of the library management team have to be sure that staff members know they are taking risks, how the decisions to take risks are made, and what happens as a result of those decisions—both the positive and the negative. In some libraries, the director is comfortable taking risks but uncomfortable sharing the information about those risks with the staff. Not all risks pay off, and some directors would rather look infallible than create an environment that supports risk taking.

If you want to change your library's environment, you will need to acknowledge and reward people who take risks. Again, that has not been the case in most libraries in the past. Promotions have gone to people who don't make waves, unsuccessful risks have been branded as failures, the risk-takers have not been given the opportunity to "fail" again, and as a result, incremental change has been the norm. Needless to say, these behaviors have reinforced the status quo.

While most libraries can't provide cash awards to staff, every library can recognize risk-takers and change agents. Be sure that staff who want promotions understand that candidates who have demonstrated that they are innovative and willing to take risks will be given preference. Publicly acknowledge and give credit to people who take risks—both those who are successful and those who are not. Make it clear that it is more important to try something new and fail than to stubbornly maintain the status quo. When you acknowledge change agents, include a brief summary of the factors that led to the decision to take the risk and what was learned as a result of the risk. Colin Powell said: "There are no secrets to success. It is the result of preparation, hard work, and learning from failure." You often learn more from analyzing a failure than you do from basking in the glow of a success.

Lorie Loe, the president of a marketing company, encourages senior managers to spread the responsibility for managing change throughout the organization and to let people close to the issues and problems make the decisions. She also offers the following suggestions for creating an organizational culture that supports risk taking and change:

Choose one routine task, and do it as if for the first time. Ask yourself: Why am I doing this? Does it have to be done this way?

Find something that is broken and fix it.

Encourage everyone to set up little experiments in improving their work. Start a "wacky idea of the week" award and give it to someone who made an interesting experiment (even if it failed) and who learned something.

Collect new ideas from everyone. Start an idea club. Ask everyone on the team to come with one new idea to improve the team's performance.

Reward risk takers. Praise them. Give them silly prizes. Have them share their experiences and lessons.

If you don't understand a policy or process, ask why. "Just because" is not an acceptable answer. If there isn't a good explanation, change it!

Tell everyone about the worst mistake you ever made and what you learned.[6]

How Can Libraries Develop Effective Managers?

The senior management team of the library cannot implement the plan without the active and informed support of the library's middle managers and supervisors. These people provide the link between the senior managers who make the decisions and the frontline staff who implement those decisions. Middle managers and supervisors will be required to become change agents, and many of them will find that new role to be challenging.

Being in the middle is never easy. Being in a middle management or supervisory position in a public library is particularly demanding. Think for a minute about the staffing patterns in the typical public library.

The majority of staff members are women. This is true in every position from pages and clerks through senior managers.

The majority of staff members are over 40 and many are over 50. The average new MLS graduate is 30 to 35 years old.[7]

The majority of staff members have worked for the library for years and sometimes decades, although they may have held varying positions within the library.

The majority of staff members have only worked in one library and tend to think that staff in every other library do things "the way we do." When people who have worked in other libraries join the staff, their comments and suggestions tend to be discounted because "they don't understand how we do things here."

There is relatively little turnover in full-time positions (although this is changing as the wave of baby boomer retirements begins).

Middle managers and supervisors typically work side-by-side with the people they supervise. They develop a camaraderie that has little to do with the standard command-and-control environment of more hierarchical institutions.

People within each work unit tend to think and act more like a family than a part of a bureaucratic hierarchy. Just as in real families, there may be one or two staff members who really irritate the others. However, just as in real families, these others reserve the right to criticize their irritating colleagues to those within the group and will band together against any outside criticism or interference.

The manager or supervisor spends every day with her subordinates and wants them to be happy. It is easier to work in a happy place than a place filled with tension and conflict. The manager also wants her subordinates to like her. It is much more pleasant to work with people who like you than it is to work with people who dislike you, particularly a relatively small group of people housed in a relatively small area.

Many managers and supervisors have had little or no formal management training. What they know, they have learned by trial and error. They think of themselves as librarians first and managers second and much prefer their librarian tasks to their managerial responsibilities.

Middle managers and supervisors typically have strong, ongoing relationships with their peers. Many middle managers and supervisors are comfortable with the status quo, and in this they reflect their subordinates. When peer pressure is exerted, it is usually intended to discourage managers from rocking the boat, and managers who persist in making changes risk being ostracized by their colleagues. It is very likely that a manager or supervisor's peers and subordinates can and will make her life far more miserable if she tries to force changes than her superiors will if she passively or actively resists making changes.

Creating the capacity for change will need to include training for middle managers and supervisors to ensure that they understand their roles as change agents and that they have the skills needed to fulfill their responsibilities. Although an initial review of the typical staffing patterns listed above would suggest this is going to be a monumental task, that is not necessarily the case. In fact, many middle managers and supervisors will be surprised to learn that they already exhibit many of the characteristics of effective change agents.

Inspired Partners, a British management consulting firm, has found that successful change agents have the following characteristics and skills:

Credibility with key sponsors and team members

Awareness of the organization's culture and the needs of the team

Enthusiasm for the project and the business overall

Reliability to do the job they say they will

Flexibility to do the job when and where needed

Good communication skills to be able to use clear language and actively listen to others

"Can do" attitude with a desire to overcome resistance[8]

Good middle managers and supervisors already have the credibility, awareness, reliability, and communication skills they need. However, some may need to be encouraged to be more flexible and to develop a "can do" attitude, and they should be praised and supported when they do so.

Most staff, whether managers or frontline staff, are unenthusiastic about changes that are forced on them. On the other hand, staff are likely to be quite enthusiastic about changes that they help to identify and design. This simply reinforces the fact that every staff member, and particularly middle managers and supervisors, should be actively involved in every step of the planning and implementation processes. Library leaders who try to get buy-in for a plan after it has been developed will have great difficulty. The planning process described in *Strategic Planning for Results* provides guidance for including staff in the planning process. This book will continue that pattern, starting in Task 2.

Occasionally, there is some confusion about exactly what being "actively involved" in the process means. Some library directors are afraid that if they encourage staff to share their ideas they will be abdicating their leadership role. Some staff members assume that any suggestions they make will be implemented. Neither assumption is true. Staff should be encouraged to express their opinions and offer suggestions throughout the process. However, staff should clearly understand their boundaries as well. Everyone will be expected to fully support and implement changes once the decisions have been made, whether they agree with them or not. This is a particularly important point for middle managers and supervisors. Middle managers and supervisors "need to recognize the effect of having a negative moment in front of individuals who may already be skeptical about the change. One negative comment or action can undo months of positive communication and progress."[9]

The other two characteristics of effective change agents that may not be common among typical middle managers and supervisors are flexibility and a "can do" attitude. Both of these characteristics are closely related to risk tolerance, which was discussed earlier. Managers are rarely flexible in an organizational culture that supports the status quo. It is hard to develop and maintain a "can do" attitude if staff input is discouraged and new ideas for new or revised services are routinely rejected.

Middle managers and supervisors won't become effective change agents solely because you tell them to, but they won't become effective change agents if you don't make your expectations clear either. Start by describing the characteristics of effective change agents and asking your managers and supervisors to evaluate themselves in each area. Work individually with each manager to identify strengths and weaknesses and to create a personal development plan. Provide training in conflict resolution, motivation, problem solving, decision making, and employee monitoring and feedback. Monitor each manager's performance regularly and provide constructive feedback. Senior managers need to model the behaviors they expect to see in their subordinates, and middle managers and supervisors should be expected to model the behaviors they expect to see in frontline staff.

If some managers or supervisors are still reluctant to effectively manage change in their units, their supervisors will have to take action. The action they take will depend on their assessment of the situation. If the manager or supervisor is unable to carry out her duties, she may need additional training and mentoring. If she is unwilling to carry out her duties, the situation may require disciplinary action.

Task 5 in *SPFR* presented information on assessing the change-readiness of your library and included a section on developing training programs for supervisors and staff.[10] You may have started a training program for the middle managers and supervisors in your library as part of that task. If not, consider initiating such a program now. You will need the active and ongoing support of every manager and supervisor to complete the *IFR* process successfully.

TASK 2: COMMUNICATE EFFECTIVELY

In this task, you will create the communication infrastructure that will be needed to bring the staff together and keep them informed and involved in the library's change efforts. The two steps in this task are normally completed by a small team of people appointed by the library director.

Step 2.1
Review the Library Communication Processes

If you are like most library managers, you probably assume that your library's internal communication processes work reasonably well, but before you initiate the *IFR* process you may want to test your assumptions. It doesn't matter whether you work in a library with ten staff members or a library with 500 staff members. Your ability to achieve the goals and objectives in your strategic plan will depend on how successful you are in engaging and involving all of the library staff in the process. Consider the typical communication patterns in most public libraries.

In small libraries with fewer than fifteen staff members, most of the internal communication is informal rather than formal. Staff talk to each other every day, and most official messages are delivered in person rather than in writing.

In midsized libraries with 15 to 75 staff members, communication is more formal. The library has an internal management structure that is set up to transmit information. Messages are often passed down verbally through the chain of command. Important messages may be put in writing, and they are often sent to staff e-mail accounts to be sure that each staff member receives the message. There may even be a staff intranet.

In larger libraries with 76 to 250 staff members, the communication process is even more formalized. Libraries of this size typically operate from a number of locations, making the chain of command's communication pattern more complex. Libraries of this size also tend to transmit more messages in writing, both electronically and in paper, in the hope that all staff will receive the same information. Thick policy manuals reside in every unit manager's office. Memoranda from the administration are posted on bulletin boards in every staff room. Groups of staff with similar responsibilities may meet regularly to discuss shared concerns (branch managers, youth services staff, etc.).

Finally, there are the metropolitan libraries with over 250 staff members. They typically use all of the communication methods used by other libraries. In smaller branches, most communication is informal and verbal. In larger branches, the more formal communication models of midsized libraries are used. The organization as a whole has a chain-of-command communication model that is often very structured. There are policy and procedures manuals, numbered memoranda that are filed for future reference, minutes from meetings, and special e-mail distribution lists. There are lots of meetings in these libraries, which allow staff to communicate with colleagues throughout the system.

As you read through these descriptions, you may have made some mental additions to reflect the communication patterns in your own library, and you may have found some things that didn't apply to you. In general, however, you probably thought that the descriptions presented a fairly accurate picture of library communication and that most libraries were doing all they could to be sure that staff had the information they needed to do their jobs. If that is the case, why should you spend valuable time assessing the library's communications?

There are several ways to answer this question. The first, and most persuasive, is that no matter how much information is transmitted from the administration, many frontline library staff members feel that no one ever tells them anything. This feeling is not limited to larger libraries. Even in very small libraries, some staff may feel left out because interpersonal relationships can affect who hears what, when, and from whom. A general discussion of the library's communication processes and procedures may provide staff with a way to share their questions and frustrations and suggest ways to improve communication in the library. Such a discussion certainly demonstrates that library managers are willing to listen and respond to staff concerns.

A second reason to assess your communications is to identify the methods and media that are most effective in your library. The methods in the descriptions above included one-on-one meetings, small group conversations, formal meetings, minutes from meetings, written memoranda, e-mail communications, policy and procedures manuals, information posted on bulletin boards, and staff intranets. Are all of these methods equally effective? Are any of them effective? Are some of them more appropriate for certain situations than others? Are you sending too many messages? Have you established ways to verify that staff are receiving the messages you are sending? Are there other ways to communicate with staff?

When managers think of communication, their focus is usually on the processes used to deliver information. A general discussion of the overall effectiveness of the library's communications will encourage managers to take a more holistic approach to the issue. What types of information should be shared with staff? Do all staff need to get all communications? Are staff receiving all of the information they need? Are they receiving too much information? Is information provided in a timely manner? Are communications designed to be easy to read and understand? Are there formal and informal ways for staff to ask questions, make suggestions, and respond to communications they receive? If you are interested in learning more about how to make sure your organization's communication processes and procedures are effective, you may want to read the "Library Communication" Tool Kit in *SPFR*.[11]

This step does not include formal surveys or focus groups. There are no worksheets to complete and no reports to write. The purpose of this step is to remind you and your colleagues that organizational communication can always be improved. The time and energy you spend evaluating and enhancing your internal communication processes before you begin to plan and implement significant changes will be more than worth the effort.

Step 2.2
Develop and Implement a Communication Plan

During Step 1.4 in *SPFR,* you were encouraged to develop a communication plan that identified the people who needed to be kept informed about a part or all of each of the tasks in the planning process and then asked them to respond to these six questions:

Why do the members of the group need to know about this task?

What do they know now?

What will they need to know [to take the action you want them to take]?

When will they need to know it?

How will you inform them?

Who will be responsible for informing them?[12]

As you can see in figure 5, you will use the same framework to develop a communication plan for *IFR.* The library's senior managers should work together to complete

---

FIGURE 5

Workform A: Developing a Communication Plan—Example

I. Task 1: Prepare for Change

II. **A.** Start Date: January 25, 2XXX **B.** End Date: February 15, 2XXX

	A. Why do they need to know about this task?	**B.** What do they know now?	**C.** What will they need to know?	**D.** When will they need to know it?	**E.** How will they be informed?	**F.** Who will be responsible for informing them?
1. Board/ Governing Authority	They need to know that the library is beginning the *IFR* process	They have approved the strategic plan and will be monitoring progress toward reaching the objectives	A brief overview of the *IFR* process and time line	At the board meeting during which they approved the plan or the following board meeting	Director's report to the board	Director
2. Senior Managers	They will be managing the *IFR* process	The strategic plan has been approved and they will be held accountable for reaching the targets in the objectives	They need to fully under–stand the *IFR* process. They need to commit to change.	Before the *IFR* process can begin	Attend a one-day management retreat on *IFR*	Director

---

the initial version of the communication plan. Then, in most libraries, one member of the senior management team will be assigned to manage the communication plan and monitor the effectiveness of the communications. She will want to record the communication decisions made by the senior managers on an electronic copy of Workform A, Developing a Communication Plan (available at http://e-learnlibraries.mrooms.net). It is an excellent idea for the senior managers to review the communication plan carefully at the beginning of each task and make any additions or modifications that are necessary. The assumptions that are made when the communication plan is completed in this step will inevitably change as the process moves forward.

What Is the Most Effective Way to Communicate with Staff?

The most effective and efficient way to ensure that all staff have the information they need to fully participate in the *IFR* process is to establish an *IFR* website on your library intranet. If your library doesn't have an intranet, you can still establish the website and make the URL available only to staff. If you used *SPFR,* you probably already have a staff planning site. That can just be expanded to include information about implementation.

This *IFR* website should include a home page that provides a brief description of the process, information about the task to currently be completed, updates about new data added to the site, and links to the pages that support each task. The site should also include fourteen subordinate pages, one for each task in the process. These pages should indicate the status of the task (working on it now, pending, completed). As each task is completed, the completed workforms from that task should be added to the site, along with any other information that seems pertinent.

If you haven't already established a planning website, don't worry. Your library webmaster can establish the basic *IFR* website in a couple of hours, and it will take very little time to post the updates and workforms. The time-consuming part of the process is actually completing the tasks and steps and the associated workforms, and you will be doing that even if you don't post the results.

The benefits of this open communication should be apparent. Everyone will have equal access to all of the current information about the process, which will significantly reduce the rumors that surround this type of endeavor. Staff will be able to see that their suggestions and comments are being reported accurately, which should help lower the paranoia levels. Some of the tasks will be completed by small groups, and those who are not involved may think that the process has stopped. The website will help them understand that the work is ongoing and provide a way for them to review the results of the small-group efforts. They will be able to easily see the decisions that have been made and the tasks and steps that remain to be completed.

These are all organizationally sound reasons for developing the *IFR* website. There is also a very pragmatic reason for doing so. It is much easier and much less expensive to maintain one website with all of the information about the *IFR* process than it is to duplicate and distribute multiple copies of completed workforms, write and disseminate memoranda providing status reports, and so on. It also guarantees that everyone will have access to exactly the same information, something that rarely occurs when you use more traditional communication methods.

What's Next?

In this chapter you made sure that the library was prepared for the discussions about changes that will be coming, and you developed a plan to be sure that all staff members had access to the information they needed to fully participate in the implementation process. In the next chapter, the actual work of the *IFR* process will begin by looking at what staff are doing now to support the library's service priorities and by exploring other activities that might be more effective.

Key Points to Remember

A strategic plan is only valuable if it is implemented.

The library must develop new services and programs to support the new priorities in the library's strategic plan.

Public libraries that succeed in the future will be led by managers who are willing and able to respond proactively to change.

You can and should acknowledge the value of services offered in the past, but you should not feel compelled to continue those services if they are no longer effective.

The library's commitment to change must be communicated in written and verbal messages and demonstrated in every decision made throughout the *IFR* process.

The library board should be kept informed about every task in the implementation process.

Strong library directors need the imagination to innovate, the professionalism to perform, and the openness to collaborate.

Staff must have the data they need to make effective decisions—and they must be required to *use* those data in the decision-making process.

Library managers who want to create a more risk-tolerant environment must model the behaviors they expect others to emulate.

Staff should be strongly encouraged to participate in this process with the understanding that their suggestions and opinions will be carefully reviewed and considered. However, everyone should also understand that they will be expected to fully support and implement the final decisions, whether they agree with them or not.

The most effective and efficient way to ensure that all staff have the information they need to fully participate in the *IFR* process is to establish an *IFR* website on your library's staff intranet.

Communicate, communicate, communicate.

Notes

1. Internet World Stats, "Internet Usage Statistics," www.internetworldstats.com/stats.htm.
2. National Center for Education Statistics, http://nces.ed.gov/pubs2008/2008301.pdf.
3. Sandra Nelson, *Strategic Planning for Results* (Chicago: American Library Association, 2008), 108–9.
4. Rosabeth Moss Kanter, "The Enduring Skills of Change Leaders," *Leader to Leader,* no. 13 (Summer 1999): 15–22. www.leadertoleader.org/knowledgecenter/journal.aspx?ArticleID=50.

5. Margaret J. Wheatley, "When Complex Systems Fail: New Roles for Leaders," *Leader to Leader,* no. 11 (Winter 1999). www.leadertoleader.org/knowledgecenter/journal.aspx?ArticleID=58.

6. Lorie Loe, "Are You Challenging the Process?" *BEK Best Practices Newsletter,* June 2005, www.bekteam .com/news/jun_05.html.

7. Denise M. Davis, "Librarian Salaries in the USA: The Impact of Revenue Redistribution on Library Recruitment," *VINE* 35, no. 4 (2005): 188–95.

8. Inspired Partners, "Change Agents: The Key to Successful Change," www.inspired-partners.com/ KBdownload4-CA.pdf.

9. Ibid.

10. Nelson, *Strategic Planning for Results,* 76.

11. Ibid., 240–54.

12. Ibid., 17–19.

Chapter 2

Explore the Possibilities

We need a sense of the value of time—that is, of the best way to divide one's time into one's various activities.—Arnold Bennett

MILESTONES

By the time you finish this chapter you will be able to

- conceptualize library services as a series of interlinking activities, each of which is supported by steps and substeps
- explore activities provided by other libraries and agencies that support the goals in the library's strategic plan
- facilitate staff meetings to identify current and potential activities that support the goals in the library's strategic plan
- explain the concepts of effectiveness and efficiency
- consolidate and organize the current and new activities suggested during staff meetings
- review the final list of activities to determine what, if anything, is missing

Mary has been director of the Tree County Public Library for four years. Prior to coming to Tree County, she was the manager of a small branch in an urban library system and the head of public services in a midsized library in another state. Because she is now responsible for all aspects of the library and because of her experiences in other positions and in other libraries, Mary usually thinks about the library's programs and services in broad, systemic terms: service priorities, resource allocation, organizational relationships, governance structure, state and national trends, and so on.

Tanya has worked as the children's librarian in the Elm Branch of the Tree County Public Library since she graduated from library school seven years ago, and it is the only library in which she has worked. Like Mary, Tanya sees the library through the lens of her own experiences, and those experiences have given her a more local view of the library. When Tanya thinks about library services, she thinks first about youth services and then about how things are done in the Elm Branch. Tanya isn't very interested in adult services or the work of the other branch libraries. Tanya likes her job and believes the work she does is very important. She sees how her work is received by the children and parents she serves, and it reinforces her belief in the value of what she does. Both Mary's systemwide point of view and Tanya's more service-specific point of view will be needed as the Tree County Public Library plans the changes that will be required to implement the library's new strategic plan.

The global picture of change held by Mary and her senior management team starts with the library's strategic plan. The plan includes goals that describe the benefits that Tree County residents will receive because the library provides services in specific priority areas, and the plan also has objectives to help board members, managers, and staff track the progress being made toward reaching the goals. In a few cases, the plan includes some indicators of the actual activities that will be required to achieve the objectives. The objective "Each year, at least 500 children will attend programs presented by library staff in off-site locations" doesn't provide any guidance on the types of programs to be presented or where to present them, but does make it clear that staff will be presenting programs somewhere other than the library. However, most objectives are less activity-specific: "By 2XXX, the number of library visits will increase by 10 percent" describes the end toward which staff will be working but provides no information about the means that will be used to reach this end. When Mary and the other senior managers begin to think about the changes that will be required to implement the plan, they will focus on identifying the programs and services that will support the goals and objectives.

In contrast, Tanya and other frontline staff members' views of change are influenced by the work they do each day. Frontline staff are rarely concerned about how what they do fits into the overall priorities of the library. They believe the work they do is important, and they can see that some of the library's users share their opinion. Furthermore, when frontline staff think about the changes that might be needed to implement the strategic plan, they know that they will be the people who actually have to change. They will have to learn new skills, become comfortable with new tools, and stop doing some things that they have enjoyed in order to find time for new responsibilities. They also know they will have to explain the changes to the public. This is a much more pragmatic and localized reaction than that of the members of the administrative team.

Activities provide the link between the global view of the library held by senior managers and the local view of the library held by frontline staff. It is at the activity or task level that the actual programs and services of the library are defined and delivered. The terms *activity* and *task* are often used interchangeably, particularly in management literature. Sometimes one term is used to define the other. That was the case in *Staffing for Results: A Guide to Working Smarter,* in which an activity was defined as "a set of tasks that results in a measurable output of things done or services delivered."[1] The terms *activity* and *task* will both be used in this book, although they will each be used in a different context. As you have seen, the information in this book has been divided into fourteen tasks. This is consistent with other books in the Results series, which also have been organized by tasks. The term *task,* then, will be used to refer to segments of the *IFR process.* The word *activity* will be used to describe the work that library employees do to produce programs or services or the programs and services themselves.

Each activity and task is made up of a series of *steps,* which are defined as "sequential actions taken in the performance of an activity or task." Each of the *IFR* tasks has been subdivided into steps, which provide you with detailed information on how to accomplish the fourteen tasks in the book. Library activities are also supported by steps. For example, if one of the activities you were responsible for implementing was the library's summer reading program, you might start by defining the following six broad steps:

> Plan the program
>
> Build the collection
>
> Publicize the program
>
> Coordinate the program
>
> Provide readers' advisory service
>
> Evaluate the program

The two most important things to remember about steps are that they are subordinate to activities and that they are sequential in nature. If you don't complete each of these steps you won't have a summer reading program, and you must complete the steps in order. You can't evaluate the summer reading program before you present it, and you can't publicize the program before you plan it.

Everything that library staff members do during the time they are at work can be classified as either an activity or a step. While you have to understand the meaning of both of these terms before you begin the *IFR* process, it is even more critical that you learn to conceptualize library services as a series of interlinking activities, each of which is supported by steps and substeps. This can be more complicated than it appears at first glance. Remember, the way a person views the library's activities is determined by her place in the hierarchy.

Mary and other senior managers tend to describe activities broadly. For managers at this level, activities might include programming, collection development, public access computing, web development, information services, and so on. Tanya and her colleagues who work in the branch libraries will have somewhat different perceptions. Tanya might describe her activities as presenting preschool story programs in the library, presenting programs at day care centers, working with students after school, selecting materials, weeding the collection, planning and presenting holiday puppet shows, managing the summer reading program, and creating bulletin boards and displays. As you move through the tasks in the *IFR* process, you will find that like Mary and Tanya, some of your colleagues think globally and others think locally. Your challenge will be to find common ground between these global and local perceptions.

Getting Started

During the first task in this chapter, Task 3, library staff will review the goals and objectives in the library's strategic plan. They will then consider the activities for which they are responsible in order to determine which of those activities support the library's new goals. Once there is agreement on the current activities that support the goals, staff will participate in brainstorming sessions to identify new or changed activities that could support the goals. During the second task in this chapter, Task 4, a team of staff members will sort and organize the activities suggested during the brainstorming sessions. By the end of Task 4, you will have created a list of activities for each goal. Some of the activities will be new, some will be current, and some will be modifications of existing activities.

TASK 3: IDENTIFY ACTIVITIES

This task is normally started soon after the library board has approved the goals and objectives for the new strategic plan. If your library used the *Strategic Planning for Results* process, the library priorities were recommended by a community planning committee. Staff had an opportunity to provide input, but the final decisions about priorities were made by the board. Draft goals and objectives were probably written by one or two senior staff members and made available to staff for review and suggested revisions.

In other words, the staff role in the planning process up to this point has been reactive, not proactive. That changes with this task. If the *IFR* process is going to be successful, all staff members must have an opportunity to participate in the process of shaping future library services and programs.

Step 3.1
Review the Library's Goals and Objectives

It is appropriate that Task 3 starts with a review of the goals and objectives in the library's strategic plan. The whole purpose of *Implementing for Results* is to determine what activities will be required to accomplish the results described in the plan and then deploy the resources necessary to implement those activities. You cannot make informed resource-allocation decisions without a clear understanding of the service priorities in your library.

This step may seem superfluous to staff members who have been intimately involved in developing the strategic plan. Those staff can probably recite the goals and objectives from memory. However, only the few staff members who were responsible for managing the planning process and developing draft documents for review have this intimate knowledge of the final product. Most staff have had little direct contact with the planning process. They probably attended a planning orientation meeting three or four months ago; they may have participated in a review and discussion of the preliminary recommendations from the planning committee three months ago; and they may have read the draft goals and objectives last month. At least some of your staff will have tuned the whole process out and only participated when they were required to. You cannot assume that everyone is familiar enough with your goals and objectives to be able to use them as a framework for reviewing their current activities and thinking about possible new or changed activities.

This step should not take long or be difficult, even in larger libraries. The first thing you will want to do is make sure that every staff member has a copy of the goals and objectives. Most libraries can fit their goals and objectives on two to four pages. Printed front and back, this won't require an inordinate amount of paper. Don't be tempted to send one copy of the goals and objectives to each unit or to post them on the library's intranet and expect the staff to download them on their own. They won't. If you want every staff member to have the goals and objectives to use during this process, you will have to provide them with paper copies.

Some library managers may resist doing this. They will say that it is too expensive, that it is a waste of time because staff won't read the goals and objectives anyway, that staff should be expected to get the goals and objectives on their own, or that the branch or unit manager can pass on the information. Interestingly, many of these same managers will spend hundreds or even thousands of dollars disseminating the results of the plan to members of the community, who have much less of a vested interest in the information than the staff do. This is not to say that you shouldn't make plans to disseminate the results of your planning process to the community. You should—but only after you have made sure that your staff members understand the goals and objectives, support them, and are ready to produce the activities needed to make them a reality.

Before you send the goals and objectives to all staff members, meet with all unit and branch managers and supervisors to answer any final questions about the planning document and to review the plans for identifying activities. When frontline staff have questions about the goals and objectives and the activity process—and they will—they will take those questions to their supervisors. You want to be very sure that supervisors have the information they need to provide complete, accurate, and positive answers to any questions that may arise.

When you send each staff member a copy of the goals and objectives, include a letter from the library director recapping the process to date, providing a brief summary of the next planning tasks, encouraging staff to participate fully, and stressing the importance of the planning process to the library. Staff will find it easier to identify the current activities that support each goal and to identify possible new activities if they are given a chance to think about them before they participate in any group discussions and if they understand that their recommendations will be taken seriously.

Note that the intent of this process is to identify current and potential activities that support the library's service goals, and not the individual objectives for each goal. If the goals were developed using the process described in *SPFR,* they describe the benefits the community will receive because the library provides a specific service response. The objectives, on the other hand, will describe the way the library will measure progress toward reaching a goal.[2] Typical library plans have five to eight service goals, each of which has three to five objectives. It is relatively easy to identify activities in the five to eight broad priority areas defined by the library goals. It is much more complicated and time-consuming to try to identify activities that support twenty or thirty objectives, particularly when it becomes clear that many activities will support more than one objective under a goal. For example, let's assume that the Tree County Public Library strategic plan included this goal: "Preschool children will develop a love of books and reading." The objectives for this goal might include

1. Each year at least 5,000 preschool children will attend programs presented or sponsored by the library in nonlibrary locations.
2. Each year, easy books and picture books will be checked out at least 125,000 times.
3. By 2XXX, at least 75 percent of the parents or caregivers who bring their children to the library will say that the library helps preschoolers to prepare to enter school.

Activities might include planning and presenting programs on early literacy for parents (objectives 2 and 3), presenting story programs for parents and young children in the evening and on weekends to teach parents how to read to their children (objectives 1, 2, and 3), and working with day care providers and pediatricians to provide "Books to Go" bags with collections of concept books for parents to read to their children (objectives 2 and 3). As you can see, each of these activities would lead to progress in at least two of the objectives above. It would be a waste of time and energy to have to go through each objective to identify activities and find that you are repeating the same activities over and over.

Step 3.2
Identify Current Activities

It is very likely that you will find that your library is already providing some activities that support most of the goals in your strategic plan. Therefore, the work in this step will begin by developing an inventory of those current activities. It makes sense to know what you are doing now before you spend time and energy imagining a whole new set of activities.

How Much Time Will This Take?

The golden rule for every aspect of planning is "keep it simple," and this certainly applies to the process of identifying activities. The *IFR* tasks and steps presented here have been field-tested over the past four years in very large urban libraries, in medium-sized county systems, and in small rural libraries. In the earliest field tests, the process was extremely detailed and time-consuming. Over time, it became clear that there was no point in creating a process to manage change that was so labor-intensive and cumbersome that it was impossible to complete while still providing some modicum of services to the public. The processes relating to identifying, organizing, evaluating, and selecting activities that are described in Tasks 3, 4, 5, 6, 7, 8, and 9 have been simplified and streamlined several times. In this final iteration, they include all of the steps necessary to identify and evaluate effective and efficient activities in the real world, but none of the steps that sound like good ideas in a theoretical or academic world but are too cumbersome to be practical.

What Is the Best Way to Involve Staff?

You will start this step by deciding who should be involved in identifying the current activities that support each of the goals. There are a number of ways to approach this step, depending on the size and complexity of your library. Remember, it is important to provide ways for all staff to participate in this process.

Small libraries. In many smaller libraries (fewer than fifteen staff members), the staff assist with or are aware of most library activities. In these libraries, you will want to involve everyone in the process of determining which of those activities support the library's goals. This can usually be done in a single staff meeting.

Larger libraries with no branches. In larger libraries with a number of departments, the process may be time-consuming. You may have to have several meetings to allow all staff to participate. If possible, schedule open meetings and encourage units to send staff from different classifications. These different points of view will be valuable during the activity discussions.

Library systems with multiple outlets. There are at least two options to consider. You could bring together all of the staff who currently provide activities that support a goal in order to identify those activities. For instance, it might be appropriate to bring all of the children's services staff from throughout the system together to identify current and potential activities that support the goals targeted at children. This process will work best in libraries with a relatively limited number of branches. You could also treat each branch and central library department (if any) as a separate unit and use the same process suggested for small libraries. This choice is based on the assumption that staff in the branch/unit assist with or are aware of most branch/unit activities. This may be more practical in library systems with many branches.

FIGURE 6
What Facilitators Do

Facilitators Organize the Work of the Group

- Define the outcomes
- Develop the agenda

Facilitators Keep the Group Focused

- Clarify and verify participants' comments
- Summarize the group's input
- Manage time during the meeting

Facilitators Involve Everyone

- Encourage participants to share their ideas
- Keep the focus on the participants and not the facilitator

Facilitators Intervene to Resolve Problems

- Make sure that participants understand the process to be used and their roles in that process
- Respond to questions about the goals and objectives
- Address interpersonal or group dynamics that negatively affect the group's ability to operate

---

Who Should Facilitate the Activity Meetings?

As every manager knows, meetings don't run themselves. Someone has to be responsible for scheduling the meeting, convening the meeting, and keeping the meeting participants focused on the work at hand. The meetings to identify current activities will require a special kind of leader, one who can facilitate a discussion rather than dominate it. For the process to be effective, the participants have to believe that the facilitator is neutral. In other words, you probably don't want to ask the youth services coordinator to facilitate the identification of activities to support the youth services goals if she is known to have strong opinions about services and programs. Figure 6 describes the responsibilities of facilitators. As you can see, the facilitator's role is to manage the process of the meeting. Facilitators do not monopolize the discussion, they do not offer content suggestions, and they do not in any way appear to be "experts." The whole point of these activities meetings is to hear from staff. If the group leader dominates the conversation and tries to drive the recommendations, the meetings will do more harm than good.

In small libraries, the planning project coordinator may be the logical person to lead the meeting unless the library director was also the project coordinator. While it is possible for the director to be a good facilitator, it is often very difficult for both the director and the participants to shift their perceptions. The director is used to directing—being in charge and making decisions. Staff are used to doing what the director says. Look again at figure 6 and you will see that there are some inherent conflicts in the role and responsibilities of directors and facilitators. If there is no library employee who could facilitate the meeting, consider asking someone from another city or county agency to help. There are probably people at the county extension service or the city planning office who have the needed facilitation skills. Their lack of knowledge of library programs and services would be a strength and not a weakness. Remember, facilitators do not provide content input or suggestions.

In larger libraries, there are more options. Often the best solution is to appoint several members of the management team to be facilitators. They can work together to plan and facilitate the meetings and to collate and tabulate the results. Consider asking them to serve as co-facilitators for the meetings. Novice facilitators may be more comfortable working in a team.

In very large systems, the most obvious solution would be to ask branch managers to facilitate meetings in each branch, but this is not ideal for exactly the same reasons that library directors probably shouldn't facilitate the meetings in small libraries. Consider pairing branch managers and asking branch manager A to facilitate the meeting in branch B and branch manager B to facilitate the meeting in branch A. Or you might want to select a group of branch managers with facilitation skills, bring them together for additional training, and then ask them to facilitate the activities meetings in the branches throughout the system.

There is yet another option that has worked in some large libraries. In these libraries, cross-functional teams were appointed to do the initial identification of current activities and to develop the list of potential activities. Then all staff were given an opportunity to review the preliminary lists and to make comments and suggest additions.

Once you have decided who will be involved in identifying current activities for each goal, you will have the information you need to schedule meetings of those people. The number of meetings that are required will be determined by the number of goals in the library plan and the number of separate groups that will be involved in the process. In small libraries, all of the library goals may be discussed in a single meeting of all staff. In larger libraries, more meetings will be required to ensure that all staff have an opportunity to participate in the process.

How Should Meetings to Identify Current Activities Be Organized?

The facilitator will open the meeting with a brief description of the purpose of the meeting and a reminder that everyone has received a copy of the library's goals and objectives. The participants will be asked to divide themselves into groups of three or four members, and each group will identify the library's current activities that support one of the goals in the strategic plan. The members of the first group will work on goal 1, the members of the second group will work on goal 2, the members of the third group will work on goal 3, and so on. If there are more groups than goals, two groups should be assigned to work on each goal. If there are fewer groups than goals, each group should work with two goals.

The easiest way to record the activities that the group members identify is to use large sticky notes. The Post-it brand produces a note that is 7⅞ by 5⅞ inches, which is perfect for this process, although you could use the more common 3-by-5-inch size if necessary. Each group should select a member whose handwriting is easy to read to be the recorder. The facilitator should encourage all of the recorders to write each activity in large letters that are legible from a distance and to write the number of the goal that each activity supports in the lower right-hand corner of the sticky note.

The facilitator will want to ensure that the participants understand that they are supposed to be focusing on *current* activities. However, she will also have to acknowledge that in the course of the discussion of current activities, someone might suggest a potential activity or a significant modification of a current activity. To be sure that those suggestions aren't lost, the facilitator should distribute a second color of sticky notes to be used to record potential activities. Sometimes group members may identify an activity that supports the goal they are discussing as well as one or more other goals. Groups should be encouraged to list the activity under this goal and make a note to be sure to include it again under the other goals it supports.

If participants identify a group of activities that seem to be related, they might want to merge them into a single activity. For example, the members of a group might identify the following activities during a general discussion of the current activities that support the goal "Children will enjoy materials and programs that stimulate their imaginations and provide pleasurable reading, viewing, and listening experiences":

> Plan and present school visits in the spring to publicize the summer reading program
>
> Buy new materials to support the summer reading program theme
>
> Coordinate craft programs for the summer reading program with the Parks Department staff
>
> Schedule special speakers for each week of the summer reading program

These could and should all be combined into the single activity "Plan and present the summer reading program." If the group also identifies the activity "Plan and present a read-to-me program as part of the summer reading program," this activity is sufficiently different to stand alone. Merging activities is not a high priority at this point, but it is just common sense to merge things that are clearly related.

The facilitator should circulate through the room as the groups are working to be sure that everyone understands the process and that all group members are participating. The groups should be given about fifteen minutes to work, and then the facilitator should check to see if they need more time. If the groups are working on more than one goal, they may need more time. While the groups are working, the facilitator should tape signs on the available walls labeled "Goal 1," "Goal 2," "Goal 3," and so on. When the groups have finished working, one member from each group should post the results on the wall under the appropriate labels.

The next part of the process is a round-robin exercise. The members of each group will move their chairs into a semicircle near the place where the activities they identified during the first phase of the process are posted on the wall. When everyone is in place, the members of each group will move to the chairs by the next goal. The people that identified activities for goal 1 will move to the chairs by goal 2, the people who identified activities for goal 2 will move to the chairs by goal 3, the people who identified activities for goal 3 will move to goal 4, and so on. The people who identified activities for the final goal in the plan will move to goal 1.

The groups will read the current activities suggested by the preceding group and then add any activities they think are missing. If they have questions about any of the activities posted by other groups, they can write those on a sticky note and post them near the activities in question. The facilitator may want to provide sticky notes in a third color for questions, and should again remind the recorder to write the goal number on the bottom right-hand corner of each question. The groups will need about ten minutes to review and add to the second goal they consider, and then each group can move on to the next goal. By the time the groups are looking at the work done by two or three other groups, there probably won't be a lot of current activities missing, which speeds up the process. It shouldn't take more than five minutes to review and add to goals later in the process. What this means in real time is that staff from a library with seven goals should be able to move through this process in about an hour (fifteen minutes for the first goal, ten for the second, and around five minutes for each of the remaining five goals, plus time for the groups to move from goal to goal).

When all of the groups have had a chance to identify activities for all of the goals, the facilitator should take a few minutes to read the list of activities for the first goal aloud. She should try to get clarification for any questions that were posted and then encourage the participants to briefly discuss the activities for each goal before moving on to the next. Questions such as these might help to initiate the discussion:

> Does the list of current activities for this goal seem complete?
>
> Are there activities that should be merged?
>
> Are there activities that are too broadly defined to be useful and should be subdivided?
>
> Are there activities that are not defined clearly?
>
> Are the activities under the right goals?
>
> Should some activities be listed under more than one goal?
>
> Are the activities clear enough so that people not in this meeting will understand them?

This will be an interesting process and should help to ensure that the final list of activities will be understood by people who did not attend the meeting. Some staff may feel somewhat threatened by this whole process and may want to use the discussion as a time to defend one or more of the activities on this list. The facilitator should remind the participants that the purpose of this meeting is to develop a comprehensive list of current activities. The activities will be reviewed and evaluated later in the process. When the groups have finished their work, there will be a list of current activities that support each of the goals under review and notes reflecting any questions or unresolved issues that were raised during the discussion.

After this part of the process, the facilitator should remove the sticky notes that list the current activities and questions about the current activities for each goal and put them in separate manila envelopes, one for each goal, checking to be sure that the goal number is written on each envelope. It is very important not to mix up the activities for the different goals when they are filed. If the facilitator is going to combine the meetings to identify current and potential activities into a single meeting, she will leave the Goal 1, Goal 2, etc., labels on the wall and leave any sticky notes that list possible activities for each goal as well. If not, she will file those for use during the meetings that are held to identify potential activities.

Step 3.3
Identify Potential Activities

When you have completed your review of current activities, you will work with library staff to identify an array of potential activities that could support the library's goals. Potential activities include both new activities and significant modifications of current activities. As a part of this step, staff will have the opportunity to explore the effect of changes in the internal and external library environments in the past ten years. It is during this step that staff at all levels will be encouraged to suggest new activities and to recommend changes in the way current activities are delivered. They will be working together to redefine their own jobs and to shape the future of the library. This is the step in the *Implementing for Results* process that staff most often describe as exciting and creative.

How Should Staff Prepare to Identify Possible New Activities?

Encourage staff to spend some time learning about what other libraries are doing to provide activities in the areas identified as priorities for your library before the meetings you hold to identify possible new activities. It can also be valuable to have staff look at the activities offered by other organizations and agencies. If a library goal is "Adults will have timely access to new and popular materials and programs that stimulate their imaginations, respond to their current interests, and provide pleasurable reading, viewing, and listening experiences," staff might explore how other libraries provide readers' advisory services, how bookstores train their staff to assist customers, and how online providers such as Amazon.com provide readers' advisory support.

The Internet provides an excellent way to help staff become familiar with different types of activities. Almost every public library has a website, and most of those websites include descriptions of the library's services. Type the phrase "public library preschool programs" into the Google search box and Google will return over a million hits. The results on the first ten pages of hits include descriptions of preschool programs from libraries all over the country—and the world. Search the phrase "emergent literacy" and you will get links to thousands of programs, some in libraries and some offered by other agencies. A search on "reading readiness" results in a different set of sites and descriptions of different types of programs.

Staff can also learn about different ways of meeting the library's goals and objectives by reading professional literature, attending state and national conference programs, and participating in online discussion groups. Some library managers arrange to have staff members visit neighboring libraries to meet with their counterparts in those libraries and share ideas. In some regional library systems, several libraries develop strategic plans at the same time. In those cases, it can be very helpful to have staff from all of the libraries meet together to discuss current and possible activities for common goals.

Creative managers in one library organized the library's annual staff day around an exploration of the six service responses that had been identified as priorities for the library during their strategic planning process. Staff in each branch (smaller branches were paired) were asked to explore one of the service responses and develop a poster session illustrating the array of activities the library might offer to support that service response. A poster session combines text and graphics to make an interesting and attractive presentation and typically includes a large visual display and printed support materials that can be distributed to people who attend the poster session. The staff working on each priority were given a freestanding tri-folding foam display board to use to mount their presentation. The poster session was held in a large room, and each group of presenters was assigned a table. Each group was given fifteen to twenty minutes to make a presentation about their service response, distribute their printed materials, and answer questions. After the formal presentations, staff were encouraged to visit the poster tables that particularly interested them to discuss potential activities in more detail. The staff day program was a spectacular success, and almost all of the library staff members became very excited about the possibilities for future programs and services. If you are interested in replicating this staff day event, you can find information about organizing and developing effective poster sessions on the Web.

How Should Meetings to Identify Potential Activities Be Organized?

The process for identifying possible new activities to support each goal will be structured very much like the process that was used to identify current activities and will probably take about another ninety minutes. You will have to decide whether you want to combine the two processes into a single meeting or if you prefer to have two separate meetings. Unless there is a compelling reason not to, it is a good idea to combine the identification of current and possible activities in the same meeting. The discussion of current activities (Step 3.2) almost always generates ideas for new activities. Once people start thinking about existing activities, it is natural to move on to "what if . . . ?" You may lose some of those good ideas if you have separate meetings to discuss current and potential activities.

PROVIDE A CONTEXT

Whether you have one meeting or two, you will probably want to have the same staff in attendance and the same person or team facilitating the meeting. Be aware of the fact that some of the staff may be nervous about suggesting new activities. What will happen to their suggestions? How will they be evaluated? Will every idea be accepted? Who will choose? Will the process be fair? Will anyone even listen to what they say? Most staff will probably be more comfortable if they have a context for their suggestions.

The best way to provide a context for the discussion of potential activities is to briefly introduce the process and criteria that will be used to evaluate both the current activities and potential activities. Task 5 in chapter 3 provides a detailed explanation of the criteria to be used to evaluate activities. In most libraries, the senior managers will be responsible for the evaluation process, and they will need to fully understand the process and criteria that will be used. However, the majority of the staff don't need such in-depth understanding. They simply need to be introduced to the criteria that will be used to evaluate activities and to have some idea of how those criteria will be applied.

In the past, if library staff evaluated an activity, they typically used *efficiency* and *cost* as their two criteria. The *IFR* process focuses instead on criteria that measure *effectiveness.* When staff use *efficiency* as a criterion for evaluating an activity, the implicit assumption is that the activity is one that should be implemented. The only issue is how to accomplish the activity with the fewest possible resources. When staff use *cost* as a criterion for evaluating an activity, the implicit assumption again is that the activity is one that should be implemented. The only issue is the availability of resources.

Effectiveness is a measure of the value of a service to the library and to the community, and this is a new way of looking at activities for many staff members. Remember the discussion of Tanya's point of view at the beginning of this chapter. Tanya believes that everything she does has value, and the feedback she receives from the people she serves reinforces her opinion. Tanya has never had a reason to consider the relative value of the services she provides in relation to the other services provided by the library, nor has she ever been asked to consider the relative value of the various activities she completes each day. Tanya has also never been asked to think about what she might do instead of her current activities. When Tanya begins to think about effectiveness, she may look at what she does in a new light.

Efficiency and cost can both be measured in absolutes: time and money. Neither measure is ambiguous, and while there may be some room for interpretation, decisions can generally be made using data. There are no similar hard-and-fast measures that must be used to measure effectiveness. This means that you and your colleagues will have to agree on the criteria that will be used to measure effectiveness in your library before you evaluate the current and potential activities that are identified during this process. Otherwise, sooner or later your discussions about effectiveness will devolve into emotional battles that no one can win.

There are three ways to measure the effectiveness of library activities. First, you consider the percentage of the audience identified in the goal who will be served by the activity. Activities that reach a higher percentage of the target audience are considered to be more effective than activities that reach fewer people. If an activity reaches enough members of the target audience to be considered effective (and that percentage is determined by each library), the next measure of effectiveness is the results produced. To be effective, an activity must contribute to reaching the targets identified in one or more objectives for the goal. If the activity reaches a high enough percentage of the target audience and supports the objectives in the strategic plan, the final measure of effectiveness is audience reaction. This is the most intangible of the three elements and is based on the belief that effective activities appeal to the intended users.

This is a very brief introduction to the criteria to be used to measure effectiveness. Be sure to read Task 5 in chapter 3 before you try to explain the effectiveness criteria to the staff. The concepts are explained in more detail and with many examples there.

ASSIGN GROUPS

When the person facilitating the meeting has completed a brief introduction that describes the effectiveness criteria, she will use the same process to run the meeting that was used in the preceding step. The participants were divided into groups of three or four members for that meeting. They can be left in their original groups, or the facilitator can shuffle the membership of the groups. If the members of each of the groups seem to be working well together, she should probably leave them alone and let them continue to work. It takes time for several individuals to become an effective group even if the individuals know each other well. Once an effective group has been formed, there is no point in disbanding it.

However, if one or more groups are not working well, the facilitator might want to move all of the participants to new groups. She can't just reorganize the dysfunctional groups—reassigning the groups is an all-or-nothing proposition. The most common reason for reassigning groups is that one or two participants are domineering and hard to work with. It is only fair to give the people who had to work with one or more difficult group members in the first part of the meeting an opportunity to work in a more pleasant and productive group during the second part. It is too bad that this will mean that some people who had a positive experience early in the meeting may have a less positive experience during this second part of the meeting, but unless you can control the behavior of the domineering group members (and the facilitator often cannot), that will be necessary.

FACILITATE THE BRAINSTORMING

The facilitator will start this part of the meeting by distributing more of the sticky notes in the color being used for potential activities and reminding the recorders to write the goal number of each potential activity in the lower right corner of each sticky note. The participants will have learned how to work within this process when they were identifying current activities, and they know that their work will be posted for others to review and amend. If the groups were not reassigned, each will already have identified a recorder who will write the suggested activities on the sticky notes. If the groups were reassigned, a new recorder will have to be selected.

The facilitator will ask the participants in each group to brainstorm a list of possible activities that might support one of the goals in the strategic plan. The members of the first group will work on goal 1, the members of the second group will work on goal 2, the members of the third group will work on goal 3, and so on. If there are more groups than goals, two groups can work on each goal. If there are fewer groups than goals, each group can work with two goals.

The biggest difference between identifying current and potential activities is in the scope of the discussion. It is relatively easy to identify current activities. After all, one or more people in the room are probably actually responsible for a part or all of the current activities that are identified. Any confusion or disagreement among the group members is likely to be about which goal is supported by an activity or how broadly or narrowly an activity should be defined. It is much more challenging to identify new activities. Before the groups start their work, the facilitator may want to provide some basic parameters for the discussion by distributing a copy of figure 7 and reviewing the rules.

Most groups will be able to brainstorm ideas about possible activities for the goals they are first assigned to work with in about fifteen minutes, although if the groups are working on more than one goal they may need more time. When the groups have finished working, one member of each group should post the results on the wall under the appropriate goal labels.

FIGURE 7

Ten Rules for Brainstorming New Activities

1. Record every idea, no matter how far out it seems. The activities will be evaluated later.

2. There are no bad ideas and there are no stupid ideas. Don't laugh or frown or groan!

3. Encourage wild and fanciful ideas. They often provide the starting point for more realistic activities later in the process.

4. Don't worry about resources right now. That will come later.

5. Build on the ideas of others. Collaborate.

6. Quantity is more important than quality at this stage of the process.

7. Don't stop to discuss or explain an idea—and don't argue about it either. Record the basic idea and move on.

8. Stay focused on identifying possible activities for the goal under review. Don't start talking about other goals.

9. Give everyone a chance to participate.

10. Have fun!!

> **CAUTION**
>
> Monitor the groups carefully to be sure that the participants don't start discussing the pros and cons of a suggested activity. This is not the time to evaluate suggestions.

The next part of the process is exactly the same round-robin exercise that was used to identify current activities. The people who identified potential activities for goal 1 will move to the chairs by goal 2, the people who identified potential activities for goal 2 will move to the chairs by goal 3, the people who identified potential activities for goal 3 will move to goal 4, and so on. The people who identified potential activities for the final goal in the plan will move to goal 1.

The groups will read the potential activities suggested by the preceding group and then brainstorm briefly and add their own potential activities to the list. Groups can post activities under more than one goal, just as they did in the current activity exercise. The facilitator should give the groups about ten minutes to review and add to the second goal they consider and then ask them to move on to the next goal. Although the members of the groups will complete their work more quickly when they review the later goals, it will probably take them more time than it did when they were identifying current activities. There were a finite number of current activities that could be identified. The number of potential activities is far greater.

REVIEW THE RESULTS AND DISCUSS THE NEXT STEPS

When the members of the groups have had an opportunity to review and make additions to potential activities for all of the goals, the facilitator should take a few minutes to read the suggestions for the first goal. If any of the suggestions are unclear, the facilitator can ask the people who made the suggestions to provide more information. The facilitator will again want to be careful to keep the discussion focused on clarifying the suggestions and not evaluating them.

After the group has reviewed all of the activities for all of the goals, the facilitator should briefly review the next steps in the process. First, in Task 4, both the current and the new activities will be sorted, merged, and organized by a small team of staff appointed by the library director. The activities will not be evaluated during this process, and the only activities that will be merged are those that are clearly similar. The final lists of merged current and new activities will be posted on the staff intranet so that staff will be able to read everyone's suggestions. When the team has completed organizing the activities, the senior managers will evaluate both the current and new activities to determine their relative effectiveness (Task 5). The effective activities will be prioritized (Task 6), and after a review of available resources, the activities for this planning cycle will be selected (Task 12). Staff will be kept informed throughout the organization and evaluation process and will have a chance to comment on the results of each step of the process.

TASK 4: ORGANIZE ACTIVITIES

Task 1: Set the Stage
Task 2: Communicate Effectively
Task 3: Identify Activities
Task 4: Organize Activities
  Step 4.1: Consolidate and sort activities by goal and cluster
  Step 4.2: Determine what is missing
Task 5: Evaluate Activities
Task 6: Establish the Priority of Effective Activities
Task 7: Identify Activities That Do Not Support the Library's Goals
Task 8: Identify Inefficient Activities and Steps
Task 9: Decide How to Address Inefficient and Ineffective Activities
Task 10: Identify Resources Available for Reallocation
Task 11: Identify Needed Resources
Task 12: Select and Implement Activities
Task 13: Monitor Implementation
Task 14: Make Change the Norm

In Step 4.1 you will consolidate and organize the lists of current and potential activities into a single list of activities for each goal that will be evaluated during Task 5 in the next chapter.

Although it is hard to imagine when you first look at the long lists of activities that were developed during Steps 3.2 and 3.3, it is probable that there are current or potential activities that have not been included on your lists. In Step 4.2 you will review the list of preliminary activities to see if there are any obvious omissions. Remember, by this point the list of activities for each goal should include all of your current activities that support the goal and all of the potential activities that might support it. It is particularly important that all of your current activities be included in the list.

These tasks will begin as soon as all of the staff meetings to identify activities have been completed. The library director usually appoints a team of three people to be responsible for these two tasks.

Step 4.1
Consolidate and Sort Activities by Goal and Cluster

When you complete Task 3, you could easily have several dozen current or potential activities to review for each goal. At first glance this may seem overwhelming, and there is no question that it can be challenging to work with so many activities. However, the process of sorting and organizing the activities is relatively straightforward and less time-consuming than you might think. When it is completed there will be a more manageable number of activities left with which to work.

Who Should Be Responsible for Merging and Sorting the Activities?

It was important to involve as many staff as possible in the identification of current and potential activities for each goal during Steps 3.2 and 3.3 in order to ensure that all staff had an opportunity to help redefine the library's services and programs. However, as you move from identifying activities to merging and sorting those activities, the need for and value of large-scale staff participation diminishes. Ask anyone who has ever been part of a group that was trying to collectively write a document and they will tell you that group editing is a nightmare. The group members end up arguing about the minutiae of semantics rather than discussing substantive content. Trying to review, combine, and organize activities in a group would be even less satisfactory than trying to write in a group because so much of the initial part of the review process will have to focus on semantics. It is much more effective and efficient to have three people work together to develop the final list of current and potential goals. It is easier to reach consensus in a group of three than it is to reach consensus in larger groups. Even a group of four can have challenges. If there are different interpretations of a word or concept in a group of three, two people generally agree and the third typically acquiesces. If there are different interpretations of a word or concept in a group of two or four, the group all too often splits down the middle, which makes reaching agreement more difficult.

The same small team of people should review and organize all the activities for all of the goals. It may be tempting to try to spread the responsibility for this step among several teams, but that will just make the process take longer. Sooner or later some person or some small group will have to make sure that the language in all of the activities is consistent and compatible. Given that, it is more efficient to have one small team work through the semantic issues for all of the activities than to have several teams coming up with different approaches to semantics that will have to be resolved to develop the final list of activities.

There is no hard-and-fast rule about which staff members should be asked to serve on the review team. It is a good idea to include one or more of the people who facilitated the meetings in Steps 3.2 and 3.3. The facilitators may have a better understanding of the intent of some of the activities listed by the groups because they also heard the groups discuss their suggestions. You might also want to ask a staff member who works with the public every day to be a member of the committee. Such a person could serve as a reality-checker for the process. The final wording of the current and proposed activities has to be close enough to the initial suggestions for staff to see the relationship.

How Should the Activities Be Organized?

The members of the review team will want to review, merge, and organize the current and potential activities for one goal at a time. If there was more than one meeting to identify current and potential activities, they will merge all of the suggestions for each goal from all of the meetings into a single list. Although some team members may want to start with the goal that has the fewest current and potential activities, it makes more sense to start with the goal that has the most activities. The members of the team will be making semantic decisions as they move forward, and it will be easier to make the initial decisions from the largest number of activities.

The team should work in a room with a blank wall that can be used to post the sticky notes that have the activities written on them. The team will start with the current activities for the first goal that they choose to review. These current activities should all be on sticky notes of the same color, and the goal number should be written in the lower right corner of each. If the notes are on different colors of sticky notes, take a few moments and write "CA" for *current activity* in the upper right corner. If the goal number is not on the sticky note, add it before the note is placed on the wall.

The team will organize the activities in a four-step process. First, the current activities for a goal will be sorted into clusters of related activities. Then the current activities in each cluster will be reviewed to make sure that they are actually activities and not steps of activities. Once the steps have been removed, the remaining activities in each cluster will be reviewed again and similar activities will be merged. Finally, the cluster labels will be reviewed one final time to be sure that they make sense for the library and accurately describe the activities within the cluster. Then the team will repeat the same four steps for new activities.

SORT THE ACTIVITIES INTO CLUSTERS

The easiest way to manage this part of the process is for one person to read an activity aloud and another to post it on the wall with similar activities. After the first few activities have been posted, themes will begin to emerge. If you were working with activities that support the goal "Adults will have timely access to new and popular materials and programs that stimulate their imaginations, respond to their current interests, and provide pleasurable reading, viewing, and listening experiences," you might find activities that relate to programming, collections, web-based services, special events, marketing, and collaboration. As you can see, these are broad clusters, but they will work for the first rough sort. When you have finished clustering similar activities, you will probably have a group of unrelated activities left over. These can be clustered together under the general heading "miscellaneous."

As you identify each broad cluster of activities, write the cluster on a sheet of paper or a large sticky note and put in on the wall at the top of the activities that fall within that cluster. It may be easy to keep two or three clusters clear in your mind, but by the time you have five or six clusters it will be much more confusing. The clusters will serve several functions now and later in the evaluation process. During this part of the process they provide a structure for organizing the initial sort of the activities. Later in the process, they will provide the senior managers with a framework for making the initial evaluations of the activities.

IDENTIFY AND REMOVE STEPS

When both the current and potential activities for a goal have been sorted into clusters, the team will complete a second and more thorough review of each cluster. Again, it makes sense to start with the largest cluster. In the example in the preceding section, that might be programming. During this second review, team members will be doing two things. They will look at each suggested activity to make sure that it is actually an activity and not a step of an activity, and they will merge obvious duplicate activities.

The team will probably find that some of the items in each cluster relate to the same activity. Consider the following items, each of which was included in a list of current activities from a suburban library:

1. Make sure that all staff are informed about all adult programs that are scheduled
2. Encourage customer feedback by asking for a written evaluation from program attendees
3. Present monthly programs on topics of interest to adults
4. Publicize adult programs in the newspaper
5. Collaborate with local agencies to present adult programs

All of these items deal with adult programming, but they are not all equal. Only one of the items is an actual activity. The rest of the items are steps that staff might take to accomplish the activity. Remember the definitions from the beginning of this chapter. An activity is "a set of tasks that results in a measurable output of things done or services delivered." Steps, on the other hand, are "sequential actions taken in the performance of an activity or task." Can you identify the activity in the above list?

In the above example, the suggestions included both the activity ("3. Present monthly programs on topics of interest to adults") and four of the steps that support the activity. Sometimes the team may find that although a variety of steps have been listed, the activity that is supported by those steps is missing. The following items were all listed during Step 3.2 in a small rural library to support the goal "Children and teens will have the materials and services they need to succeed in school":

Contact the school district to discuss collaborating on a homework help website

Check homework help links regularly to make sure they are working

Meet with web designer to discuss adding a link from the school district's website to the library website

Review homework help websites from other libraries for ideas

Publicize the library's homework help website in the local paper

Make a presentation at the PTA about the library's homework website

Count the number of hits on the various links on the homework help website

As you review the items on this list you may be reminded of the old saying, "There must be a pony in here somewhere. . . ." A lot is happening, but it isn't explicitly clear to what purpose. In this instance, the "pony" is a homework help website. The suggested "activities" are all steps. As noted earlier, steps are the sequential actions taken in the performance of an activity. As a general rule of thumb, anything that relates to planning, publicizing, implementing, or evaluating a program or service is a step. The program or service itself is the activity. As you can see, each of the steps in the above list falls into one of the four clusters of steps:

- Planning
    Contact the school district to discuss collaborating on a homework help website

Meet with web designer to discuss adding a link from the school district's website to the library website

Review homework help websites from other libraries for ideas

- Communicating

  Publicize the library's homework help website in the local paper

  Make a presentation at the PTA about the library's homework website

- Implementing

  Check homework help links regularly to make sure they are working

- Evaluating

  Count the number of hits on the various links on the homework help website

The review team members in this library knew that the library had a very basic homework help web page, and so they were able to write the activity "Expand and enhance the library's homework help website" and remove the suggested steps from the activities list. They did not, however, discard those steps. Instead, they put the sticky notes with the steps behind the sticky note with the activity. Although the list of steps is not complete, it provides an excellent starting point for developing a plan for implementing this activity if it is one of those that are finally selected.

MERGE AND COMBINE DUPLICATES

The review team will probably catch obvious duplicates when they are looking for steps. It is not hard to see that the activities "adult book clubs," "book discussion groups," and "reading groups" probably all refer to the same activity and should be combined into a single activity. However, the relationship among activities is not always that clear. This is where semantics comes into play, and this is where the members of the review team will have to use their own judgment. There are clear guidelines for identifying steps. There are no such guidelines for identifying and merging duplicate activities, although there is one basic rule: the team members should never forget that their responsibility is limited to merging and organizing the activities suggested by staff. They are not responsible for making any value judgments about those activities. They will have to be careful to guard against the tendency to combine a "realistic" activity with a slightly similar "unrealistic" activity. "Provide equipment and training for teens to shoot and edit their own films for a teen film festival" is *not* the same activity as "Host teen film night programs." The review team members may think that the first is impossible and the second is doable, but it is not their call to make. Every activity will be evaluated during the next task.

The preceding example was fairly easy to understand, but what would you do if you had to decide whether or not to merge the following activities?

Lap-sit programs

Story programs for two-year-olds

I Can Read story programs for four-year-olds

Bedtime story programs

Preschool story programs to occupy children whose mothers are attending programs

These activities all have three major things in common. They are all *programs* designed for *preschool children* which will be presented in the *library.* They also have three major areas of difference. They are designed for *different ages* of preschoolers, they are presented at *different times,* and they have *different purposes.* There is no right or wrong answer about merging these activities, but there are some things to consider. Do these activities support a goal that is targeted toward preschool children, or do they support a goal with the broader target of all children? If they support a preschool goal, it may make sense to leave them separate. If they support a goal that focuses on all children, you may want to combine them in the single activity "Present preschool story programs in the library." If you do combine the activities, be sure to paper-clip the sticky notes for each suggested activity to the back of the combined activity. Generally speaking, if the team members have any doubts about whether two or more activities should be merged, they should probably leave the activities separate. The senior managers will be making the final decisions, and they should have an opportunity to consider all of the activities that were suggested during Steps 3.2 and 3.3.

If there was only one meeting to identify current and potential activities in your library, semantics may not be a big issue. If there were multiple meetings, however, you are likely to find that staff have used different words to describe the same activity. The following items were all submitted during Step 3.2 by the staff of one library to support the goal "Adults will be able to find, evaluate, and use information":

Database instruction for customers

Instruct customers to use electronic resources

Set aside one evening weekly for online reference instruction

Show customers of all ages how to use e-resources

Provide regular branch electronic training sessions

Improve database training that increases depth of knowledge for users

Provide instruction on the use of the resources provided by the state

Self-taught database instruction (tutorials)

Develop a template to help patrons learn how to search for answers more effectively

Train adults to use databases instead of Google

Teach people to use library electronic resources

All of these items use different words to describe the same activity: "Provide instruction to help adults use the library's databases." They should be merged into that single activity. Again, the various suggestions should be collected and paper-clipped to the back of the sticky note with the final wording of the activity.

There is yet another thing to keep in mind. You can't assume that staff in even the smallest libraries or library units mean the same thing when they talk about current or proposed activities. There are many areas of potential confusion, a few of which are listed here:

What are information services?

What are displays?

Are seniors always included in the term *adults?*

Are young adults teenagers or adults in their early twenties?

Do families always have children living at home?

What does *cosponsored* mean?

When we say training, do we mean training for the staff or for the public?

Are volunteers always included in the term *staff*?

Are volunteers ever included in the term *staff*?

Is programming always a formal activity that has a scheduled time and duration?

What is homework help?

Obviously, the activity review process will go much more smoothly if everyone has the same understanding of the words being used. The members of the review team don't need to develop a glossary or internal dictionary to deal with this issue. They just need to be sure that they use terms consistently throughout the review and organization process. This is why it is so important to have a small team of the same people work on the activities for all of the goals. It makes it much easier to be consistent.

If the team gets bogged down in circular discussion about how to describe an activity, they might want to consider whether or not the difficulty has to do with terminology. A few questions can usually resolve any confusion and help people come to agreement on the meaning of the term in question. If they find that there is obvious confusion about how a term is used throughout the library, they may want to spell out the meaning of that term for everyone in writing.

REVIEW AND REVISE CLUSTERS AS NEEDED

When all of the current activities in each cluster have been reviewed, members of the review team should take a few minutes to look at the cluster labels again. At the beginning of this chapter you were introduced to Mary, the library director, and Tanya, the children's librarian. Mary had a global view of the library's activities and Tanya had a much more local view. In this process, which point of view will be most effective? Do you want your clusters to be broad and general or narrow and focused? Do the cluster labels accurately reflect the activities within the clusters? Are the clusters consistent across all of the goals? Again, these are judgment calls, and staff in different libraries will reach different conclusions. There are certainly a lot of different ways to categorize activities, and the members of the review team will have to find an approach that will make sense to staff who will see their final product.

When the review team has completed merging and organizing the current activities for a goal, they should move on to merging the potential activities for that goal using exactly the same process they used for the current activities. It will probably be a little easier to work with the potential activities because the team members will have already identified general activity clusters and resolved a number of semantic issues during their discussion of the current activities. The potential activities should have been written on sticky notes that are a different color than the notes used for the current activities, and they should have the goal number written in the lower right corner. If one or both of these things have not been done, be sure to label the sticky notes with the potential activities carefully before beginning. Write "NA" for *new activity* in the upper right corner and add the goal number to the lower right corner. You will need to be able to differentiate current and new activities when you record them at the end of the review.

The review process may be somewhat iterative. As you work through the activities that support each of the goals in the plan, you will probably identify additional clusters of activities. Some of those clusters might be more appropriate for the activities in goals that have already been reviewed than the initial clusters that you developed. You are encouraged to go back and refine your earlier work as needed. Ideally, all of the activities for all of the goals will be placed into comparable clusters. In other words, you won't want to use the cluster "information services" for the activities in one goal and the cluster "reference services" for similar activities in another goal. If you decide at some point in the process to have two clusters of programming to reflect programs presented in the library and those presented in off-site locations, you will need to make sure that all of the activities relating to programming are subdivided into those two clusters.

How Should the Results of the Team's Work Be Reported?

When all of the activities for all of the goals have been reviewed, the final list of activities for the clusters for each goal should be recorded onto electronic copies of Workform B, Identifying and Evaluating Activities by Goal and Cluster (available at http://e-learnlibraries .mrooms.net). In the example in figure 8, you can see that the workform has been used to record programming activities for the goal "Preschool children will develop a love of books and reading." Throughout the review and merging process you have been encouraged to cluster steps of activities together and paper-clip them to the back of the activity sticky note and to do the same thing with a group of activities that were merged into a single activity. As you can see in figure 8, column B provides a place for you to record if the activity includes such attachments. In column C, each activity is labeled "current" or "new." New activities include both activities that the library has never performed and proposed activities that are substantial modifications of current activities. The double line between column C and column D indicates that the columns will be completed by two different groups. Column D will be used by senior managers in Step 5.2.

When all of the activities for a cluster have been recorded on Workform B, put the sticky notes for that cluster in a properly labeled manila envelope and staple the completed workform to the envelope. When all of the activities for all of the clusters for a goal have been recorded, put all of the manila envelopes for that goal together in a file. This will make it easy for the senior managers to find additional information if they need it when they are evaluating the activities in the next task.

Step 4.2
Determine What Is Missing

The final step in this task takes very little time to describe, but it is important. Up to this point in the process, the review committee has been working with activities that were suggested by staff during open meetings, which were probably facilitated by other staff members. In most libraries, the process will have worked well and you will have a relatively complete list of current activities and a reasonably creative list of potential activities. Take careful note of the qualifiers in the preceding sentence: "relatively" complete

I. Goal: Preschool children in Tree County will develop a love of books and reading.

II. Objectives: 1. Each year, at least 5,000 preschool children will attend programs presented or sponsored by the library in nonlibrary locations.

               2. Each year, easy books and picture books will be checked out at least 125,000 times.

               3. By 2XXX, at least 75 percent of the parents or caregivers who bring their children to the library will say that the library helps preschoolers to prepare to enter school.

III. Cluster: Children's Programming

A. Activity	B. Other Information	C. Type		D. Effectiveness			
		1. Current	2. New	1. Audience	2. Results	3. Reaction	4. Total
1. Present an average of four story programs a week for preschool children in the branch libraries (typically two on Tuesday and two on Thursday)	✓	X					
2. Plan and present monthly puppet shows using puppets hand-created by staff		X					
3. Plan and present a Read to Me program as part of the Summer Reading Program		X					
4. Present story programs in day care centers	✓		X				
5. Present bedtime story programs in parks and recreation centers			X				

and "reasonably" creative. The implication is that there may be room for improvement in both lists.

Take some time to carefully review the suggested clusters for each goal. Do the clusters include all of the types of activities that are currently being done in the library that support the goal? Can you think of other clusters of activities that might support the goal? Look at the activities within the clusters. Do the current activities include everything within that cluster of activities to support the goal? Do the new activities sound like activities that should be offered in a twenty-first-century library, or are they more suited to the mid-twentieth century?

Do the activities that support each of the goals provide services to appropriate target audiences? If the goals in your plan refer to specific target audiences, this may not be an issue. However, if your plan includes a preponderance of goals that start with the phrase "All residents will . . . ," you may find that some of the people who should be included in that general descriptor have been forgotten. There are several reasons why this may happen. The staff who suggested the activities in Steps 3.2 and 3.3 may have been predominantly adult services staff or predominantly children's services staff. Whichever the case, the staff would probably have focused on activities that served audiences they were familiar with.

Even if the right mix of staff was involved in suggesting activities, you may still find that most of the activities on your list focus on serving adults and children, often specifically preschool children. There may be a limited number of activities designed for audiences that have been traditionally difficult to serve. These audiences might include teens, small business owners, and people with less than a high school education, among others. You may also find that there are few activities targeted to audiences that you have never served before. For example, if your community has a growing number of people who speak English as a second language but has not yet begun serving them, there may be few activities that serve that group.

If you identify additional current activities that support one or more goals, you can add them to the appropriate cluster. However, if you or colleagues on the review team think the new activities that have been suggested are too limited, you might want to ask that a small team of staff be appointed to do more research to identify new options. Ideally, the team would include some new graduates and some librarians who have worked in other libraries, as well as some of the most innovative of the library's long-term staff. This team could be given a week to submit their suggestions to the review team, which would then add them to the appropriate clusters.

This is a key point in the whole process. The activities that the library ultimately implements will be selected from among the activities that are recorded on Workform B. If those activities are limited in scope or imagination, the activities the library offers in the future will be less effective than they could have been. Take the time needed here to be sure that the final choices will allow the library to fully implement the strategic plan.

What's Next?

In this chapter, all staff participated in a process to identify current and new activities that support the library goals. Then a small team of staff sorted, merged, and organized those activities. In the next chapter, the library's senior managers will decide what criteria they will use to evaluate the effectiveness of both the current and new activities and apply those criteria to each activity. They will then use a second set of criteria to prioritize the activities they have determined to be effective.

Key Points to Remember

One's view of the library is determined by one's place in the hierarchy. Library directors and senior managers tend to view the library from a global viewpoint. Frontline staff have a more local point of view.

Everything that library staff members do during the time they are at work can be classified as an activity or a step.

Make sure that unit managers and supervisors have all of the information about the implementation process they need to provide complete, accurate, and positive answers to any questions that may arise.

You will be identifying current and potential activities that support the library's service goals and not the individual objectives for each goal.

Encourage staff to look at the programs and services offered by other libraries and agencies to get ideas for new activities that could support the library's goals.

Appoint a team of three people to merge, sort, and organize the activities that were identified during the staff meetings.

The same team should review all of the activities for all of the goals.

Divide the activities into clusters of similar activities. This will greatly simplify the review process.

Words matter. Use terminology consistently when sorting, merging, and organizing the activities.

Revise your communication plan to be sure that you keep all stakeholders informed as you move through the steps in this chapter. Keep the implementation site on the staff intranet current and post the final copies of all workforms for staff review.

Notes

1. Diane Mayo and Jeanne Goodrich, *Staffing for Results: A Guide to Working Smarter* (Chicago: American Library Association, 2002), 7.
2. Sandra Nelson, *Strategic Planning for Results* (Chicago: American Library Association, 2008), 91.

Chapter 3

Identify Essential Activities

Efficiency is doing things right; effectiveness is doing the right things.—Peter Drucker

MILESTONES

By the time you finish this chapter you will be able to

- estimate the number of people who are likely to use a library activity
- determine if an activity will help the library to achieve one or more targets in the objectives in the strategic plan
- evaluate the probable audience reaction to an activity
- divide the current and new activities that support the library's goals into two groups: those that are effective and those that are ineffective
- determine the priority of effective activities
- review the effective activities with the highest priority to be sure that they include everything needed to fully implement your strategic plan

Greg is the head of public services at the Tree County Public Library. He has worked at the library for thirty-four years and was a reference librarian and the manager of two different branches before being promoted to his current job nine years ago. The Tree County Public Library has developed a number of strategic plans during Greg's long tenure, but the recently completed plan was the first since Mary became the director four years ago and the first that used the Results planning process. Greg has been supportive of the Results planning process from the beginning and has worked closely with Mary to manage the process. In the early stages of planning, when some staff were concerned about asking community leaders to help identify the library's priorities, Greg was able to help them understand why this was so important. Later in the process, Greg met with each branch manager individually to review the draft goals and to be sure that the branch manager understood the purpose of the measures in the draft objectives and how the targets for each of the objectives were determined.

Greg attended all of the meetings held to identify current and potential activities (Steps 3.2 and 3.3) as an observer and has been impressed by how involved the staff have been in the process and how creative many of the suggestions have been. As far as Greg is concerned, the process is working extremely well and the results will be worth all of the work the staff has done. Therefore, when Greg first looks at the final lists of merged and sorted activities created by the review team in Steps 4.1 and 4.2, he expects to be enthusiastic and excited. Instead he just feels overwhelmed. His excitement and enthusiasm fade as he reviews the items on the list. It seems clear to Greg that the staff are already doing so many things to support each of the library's new goals that there is little point in thinking about new activities. The more Greg thinks about the adding of new activities to the already overcommitted staff, the more discouraged he becomes.

Greg's experience is not unique. Many people find planning exciting. In the planning phases of anything the possibilities seem endless. When you first start planning a trip to Europe, it may seem like seeing five countries in seven days is a great idea. When you are in the early stages of planning a dinner party, you may think it would be elegant to serve three separate courses. However, as everyone knows, there is a big difference between planning and doing, and people often have second thoughts as they move from possibilities to probabilities to realities. Maybe visiting five countries in seven days isn't the best idea. Maybe serving a buffet dinner would be better. Then again, maybe not. How do you decide?

Both of the decisions in the preceding paragraph are individual decisions, and different people will make different choices based on their own personal criteria. A college student who has seven days in Europe may want to see as much as possible on her first trip. For her, five countries in seven days sounds like fun. An older woman who has been to Europe often may want to spend seven days exploring the treasures of the Louvre. For her, five countries in seven days sounds dreadful. A woman hosting a neighborhood party may decide on a buffet so she can enjoy her dinner guests instead of stressing over preparing and serving three separate courses. A businessman and his wife who are entertaining important clients may want to make the effort to impress them with a three-course meal. The decisions the people made in these examples were not random. They were based on what was important to the people who were making the decisions at the time the decisions were made.

Greg and his colleagues have reached a point in the planning process when they will be making real decisions that may have a profound effect on the services and programs that the library offers, but they haven't yet identified the criteria they will use to make those decisions. This leaves them with two options. They can work together to identify the criteria they will use to evaluate the current and potential activities on their list, or they can base their decisions on their personal values, their past experiences, and their hopes and aspirations.

Greg is discouraged because in the past the library's senior managers had chosen the second option, and Greg has suddenly been reminded of the discussions about new activities that accompanied the last two strategic plans. Although the processes used in those planning efforts weren't as linear as the Results process, Greg and his colleagues did identify a variety of activities that could be implemented to support the goals in the earlier plans. They then argued about them for several months and finally agreed to implement the two or three activities they would all support. None of these activities was as effective as they had hoped they would be, and most dwindled to little more than token services over the years.

The only way to avoid repeating the mistakes of the past is for Greg and his colleagues to develop—and agree to abide by—a set of external criteria to be used to evaluate the current and potential activities. The criteria need to be developed before the evaluation process begins. This will allow people to discuss the criteria that will be used in the abstract rather than becoming sidetracked by trying to protect the status quo.

Most libraries use a combination of criteria to evaluate the current and potential activities that support the goals in the library's plan. The first and by far the most important criterion to consider is effectiveness. The Drucker quotation at the beginning of this chapter says that "efficiency is doing things right; effectiveness is doing the right things." In other words, effectiveness is a measure of value. Library staff have always been interested in efficiency but have rarely spent much time thinking about effectiveness in the past.

When Greg looked at the list of current and potential activities that had been identified during Steps 3.2 and 3.3, he saw many current activities. His immediate reaction was that staff were already doing everything they could to support the new goals. Implicit in that reaction is the assumption that all of the current activities are equally effective and that all of those current activities are more effective than any of the potential activities that had been identified. As with many unspoken assumptions, just seeing it in black and white makes it clear that the assumption is absurd. Obviously some current activities provide more value than others. Equally obvious, some of the potential activities may be more effective than any of the current activities.

You will consider efficiency in chapter 4 and again in chapter 6 when you select final activities, but it is not a part of the initial evaluations of the current and potential activities that support your goals. You will only evaluate the efficiency of activities *after* you have agreed they are effective. If "Succeed in School" isn't one of the library's priorities, then there is little point in trying to establish a more efficient way to receive advance notice of homework assignments from teachers.

This brings up another crucial point. The evaluation of activities will not be complete until you have identified not only the current activities that support the library's goals, but also the current activities that *do not* support those goals. Greg is concerned that the staff are already fully occupied and he is correct. The only way to free time for staff to spend on new activities is to have them reduce or eliminate the amount of time they are spending on ineffective activities and activities that support services that are not a current library priority. You will be considering those activities in the next chapter.

Getting Started

Completing the two tasks in this chapter will be challenging. However, the effort they require will pay big dividends. Every cook knows that you can't make fine meals with inferior ingredients. The same principle applies to your library. You can't be an excellent library if you start with mediocre services and programs.

During Task 5 the library's senior managers will agree on the criteria to be used to evaluate the current and potential activities identified during Task 3 and organized during Task 4. In Task 6, they will use the evaluation criteria they have developed to divide the activities into two lists: activities that are effective and activities that are not effective. The final decisions about activities will be made during Task 12 in chapter 6 after a careful review of available resources.

TASK 5: EVALUATE ACTIVITIES

Task 1:   Set the Stage
Task 2:   Communicate Effectively
Task 3:   Identify Activities
Task 4:   Organize Activities
Task 5:   Evaluate Activities
   Step 5.1: Determine criteria for evaluation
   Step 5.2: Evaluate current and potential activities
Task 6:   Establish the Priority of Effective Activities
Task 7:   Identify Activities That Do Not Support the Library's Goals
Task 8:   Identify Inefficient Activities and Steps
Task 9:   Decide How to Address Inefficient and Ineffective Activities
Task 10: Identify Resources Available for Reallocation
Task 11: Identify Needed Resources
Task 12: Select and Implement Activities
Task 13: Monitor Implementation
Task 14: Make Change the Norm

Step 5.1 can be completed while the review team is merging and organizing activities in Task 4. It is easiest to reach consensus about the criteria that will be used if the discussion can focus on the best ways to measure the value of a library activity in broad, general terms. It is very difficult to start with a list of specific activities and try to extrapolate the criteria that could be used to evaluate those activities. If you take that approach, the process is continually derailed by the power of the status quo, which gets in the way of objective thinking. Step 5.1 is almost always the responsibility of the library's senior managers.

Step 5.2 can be completed as soon as the criteria have been established in Step 5.1. The library's senior managers will complete this step as well.

Step 5.1
Determine Criteria for Evaluation

Most libraries operate with relatively limited budgets. As a result, library managers have a tendency to "think poor" and are inclined to make decisions based on costs rather than effectiveness. This has led to libraries offering a hodgepodge of small services that have little relationship to one another—or to the library's priorities. Grand ideas, even those that would clearly be good for the library and community, are rejected out of hand as "too expensive." The truth, of course, is that in the present time of rapid and continuous change, it is too expensive to continue to provide disconnected and unrelated services and programs. As Dan Walters, director of the Las Vegas-Clark County Public Library (NV), said: "The real challenge for public libraries is being fluid enough to move quickly to remain relevant in terms of having a mix of services that are truly valuable for our customers. Public libraries are not the most flexible of institutions; you could say that generally about the public sector."[1] The entire planning process to this point has been focused on helping the managers, the staff, and members of the library board to identify the "mix of services that are truly valuable" to their customers, and this concept is the key to the criteria to be used to evaluate the effectiveness of current and potential activities.

How Can the Library Measure Effectiveness?

Effectiveness can be measured in a variety of ways, and you and your colleagues will have to agree on the measures you wish to use. The three measures recommended in *IFR* are

1. The number of people served
2. The results produced
3. The audience reaction

These three criteria are listed in priority order. When you apply them, you first determine if an activity is used by enough people to be considered effective. If it does not, then it is moved to the list of activities that are ineffective. If it does, then you move on to the second criterion, the results produced. If the activity will not help to reach the targets in one or more of the objectives for the goal the activity is supposed to support, it is moved to the list of activities that are considered to be ineffective. If it does, you move on to the third and final criterion, audience reaction. This criterion is not typically used to eliminate activities. Instead it is used as a way to determine the relative value of a number of activities that meet the first two criteria. Each of the three criteria is described in more detail below.

NUMBER OF PEOPLE SERVED

The *IFR* effectiveness measures are based on the belief that an activity that is used by many people is more effective than an activity that is used by a few people. The rationale is simple. Public libraries are funded with public dollars from every taxpaying resident of the library's service area. Therefore, activities that reach more of the people who are paying the bills are more effective than programs that only reach a few people. This is the most important of the three criteria and one that must be understood and endorsed not just by the library's senior managers but by the members of the library board as well. The ultimate purpose of the *IFR* process is to reallocate resources to support the goals in the library's strategic plan. The library board will be involved in that reallocation process, and it is critical that they understand and agree to the criteria used to make the reallocation decisions.

In an ideal world, every community resident would take advantage of all of the library's services that have been developed specifically to serve him or her. In the real world this doesn't happen, so how do you decide how many people have to use an activity before it can be considered effective? The final decision will be made by the library's senior managers, but *IFR* recommends the following scale, in which a score of 1 is very effective and a score of 5 is very ineffective. Activities must receive a score of 3 or higher to be considered effective.

1 = 25% of the target audience uses the activity in a one-year period

2 = 12% of the target audience uses the activity in a one-year period

3 = 5% of the target audience uses the activity in a one-year period

4 = 3% of the target audience uses the activity in a one-year period

5 = 1% or less of the target audience uses the activity in a one-year period

Some staff start to hyperventilate the minute they see this scale. "How can any activity be considered to be effective?" they will ask. "We will never reach 25 percent of the target audience. There are 100,000 people who live in our service area. We can't do an activity for 25,000 people!!" Note that their immediate reaction is to assume that at least 25 percent of the target audience must use the activity one time. This is untrue on two levels. The suggested measures all include the phrase "within a one-year period," and to be effective, *IFR* recommends that an activity score be at least a 3, which means that a minimum of 5 percent of the target audience should use the service during a one-year period.

Understanding that the time frame for serving the target audience is one year and recognizing that only 5 percent of the target audience needs to use the activity for it to be considered effective should help resolve staff concerns but often doesn't. Many staff are inclined to think of the people who use the library as a single target audience, which means they assume that an effective activity in a community of 100,000 must be used by at least 5,000 people. That is a lot of people to serve with a single activity, even over the period of a year.

These staff tend to forget that most library activities are designed to serve specific target audiences rather than the generic *all residents.* In fact, most activities have target audiences that are even more specific than *children, teens,* or *adults.* Consider the activity "Present story programs in day care centers throughout the county." In a county with 100,000 people, there are probably around 4,000 children between the ages of three and five. If the county is typical, about 50 percent of those children attend day care programs.[2] The total target audience for this activity would be the number of preschool children in day care—approximately 2,000 children. To be effective, the activity would have to be used by at least 5 percent of those 2,000 children, or 100 children, which shouldn't be a stretch. If staff present programs at two day care centers a month and each day care center serves 30 children, at the end of twelve months the staff will have presented 24 programs to 720 children. That is 36 percent of the target audience, well over both the minimum of 5 percent and the 25 percent that is considered to be very effective.

Senior managers often wonder how to apply this criterion to activities that have been traditionally presented to small audiences. For example, literacy services are typically offered one-on-one or in very small groups. If "Learn to Read and Write: Adult and Family Literacy" is a service priority in the Tree County Public Library, identifying activities that will be used by at least 5 percent of the target audience over the course of a year may be challenging. The fact that this service response is a priority for the library suggests that there are a relatively large number of people in the area served by the library who need literacy training. This was verified when staff talked to the Tree County Literacy Council and discovered there are 12,000 adults in Tree County who are functionally illiterate and another 8,500 adults who speak English as their second language and need literacy tutoring as well. This means that the target audience for any literacy programs will be 20,500 people. Five percent of that potential target audience is 1,025 literacy students, which is typically many more students than most library literacy programs serve. How can any activity that supports a literacy goal be considered to be effective?

The Tree County Public Library's senior managers have two choices when they review literacy activities. The first is to disregard this criterion on the grounds that literacy services are unique. The second is to take a fresh approach to the library's literacy services. Perhaps rather than supporting in-house literacy activities that serve twenty or thirty people a year, the library's managers should consider activities that include significant collaboration with the county literacy council and the school district's adult basic education program. For the same amount of staff time and other resources, the library could make a significant contribution to helping many more than twenty or thirty literacy students in a year. An experienced library director once offered this advice to a young administrator: "Every time you make a decision, think about how it would look on the front page of the paper." Would you rather have a front-page article about the twenty people that used the library's literacy services or the thousand people that used the combined services of the public library, the literacy council, and the adult basic education program?

The literacy example brings up another problem that some staff have with using the percentage of the target audience who use the activity as the first criterion to determine effectiveness. These staff members have a philosophic bias toward activities that provide intensive services to a relatively narrow audience. Adult reading clubs often serve the same fifteen or twenty people throughout the year. The participants really love the activity, and the library staff member who leads the discussion often loves it too. However, the amount of staff time spent providing extensive services to the few people who attend the book club could be reallocated to support activities that reach many more people.

This principle also applies to the preschool services offered in many libraries. The same parents or caregivers bring their children to the story programs held in the library week after week. The children, the parents or caregivers, and the children's librarians all enjoy the programs very much. The children's librarians say that the story programs are more beneficial for children who attend regularly than for children who only attend sporadically, and that may be true. However, it is equally true that *all* parents are paying taxes to support the library. Providing preschool story programs at times and in a place that automatically limit participation to parents or caregivers who can regularly bring children to the library during the workday means that the vast majority of preschool children receive no benefit from the library.

If the senior managers decide that an activity is unlikely to be used by a large enough percentage of the target audience, that activity will be moved to a list of ineffective activities. If the activity is likely to be used by enough people, the senior managers will evaluate it using the second criterion, *results produced.*

RESULTS PRODUCED

In the Results process, objectives are defined as "the way the library will measure its progress toward reaching a goal. . . . Every objective contains the same three elements: a measure, a target, and a date or time frame by which time the target should be met."[3] Results produced is a measure of the degree to which an activity will contribute to reaching a target in one or more objectives for the goal that the activity supports. Activities that contribute to more than one objective for the goal produce greater results than those that just contribute to one objective.

Like the first criterion, this criterion is measured using a five-point scale with a score of 1 being high and a score of 5 being low, and again like the first criterion, an activity must score at least 3 to be considered effective.

1 = Very high	4 = Low
2 = High	5 = None
3 = Moderate	

The first thing that most people notice when they look at the rating scale for results produced is that, unlike the rating scale for target audience, this scale does not contain numerical indicators. Although that may suggest that this criterion is more subjective than the first, this is not the case. Evaluators will be using the numerical indicators they have already incorporated into the objectives for each goal as the bases for evaluating the activities.

In an example in chapter 2, the Tree County Public Library strategic plan included the following goal and objectives:

Goal: Preschool children in Tree County will enter school ready to learn.

1. Each year at least 5,000 preschool children will attend programs presented or sponsored by the library in nonlibrary locations.
2. Each year, easy books and picture books will be checked out at least 125,000 times.
3. By 2XXX, at least 75 percent of the parents or caregivers who bring their children to the library will say that the library helps preschoolers to prepare to enter school.

When the senior managers in Tree County are evaluating an activity that supports this goal to determine if it will produce the desired results, they will consider whether the activity will attract a large number of preschool children, will encourage parents to check out a lot of easy and picture books, or will make parents and caregivers believe that the library is their partner in preparing their children to go to school—and the managers will give their highest ratings to activities that will affect two or three of those targets. The activity "Present puppet shows for all major holidays" might be scored as 3 because it will attract a lot of children, but it probably won't have much effect on circulation or parent and caregiver perceptions. The activity "Place deposit collections in local day care centers" might be scored as 2 because it will increase circulation and encourage day care providers to see the library as a partner in preparing preschool children for school. The activity "Give the parents of each new child born in Tree County hospitals a library card for the child, a free book, and an invitation to attend monthly Born to Read programs" might be scored as 1 because it will reach a lot of children, it has the potential for raising circulation considerably, and it will encourage some parents to see the library as a partner in helping their children to become readers.

On the other hand, the activity "Develop and install theme-related bulletin boards each month" should probably be scored as 5. The senior managers evaluating this activity might have thought it would serve many people because everyone coming into the children's department would see the bulletin board displays, and therefore the managers gave it a score of 2 or 3 when applying the first criterion. However, when the senior managers begin looking at the results that this activity is likely to produce, it should quickly become clear that this is not an effective activity.

Theme-related bulletin boards are not programs, and so they don't apply to the first objective. Theme-related bulletin boards rarely have any effect on circulation and won't help to reach the targets in the second objective. Children's staff may disagree with this and say that when they include a display of books with the bulletin board, the books circulate. This is quite true, but almost all books included in any display—with or without a supporting bulletin board—circulate. Anyone who strongly believes that a theme-related bulletin board has a significant effect on circulation should be encouraged to actually test that hypothesis. Discontinue the practice of creating monthly theme-related bulletin boards. Put up an attractive generic bulletin board display and leave it unchanged for six months. Then check to see if circulation has been affected. It won't have been. In fact, it is likely that only a very few people will even have noticed that the bulletin board has been unchanged. That leads to the final objective for this goal, which is that parents and caregivers will believe that the library helps preschool children enter school ready to learn. Even the most avid bulletin board supporter will be unable to say that bulletin boards will help to reach the target in this objective.

If the senior managers decide that an activity is unlikely to contribute to reaching the targets in one or more objectives, that activity will be moved to a list of ineffective activities. If the activity will contribute to reaching those targets, the senior managers will evaluate it using the final criterion, *audience reaction.*

AUDIENCE REACTION

This is the most intangible of the three criteria used to evaluate activities and is based on the logical assumption that effective activities appeal to the intended users. The more appealing the activities are, the more likely they are to be effective. This measure is only used to evaluate activities that have already met or exceeded the minimum in the first two criteria. Like the first two criteria, this criterion is measured using a five-point scale, with a score of 1 being high and a score of 5 being low, and again like the first two criteria, an activity must score at least a 3 to be considered effective.

1 = Users will love it

2 = Users will like it a lot

3 = Users will think it is OK

4 = Users will not care much

5 = Users will not care at all

In this criterion there are no numerical indicators. Instead, the people evaluating activities will have to make decisions based on their collective knowledge about the people in their community and about library activities that have been popular in the past. Virtually every activity that will be used by at least 5 percent of the target audience and will contribute toward meeting a target in at least one objective will also receive a score of at least 3 in this criterion. Activities that the members of the target audience don't care about are not used by a lot of people and don't contribute to meeting targets. The real issue that evaluators will be considering is that of the relative popularity of the effective activities.

In the preceding example, three activities received scores of 3 or higher:

Give the parents of each new child born in Tree County hospitals a library card for the child, a free book, and an invitation to attend monthly Born to Read programs (results produced score = 1)

Place deposit collections in local day care centers (results produced score = 2)

Present puppet shows for all major holidays (results produced score = 3)

When the evaluators consider audience reaction, they might score "Present puppet shows for all major holidays" as 1. The audience for this activity is the parents of preschool children and they typically love puppet shows, particularly during holidays when they want to spend time with their children.

"Place deposit collections in local day care centers" might be scored as 2. The audience here is day care providers, many of whom will like the deposit collections. However, the collections will require more work for day care workers and may not be universally popular.

The final activity, "Give the parents of each new child born in Tree County hospitals a library card for the child, a free book, and an invitation to attend monthly Born to Read programs," received a score of 1 in *results produced* but might well be scored as a 3 in the *audience reaction.* There is no question that some parents will love the activity. There is also no question that some parents won't care at all. In most communities, the majority of parents will think the activity is OK but not wonderful. After all, new parents have a lot to think about besides early literacy initiatives.

What Process Should Be Used to Identify the Effectiveness Criteria?

The library's senior managers are responsible for identifying the criteria to be used to evaluate effectiveness. This can normally be done in a single meeting if the managers have read Tasks 3, 4, and the first part of Task 5 and clearly understand why it is important to evaluate the effectiveness of activities before considering their efficiency or cost.

The library director should lead the discussion. First, the group should consider the three criteria reviewed earlier in this step. Do these criteria seem reasonable for your library? Are there criteria you would like to add? If so, what and why? Once you have all agreed on the criteria to be used, you will next discuss the relative priority of the criteria. *IFR* recommends that the number of people served be used as the first criterion, results produced as the second criterion, and audience reaction as the third. Do you and your colleagues agree? If not, why not, and what order would make more sense in your library? Finally, you will need to decide what numerical indicators you want to use when evaluating the number of people served by an activity.

Managers in most libraries decide to use the criteria recommended in *IFR* in the priority order that is suggested. Typically, the only real discussion centers around what percentage of the target audience should use a service before it can be considered effective. Some managers may be tempted to adjust the minimum percentage of users needed to consider an activity effective. *IFR* recommends that at least 5 percent of the target audience should use the service for it to be considered effective. Although it may be tempting to lower that percentage to 4 or even 3 percent, there are at least three excellent reasons for not doing so.

First, it is in the library's best interest to make a continued and sustained effort to serve as many people within the library's service area as possible. Most libraries are funded with tax dollars. Members of the public are fighting increases in local taxes in many communities across the country. People will be more willing to support the library financially if they believe that the library's programs and services reach many people in all parts of the community.

Second, and perhaps even more important, it is only fair to give people what they pay for. In most communities, all taxpayers pay for library services, whether they use them or not. They have a right to expect that the library will design and deliver services and programs that meet their needs. You expect that there will be motor vehicle inspection stations conveniently located throughout the community, and you would be upset if all of the inspection stations were located in one area. You expect that the police will respond to calls about all types of crime all over the community, and you would be very angry if the police decided to respond only to calls about burglaries because the policemen liked investigating burglaries more than dealing with vandalism or prostitution. You expect that the Fire Department will respond to all types of fires, not just big fires in the business district that get lots of publicity. You expect the Parks and Recreation Department to offer programs that are open to all children at times that are convenient for the children and their parents, rather than programs with limited audiences offered at times that are convenient for the parks and recreation staff, but not the parents and children. The public has the same expectations for the library.

The third reason is one that may take a while to become apparent. Although library staff may have some initial concerns about focusing on activities that attract many users, most will soon realize that it is much more rewarding to put energy and enthusiasm into developing and implementing an activity that is heavily used than it is to put that same energy and enthusiasm into an activity that is largely ignored by the target audience. In the long run, this approach will be very good for staff morale.

When the senior managers have agreed on the criteria that they think should be used to evaluate the effectiveness of activities, the library director should share the criteria with the members of the library board. The board may not take formal action on the criteria, but it will be important that all board members review and understand each of the criteria—and that they are willing to support the actions the managers take based on those criteria. When the board has reviewed the criteria, they should be put in writing and posted on the staff planning intranet. Figure 9 is an example of the criteria that will be used to evaluate the Tree County Public Library's activities.

Step 5.2
Evaluate Current and Potential Activities

It is finally time for the library's senior managers to begin to make decisions based on the information that came from the staff meetings in Steps 3.2 and 3.3 and the work done by the review team in Task 4. While it may seem that the activities process has been going on for a long time, in reality it typically only takes one or two weeks to identify current and potential activities, and another week or two for the review committee to sort, merge, and organize those activities. The senior managers will be identifying the evaluation criteria (Step 5.1) and sharing the final criteria with the board at the same time that the review team is working. It is not unreasonable to expect to be ready to begin Step 5.2 less than a month after the first staff activity meetings. Remember, the first meetings to identify current and potential activities could have been scheduled as soon as the board approved the goals and objectives in the library's strategic plan. This illustrates again that sometimes it takes as long to describe a process as it does to complete it.

During this step, senior managers will use the numerical rating scale they developed in the preceding step to identify the effective and ineffective activities for each goal. This is an interim step and not the final review of the activities. That will occur during Step 6.2,

FIGURE 9
Tree County Public Library Effectiveness Criteria

The Effectiveness Criteria and Scales

Target Audience	Results Produced	Audience Reaction
1 = 25% of the audience	1 = Very high	1 = Users will love it
2 = 10% of the audience	2 = High	2 = Users will like it a lot
3 = 5% of the audience	3 = Moderate	3 = Users will think it is OK
4 = 3% of the audience	4 = Low	4 = Users will not care much
5 = 1% or less of the audience	5 = None	5 = Users will not care at all

More Information about the Criteria

Target Audience

Number of People Served: The target audience for most activities is defined demographically (usually by age) or by condition (illiterate, new parent, etc.). The *potential* target audience for most activities should be all people who fit within the demographic or condition profile. This is a measure of the percentage of the total *potential* audience who will be reached by the activity at least once. Programs that serve the same people repeatedly are less effective than those in which the audience varies.

> **If an activity ranks 4 or 5 on the *Target Audience* scale, it is not effective. No further evaluation is necessary. If an activity ranks 1, 2, or 3, evaluate the *Results Produced*.**

Results Produced

Services: The services provided by the activity must contribute to producing a result identified in one or more objectives for the goal this activity addresses. This is a measure of the degree to which an activity will meet the measure of progress in one or more objectives. Activities that contribute to more than one objective for the goal produce greater results than those that just contribute to one objective.

> **If an activity ranks 4 or 5 on the *Results Produced* scale, it is not effective. No further evaluation is necessary. If an activity ranks 1, 2, or 3, evaluate the *Audience Reaction*.**

Audience Reaction

Emotional Response: This is the most intangible of the three elements. Effective activities appeal to the intended users. The more appealing the activities are, the more likely they are to be effective. This measure is only used to evaluate activities that have already been determined to serve the target audience and contribute toward producing the desired results.

when the senior managers will carefully evaluate all of the effective activities for all of the goals and determine the relative priority of each.

Why Should the Senior Managers Be Responsible for This Step?

The importance of staff involvement at every phase of the planning and implementation process has been a consistent theme throughout both *Strategic Planning for Results* and the first part of this book. That has led some people to wonder why this step is completed by the library's senior managers rather than by another team or committee. The answer is simple. Just because a library uses an open process that encourages all staff to participate does not mean that the library director and the senior management are absolved of all responsibility for the results of that process. Ultimately the library director will be held accountable by the library's governing body for meeting the targets in the objectives in the strategic plan. The director, in turn, will make her senior managers responsible for overseeing the implementation of the activities that led to meeting those targets. Responsibility and authority go hand in hand. Decisions that will shape the future of library services must be made by those who have the authority to make those decisions and who will be held responsible for the consequences of them.

In truth, most decisions about major new or changed activities have always been made by the library's senior managers. What is unique about the *IFR* process is that when they meet to discuss the implementation of the strategic plan this time, the senior managers will be working with a wealth of information. They will have the creative suggestions that came from the staff members who will actually have to implement the current or new activities that are ultimately selected. Those suggestions will have been reviewed and organized into clusters by a cross-functional team. Finally, the senior managers will have the evaluation criteria they developed during Step 5.1. The senior managers will have all of the information they need. Now they must use that information to begin to make decisions.

What Should the Senior Managers Do to Prepare for the Evaluation Process?

It may take several meetings for the senior managers to review and act on all of the current and proposed activities for each of the goals in the plan. At the beginning of the first meeting, the participants should discuss the process they will use for their deliberations and agree on some ground rules. Fortunately, they will have already agreed on the criteria to be used to determine if an activity is effective. The first and most important ground rule will be that everyone will abide by the decisions that were made during Step 5.1.

A second ground rule should be to keep the discussion focused and on target. If they aren't careful, there is a real danger that the senior managers will become bogged down in minutiae. It is far too easy to go from discussing the effectiveness of programming for adults to comparing the merits of presenting programs for adults in the library versus presenting adult programs in off-site locations, to listing recent programs for adults, to analyzing why a recent adult program was less successful than expected, to speculating on what might have been done to make that program successful, to arguing over whether the problem was poor planning, or a lack of publicity, or poor scheduling. By this point the discussion is about as useful as trying to decide how many angels can dance on the head of a pin. The real issues were those raised first: is adult programming ever effective, and if so, are adult programs more effective when presented in the library or are they more effective when presented in off-site locations? While there may be value in determining why a particular program presented in the past succeeded or failed, this is neither the time nor the place for that discussion.

The third ground rule addresses disagreements. It is unlikely that every senior manager will agree on the effectiveness scores for every cluster or activity under review. When

CAUTION
Stay focused on evaluating the effectiveness of current and new activities. Don't get involved in debates about past activities.

the inevitable disagreements occur, it will be helpful to have established a clear process for reaching a resolution. For some groups of senior managers this will not be a problem. They may already have formal or informal processes for resolving conflicts. They will just need to verbally articulate that process and move forward. However, other groups may not have established rules for dealing with conflict.

You will know if your group has conflict resolution issues. The symptoms are obvious. One member of the group likes to argue and insists on debating every decision. Another is so afraid of conflict that she will agree with the side that seems to have the most support. Yet another is always negative about everything. Perhaps there is a member who is firmly convinced that she knows the one right answer to every question all of the time. Some groups include a subgroup of people who have been around a long time and are convinced that nothing will ever change. These are just some of the personality conflicts or value differences among the group members that can get in the way of effective teamwork. Fortunately, only the most dysfunctional of groups include people with all of these characteristics. In most groups, conflict resolution problems are less severe.

The best way to address potential conflicts is to agree on ways to reach consensus before any conflicts occur. "Consensus building is a process by which group members seek a mutually acceptable resolution to the issue under discussion. Note that *consensus* does not mean that everyone agrees that the solution is the best of all possible answers. A group has reached consensus when everyone can and will support the decision."[4] This quotation is from the tool kit "Groups: Reaching Agreement" in *Strategic Planning for Results*. The tool kit includes specific suggestions for helping groups reach consensus. If you think your group has conflict resolution issues, the tool kit may have the information you need to address those issues.

What Is the Best Process to Use When Evaluating the Activities?

In most midsized libraries, the meetings in Steps 3.2 and 3.3 result in dozens of current or potential activities for each goal. Even after the review team has sorted, merged, and organized all of them, there may be two or three or even four dozen activities for the senior managers to review for some goals. However, those activities have been organized into clusters of similar activities, and there are probably no more than eight or ten clusters for each goal.

The senior managers will be working from the copies of Workform B that were partially completed by the review team in Steps 4.1 and 4.2 (see figure 8 in chapter 2). The review team sorted the current and potential activities for each goal into clusters and recorded all of the activities in each cluster on separate copies of the workform. The senior managers will probably want to start their review with the goal that has the most clusters and the most activities for the same reason that the review team started with the goal that had the most activities. Decisions made early in the process may affect later decisions, so earlier decisions should be based on the largest amount of data.

START BY REVIEWING THE CLUSTERS FOR A GOAL

In today's fast-paced library management environment, managers rarely have the time to step back and look at the big picture. This evaluation process provides that opportunity by encouraging managers to consider the effectiveness of clusters of activities before they focus on individual activities.

When Mary, Greg, and the other Tree County Public Library senior managers began their evaluation process, they started with activities that supported the goal "Adults will have timely access to new and popular materials and programs that stimulate their imaginations, respond to their current interests, and provide pleasurable reading, viewing, and listening experiences." The members of the review team had sorted the activities that supported this goal into the following clusters: regularly scheduled programs in the library, regularly scheduled collaborative programs presented in off-site locations, special events (both in-house and off-site), web-based programs and services, collection management, merchandising the collection, and marketing.

The majority of the current and potential activities were in the first three clusters that addressed programming. Regularly scheduled in-house programming activities included book clubs, program series on health-related programs for seniors, financial planning programs for all adults, various hobbies, and sports-related program topics. The off-site programming activities included collaborating with the hospital to provide diet and exercise programs, collaborating with the senior center to provide programs on historical topics of interest like World War II or the Civil War, and collaborating with the garden club on a series of gardening programs. The special event activities included a "One Book, One Tree County" program and author presentations.

Each of the senior managers had received the partially completed copies of Workform B for each goal prior to the meeting. When Mary opened the discussion for the "Adults will have timely access to new and popular materials and programs . . ." goal, several people immediately started to talk about the relative effectiveness of the various program topics in the activities within each cluster. Mary stopped them before they could become too focused on details and asked them to first consider the more fundamental question of the overall effectiveness of the three clusters of programming for adults. If the senior managers decided that presenting one or more clusters of adult programs wasn't effective, there would be little point in evaluating each activity within that cluster.

<table>
<tr><td>

CAUTION

If you decide a cluster of activities is ineffective for a specific goal, then all of the activities within that cluster are ineffective. There is no need to review each activity in the cluster individually.

</td></tr>
</table>

The group spent a productive twenty minutes applying the effectiveness criteria to the three general types of adult programming offered by the library. The first criterion was the percentage of the target audience that used the activity. They acknowledged that attendance of the adult programs they offered in the library was typically very small, and the total attendance of such programs was less than one percent of the adults in Tree County. They then went on to evaluate adult programs presented in collaboration with others in off-site locations. Again they started with the first effectiveness criterion and tried to estimate the number of people within the target audience who would actually attend those programs. Again the estimates didn't come close to the required 5 percent. Finally, they looked at special event programming. The library's "One Book, One Tree County" had been very popular. Last year over 5,000 people (7 percent of the adults in the county) participated in the program. The few author programs the library had presented also drew standing room-only crowds. Clearly, at least some special event programs were used by enough people to be considered effective. At the end of the discussion about the programming clusters, the senior managers agreed that the only adult programming that might effectively support this goal was special event programming. The activities within the other two clusters were all ineffective and there was no need to spend time discussing each individual activity. On the other hand, each of the activities within the special events cluster would need to be evaluated individually to determine their effectiveness.

Before moving on to review the activities within the other clusters for this goal (web-based programs and services, collection management, merchandising the collection, and marketing), Mary and the group applied the effectiveness criteria to each cluster. However, they found that the activities within each of those clusters were so diverse they had to be evaluated separately.

RATE THE ACTIVITIES WITHIN EACH CLUSTER

When all of the clusters for a goal have been reviewed, the managers will have determined that some clusters are ineffective, other clusters are effective, and yet others include activities that are too diverse to be evaluated collectively. They will not need to review and evaluate the individual activities in the clusters that were determined to be ineffective. Some managers may want to do just that, but the director should remind those managers that if the group has decided that adult programs presented in the library are ineffective, there is little point in discussing specific adult programs to be presented in the library. Instead, the group's energies should be spent considering the relative effectiveness of individual activities in the clusters that are effective or that are too diverse to be easily categorized.

Most of the time, the members of the senior management team will be in general agreement about the effectiveness of an individual activity. Some of the group might think the activity should have a score of 2 in one criterion and others might think it should have a score of 3, but they all agree that it meets the specific criterion. There is little point in trying to get people to reach complete agreement on a specific number. If everyone thinks the activity should receive a score of 3 or above, average their scores and move on. There is no way to make this seem like a quick process, but there are lots of ways to make it seem endless. Debating over relatively insignificant differences in numbers is one of them.

If there are questions about a specific activity, there may be more information for you to review. Column B in Workform B (see figure 10) is labeled "Other Information." If there is a check mark in this column, the review team has attached notes with the activity steps, other wording for the activity, or questions to the main activity note. You can read through the attachments to see if they help clarify the issues. If you are still confused, you can ask one of the people who was on the review team for clarification.

As you evaluate each activity, record the scores for each criterion in the columns D.1–D.3 on Workform B (see figure 10 for an example). If the group agrees that an activity does not meet one or more of the evaluation criteria (e.g., if it receives a score of 4 or 5 in *any* of the three criteria), write the abbreviation "INEFF" (Ineffective) in the total column (D.4) on Workform B. When you have finished evaluating the activities in a cluster, total the scores for each activity that was deemed to be effective. Your totals should range from a high of 3 for activities that scored 1 in each criterion to a low of 9 for activities that scored a 3 in each criterion.

When you complete evaluating the activities clusters for the first goal and before you move on to the second, take a few minutes for a final review of all the activities that you decided would be effective. Will implementing these activities, or a selection from

CAUTION

If everyone agrees that an activity should have a score of 3 or above in a criterion, don't worry about reaching consensus on the exact number. Average the group's scores and move on.

I. Goal: Preschool children in Tree County will develop a love of books and reading.

II. Objectives: 1. Each year at least 5,000 preschool children will attend programs presented or sponsored by the library in nonlibrary locations.

2. Each year, easy books and picture books will be checked out at least 125,000 times.

3. By 2XXX, at least 75 percent of the parents or caregivers who bring their children to the library will say that the library helps preschoolers to prepare to enter school.

III. Cluster: Children's Programming

A. Activity	B. Other Information	C. Type		D. Effectiveness			
		1. Current	2. New	1. Audience	2. Results	3. Reaction	4. Total
1. Present an average of four story programs a week for preschool children in the branch libraries (typically two on Tuesday and two on Thursday)	✓	X		3	3	2	8
2. Plan and present monthly puppet shows using puppets hand-created by staff		X		3	5		INEFF
3. Plan and present a Read to Me program as part of the Summer Reading Program		X		2	1	1	4
4. Present story programs in day care centers	✓		X	1	1.5	2	4.5
5. Present bedtime story programs in parks and recreation centers			X	4			INEFF

among them, ensure that the library will meet the targets in the objectives that support this goal? Do these activities serve all of the groups within the target audience? If the goal is "Children and teens in Tree County will have materials and programs that excite their imaginations and provide pleasurable reading, viewing, and listening experiences," do the activities provide services to young children, older grade-school children, middle-school children, and teens? Do any of the activities serve children or teens who speak English as a second language? Do the activities include all aspects of the goal? For this goal, you would want to have some activities that relate to reading, others to viewing, and yet others to listening. Does everyone agree that the activities on the list reflect all current activities and an exciting and interesting mix of new activities?

If there are any questions about the quality or quantity of the remaining activities, the library director should not hesitate to ask one or two senior managers to work together to identify additional activities to bring back to the group for review. Remember, the director and senior managers have both the authority and responsibility for implementing the strategic plan. They will be held accountable for the success of the activities that are selected.

Work through all of the goals in your plan using this process. Start first by reviewing the clusters to decide if you can evaluate the relative effectiveness of each cluster. Then, if necessary, evaluate the individual activities within each cluster. You will probably find that the activities that support a number of the goals have been divided into similar clusters. When the senior managers in Tree County started reviewing the clusters of activities that supported the goal "Adults in Tree County will have the skills and resources they need to identify career opportunities that suit their individual strengths and interests," they discovered that the majority of the activities were in three clusters: regularly scheduled programs in the library, regularly scheduled collaborative programs presented in off-site locations, and special events. These were the same clusters they had reviewed when they were considering the activities that supported the earlier goal "Adults will have timely access to new and popular materials and programs. . . ." As you may remember, they decided that the only programming cluster that was effective for the earlier goal was the cluster relating to special events. When they consider the three programming clusters for this career goal, they may decide that collaborative programs presented in conjunction with the employment center maintained by the county Human Resources Department will be the most effective cluster of activities. The important thing to remember is that in this step you are looking at the clusters and activities in relation to a *single* goal. You will take a more holistic view of the clusters and activities in the next task.

Don't try to complete this step in one meeting. This is intensive work and it can be tiring. Break your deliberations into two-hour segments and plan to deal with activities that support two goals in each meeting. Schedule the meetings relatively close together, perhaps every other day for a week. This will give the participants time to reflect on the activities to be reviewed before each meeting and ensure that the meetings are close enough together to provide continuity.

How Should the Decisions Made by the Senior Managers Be Recorded?

When the senior managers complete their evaluation, a staff member who is skilled in working with spreadsheets should be asked to enter all of the decisions reached by the senior managers into electronic copies of Workform B. This will result in a separate workform for every cluster of activities that supports every goal in the strategic plan—and that is a lot of workforms. Before the senior managers can complete their review of the activities, all of the copies of Workform B for each goal should be consolidated onto a copy of Workform C, Consolidating and Sorting Activities by Goal (see figure 11).

When all of the activities for a goal have been consolidated onto a single copy of Workform C, the activities for that goal should be sorted in ascending order by their total effectiveness score. The activities for each goal with the lowest scores (most effective

I. Goal: Preschool children in Tree County will develop a love of books and reading.

A. Activity	B. Type		C. Effectiveness Total
	1. Current	*2. New*	
1. Plan and present a Read to Me program as part of the Summer Reading Program	X		4
2. Present story programs in day care centers		X	4.5
3. Provide access to the Tumblebook Library: E-Books for Kids	X		5
4. Provide "Books to Go" bags, each with a collection of related materials (concept books, bilingual reading kits, picture books about animals, etc.)		X	5
5. Give the parents of each new child born in Tree County hospitals a library card for the child, a free book, and an invitation to attend monthly Born to Read programs		X	6
6. Present an average of four story programs a week for preschool children in the branch libraries (typically two on Tuesday and two on Thursday)	X		8
7. Produce regular podcasts of librarians reading stories for children and make them available through the library's website and for download in the library		X	9
8. Create themed bulletin boards each month in the children's areas of all branches	X		INEFF
9. Plan and present monthly puppet shows using puppets hand-created by staff	X		INEFF
10. Present bedtime story programs in parks and recreation centers		X	INEFF

activities) will be displayed first. All of the activities that were rated "INEFF" for *ineffective* will be grouped together after the numerical listing of effective activities. There are more complete instructions for sorting the activities for each goal with the workform.

Workform C is an interim workform with one purpose—to consolidate and sort the activities for each goal. The senior managers still have to determine the priority of the effective current and new activities which support that goal and decide how to address the current activities for that goal which are ineffective. Therefore, the staff member who created a copy of Workform C for each goal will copy the consolidated and sorted data onto two new workforms. The effective current and new activities for a goal will be copied onto Workform D, Determining the Priority of Effective Activities by Goal (see figure 12), which will be used in the next task. The current ineffective activities for each goal will be copied onto Workform E, Addressing Current Ineffective Activities That Support Each Goal (see figure 13), which will be used in Task 9 in chapter 4. The ineffective activities that are new will not be copied to Workform E, because no action will need to be taken to address them. They are not currently being provided by the library and they will not be. (Electronic copies of Workforms D and E are available at http://e-learnlibraries.mrooms.net, and the workforms will be discussed in more detail in Steps 6.2 and 9.1.)

FIGURE 12
Workform D: Determining the Priority of Effective Activities by Goal, Part I—Example

I. Goal: Preschool children in Tree County will develop a love of books and reading.

II. Objectives: 1. Each year at least 5,000 preschool children will attend programs presented or sponsored by the library in nonlibrary locations.

2. Each year, easy books and picture books will be checked out at least 125,000 times.

3. By 2XXX, at least 75 percent of the parents or caregivers who bring their children to the library will say that the library helps preschoolers to prepare to enter school.

A. Activity	B. Type		C. Effectiveness Total	D. Priority
	1. Current	2. New		
1. Plan and present a Read to Me program as a part of the Summer Reading Program	X		4	
2. Present story programs in day care centers		X	4.5	
3. Provide access to the Tumblebook Library: E-Books for Kids	X		5	
4. Provide "Books to Go" bags, each with a collection of related materials (concept books, bilingual reading kits, picture books about animals, etc.)		X	5	
5. Give the parents of each new child born in Tree County hospitals a library card for the child, a free book, and an invitation to attend monthly Born to Read programs		X	6	
6. Present an average of four story programs a week for preschool children in the branch libraries (typically two on Tuesday and two on Thursday)	X		8	
7. Produce regular podcasts of librarians reading stories for children and make them available through the library's website and for download in the library		X	9	

FIGURE 13
Workform E: Addressing Current Ineffective Activities That Support Each Goal, Part I—Example

A. Current Ineffective Activity	B. Decision	
	1. Option	2. Notes
1. Create themed bulletin boards each month in the children's areas of all branches		
2. Plan and present monthly puppet shows using puppets hand-created by staff		

TASK 6: ESTABLISH THE PRIORITY OF EFFECTIVE ACTIVITIES

The two steps in this task build on the decisions made in Task 5 and will also be completed by the senior managers. Although the senior managers can begin this task as soon as they have completed Task 5, it may be helpful to wait until after the three tasks in chapter 4 have been completed. Some managers may feel more comfortable considering new and expanded activities if they know there are current activities that can be reduced or eliminated and current inefficiencies that will be addressed.

In Step 5.2 the library's senior managers evaluated clusters of activities for each goal separately. At the end of that step the decisions they made were consolidated and the activities for each goal were sorted into two groups, those that were effective and those that were not. The effective activities for each goal were recorded on separate copies of Workform D, and those are the workforms the senior managers will be working with in this step (see figure 12).

Up to this point in the process, there has been no discussion of the specific resources that will be required to implement any of the effective activities. Those discussions will obviously have to happen before any final decisions about activities can be made, and you will have them during Tasks 10 and 11 in chapter 5. However, there is little point in spending the time to identify the resources needed for an activity that is unlikely to be implemented, and even a cursory review of the effective current and new activities on Workform D for each goal will make it clear that while they may all be effective, they are not all *equally* effective.

During this task you will determine the relative priority of the effective activities for each goal. Then, during Task 11, you will start by identifying the resources required to implement the activities with the highest priority first. If you discover that you have enough resources to implement additional activities, you can consider the activities with lower priorities. If not, you won't have wasted your time thinking about them.

Step 6.1
Review the Criteria for Establishing Priority

Before you can determine the relative priority of the activities you and your colleagues have agreed are effective, you will have to decide on the criteria you will use to establish priority. Most of the criteria recommended in earlier tasks included numerical indicators, which allowed you and your colleagues to assign a numerical score to each activity. The five criteria used in this step are not so easily managed. Although the criteria are listed below in order of their relative importance, you and your colleagues will probably apply them holistically. That is to say, you will read through a group of activities and have a general discussion about which of them seem to best exemplify these criteria, rather than trying to apply the criteria to each activity. You will learn more about applying these criteria in Step 6.2, but before you and your colleagues can apply the criteria, you will need to understand them. The five criteria you will use to establish the priority of the effective activities that support the library goals are

- effectiveness
- capacity
- efficiency
- staff reaction
- opportunity

EFFECTIVENESS

Yes, the first criterion is effectiveness again. In Step 5.2 you considered the effectiveness of the clusters and activities in relation to a single goal. Now you will consider the effectiveness of each cluster or activity in relation to all of the goals in the strategic plan. An activity that received a perfect effectiveness score of 3 but supports the goal in your plan with the lowest priority may not be as effective as an activity with a score of 6 or 7 that supports the goal with the highest priority.

Some activities will support more than one goal, which will probably make them more effective than activities that relate to only a single goal. The activity "Develop and maintain an effective readers' advisory service" could apply to goals relating to the service responses "Stimulate Imagination," "Satisfy Curiosity," and "Make Informed Decisions," among others. This activity would be more effective than the activity "Create 'what to read after you have read [best-selling author's name]' bookmarks," which only applies to "Stimulate Imagination."

CAPACITY

When you consider capacity you will be looking at four different factors: resource balance, target audiences, the mix of current and new activities, and timing. As you will see when you read the detailed descriptions of these factors below, capacity issues tend to focus on balance.

Resources. The final activities you select should require a relatively balanced use of the library's four types of resources: staff, collections, facilities, and technology. Although most activities may require some of each of these types of resources, every activity typically requires more of one type of resource than others. For example, while the activity "Present puppet shows during major holidays" may require library space, its overall effect on the library's facility resources is minimal. The resource affected most by this activity is staff. On the other hand, while the activity "Place deposit collections in day care centers" will require some staff time, the most significant ongoing resource required will be collection dollars. The activity "Create a popular materials area that includes new and high-demand books and media items" will also require some staff time to plan, but the staff impact will be minimal compared to the effect of this activity on the library facility. The activity "Provide wireless access to the Internet in all library facilities" will also require some planning time, but will have a far greater effect on the library's technology resources than on the library's staffing resources.

You will be able to implement far more of your effective activities if you select activities that use a mix of resources. Otherwise, you may find that when you have fully allocated your staff resources, you still have significant collection, facility, or technology resources available that can't be used. Occasionally, library managers find themselves focusing on activities relating to the collection rather than selecting activities that use other resources. This happens most often in libraries in which the priority has shifted from "Get Facts Fast" and "Succeed in School" to the service response "Stimulate Imagination." There is no question that a shift of this magnitude has major collection implications, but there are many activities that require staff, facility, and technology resources that would also be effective.

Target audiences. You want to be sure that the activities you select provide a reasonable balance of services to all target audiences. In Step 4.2 and again in Step 5.2, you and your colleagues were encouraged to be sure that the activities under review served all of the people in your community. Now you need to be sure that all of those people are served by the activities you select as the highest priority.

Current and new. The final activities you select should include a combination of current and new activities. It would be a mistake to assume that all of your current activities that support one of the goals in the strategic plan are equally effective, but it would also be a mistake to assume that any new activity is automatically more effective than any current activity. Every library will be incorporating new activities into an existing group of effective activities, and staff need to know that their current work is as valued as the new work they will be doing.

Timing. If you used *Strategic Planning for Results,* it probably took three or four months to go from the time you started the process to the time that the board approved the goals and objectives. It will take you another two or three months to complete the tasks in *Implementing for Results.* In other words, most libraries will spend a minimum of six months preparing to implement. By the time you are through with *IFR,* some staff will be eager to see changes, and others (the more pessimistic) will have decided that nothing will ever happen.

Therefore, you will want to be sure that your highest-priority activities include a combination of new activities that can be implemented quickly and activities that may require more time. The activities that can be implemented quickly will probably be modifications of existing activities, or activities that will not have a huge long-term impact on library services. That's fine. The point is for staff to see that something new or different is happening. While staff focus on those activities, plans for implementing activities that will require more effort and produce more results can continue.

Finally, you will want to select some one-time activities and some ongoing activities that will require consistent resources. This will allow you to provide a consistent level of services interspersed with exciting special events.

EFFICIENCY

This is the first time you will be looking at the efficiency of the activities that are still under consideration. As you may remember, the Drucker definition of efficiency is "doing things right." Senior managers in every library will interpret this definition in a slightly different way, but there are common elements that tend to make some activities more efficient than others. Efficient activities take full advantage of technology, minimize staff time required, or streamline procedures; or they provide opportunities for partnerships or to use volunteers. Many efficient activities do two, three, or even four of these things.

Activities that take full advantage of technology are almost always more efficient than activities that must be done manually. The activity "Provide podcasts of librarians reading stories for preschool children" is more efficient than the activity "Present bedtime story programs." The first activity uses technology, it frees staff time, and it provides opportunities for self-service. Not all activities that minimize staff time use technology. The activity "Create book bags containing a dozen easy books with a common theme" should make it easier for parents to select books without the assistance of a librarian, which frees the librarian for other tasks. This activity also provides opportunities for self-service. The activity "Allow users to pick up their holds from open shelves" streamlines the holds and provides opportunities for self-service.

STAFF REACTION

When you were evaluating the current and new activities to decide which were effective in Step 5.2, one of the criteria you used was *audience reaction*. Nowhere in this process have you considered *staff reaction*. Now is the time to do that. All other things being equal—which means that the activities still under consideration are effective, they use a balance of resources, and they are efficient—it makes sense to place a higher priority on activities that staff will receive with enthusiasm. Let's say that you are trying to decide the relative priority of these two activities: "Work with the staff from the Parks Department to plan and present a summer series of puppet shows in the park" and "Plan and present a summer series of puppet shows in the library courtyard." There is little question which of these most library staff would prefer. The second would win any vote by a large margin, and it should be given a higher priority than the first for that reason. This criterion won't come into play all that often, but when there is a real choice, select the activities that the staff will prefer.

OPPORTUNITY

This is the final criterion you will consider and the one that is least important. However, if all of the other criteria have been met and you are still trying to determine the relative priority of a group of activities, you might want to give preference to activities that provide the library with opportunities. There are different types of opportunities, and their value will differ depending on the circumstances in individual libraries. Staff in some libraries are looking for ways to build strong partnerships and will select activities to make that possible. Staff in other libraries might be looking for activities that will help them to get more coverage in the local media. Yet other staff may be interested in activities that will provide support for an award or other recognition.

Step 6.2
Apply the Criteria to the Effective Activities

During this step you will determine the priority for each of the effective activities for each goal. You will be dividing the activities into three groups:

> *Essential Activity (A).* The activity must be implemented to reach the targets in the objectives for the goal.

Desirable Activity (B). The activity would make significant contributions to meeting the targets in the objectives for the goal.

Supplementary Activity (C). The activity would have a modest effect on meeting the targets in the objectives for the goal.

You will base your decisions on the criteria described in Step 6.1 (see figure 14).

You and your colleagues reviewed and discussed all of these activities in the preceding task. You developed a common understanding of the meaning of each activity and you shared your opinions about them with one another. You each have the information you need to decide what you think the priority of each activity should be before you meet to share your opinions. Therefore, every senior manager should receive a copy of Workform D for each goal and be asked to assign a priority to each activity on the workform.

When everyone has completed their preliminary assessments, you can meet to share your priority recommendations. In many cases, all of you will agree on the appropriate priority for an activity and there will be no need for any further discussion. When there is

---

FIGURE 14
Criteria for Determining the Priority of Effective Activities

---

Effectiveness

- Contribute to achieving more than one objective under the goal
- Contribute to achieving objectives under more than one goal

Capacity

- Use resources in all four resource areas
- Provide a reasonable balance of activities to all target audiences
- Include a mix of current and new activities
- Combination of activities that can be implemented relatively easily to see quick success and activities that will require more time to complete
- Combination of ongoing activities that will require consistent resources and one-time activities that will require short-term resources

Efficiency

- Take full advantage of technology
- Minimize staff required
- Streamline procedures
- Provide opportunities for self-service

Staff Response

- Will be received by staff with enthusiasm

Opportunities

- Provide opportunities for partnerships
- Provide opportunities to use volunteers effectively
- Provide an opportunity for the library to win an award or other recognition
- Will produce positive media coverage

FIGURE 15
Workform D: Determining the Priority of Effective Activities by Goal, Part II—Example

I. Goal: Preschool children in Tree County will develop a love of books and reading.

II. Objectives:
   1. Each year at least 5,000 preschool children will attend programs presented or sponsored by the library in nonlibrary locations.
   2. Each year, easy books and picture books will be checked out at least 125,000 times.
   3. By 2XXX, at least 75 percent of the parents or caregivers who bring their children to the library will say that the library helps preschoolers to prepare to enter school.

A. Activity	B. Type		C. Effectiveness Total	D. Priority
	1. Current	2. New		
1. Plan and present a Read to Me program as a part of the Summer Reading Program	X		4	A
2. Present story programs in day care centers		X	4.5	A
3. Provide access to the Tumblebook Library: E-Books for Kids	X		5	A
4. Provide "Books to Go" bags, each with a collection of related materials (concept books, bilingual reading kits, picture books about animals, etc.)		X	5	A
5. Give the parents of each new child born in Tree County hospitals a library card for the child, a free book, and an invitation to attend monthly Born to Read programs		X	6	B
6. Present an average of four story programs a week for preschool children in the branch libraries (typically two on Tuesday and two on Thursday)	X		8	C
7. Produce regular podcasts of librarians reading stories for children and make them available through the library's website and for download in the library		X	9	C

disagreement about a priority, the people with differing views should briefly describe the reasons for their opinions and all of the senior managers should vote. The priority ranking with the highest number of votes will be assigned to the activity. Sometimes you may decide that a current activity is supplemental as it is currently configured, but that it could be modified to become desirable or even essential. If this happens, revise the activity and assign the new priority.

Don't waste a lot of time trying to reconcile irreconcilable positions. Keep in mind that all of the activities that are now under review have already been evaluated and deemed to be effective. You and your colleagues have decided they will all support the goals in your strategic plan. What you are doing in this step is using additional criteria to determine the relative priority of your effective activities. This is *not* a time to revisit your earlier deci-

CAUTION

Keep the discussion focused on the relative priority of the activities. Do not try to second-guess the decisions that were made in Step 5.2.

sions about effectiveness, and the person leading the process (probably the library director) should stop any such discussion immediately.

You should be able to determine the priority of all of the effective activities for all of the goals in a single meeting. At the end of the meeting, ask someone to sort the activities for each goal one final time on Workform D. In this last sort, all of the priority A activities will be grouped together, all of the priority B activities will be grouped together, and all of the priority C activities will be grouped together (see figure 15).

The current and new activities in the A group will be the activities that you continue or initiate. You will be assigning significant resources to support these activities in Tasks 11 and 12. Before you move on to the next tasks in this process, you and your colleagues should review the final activities one more time. Taken together, do they reflect the priorities in your strategic plan? Do they provide services to all of the target audiences in your community? Do they retain the best of your current activities while adding a mix of creative and innovative new activities? Would you be proud to be a manager in a library that offered these activities? If the answer to all of these questions is "yes," then you deserve congratulations for a job well done. If you have any doubts about the activities, now is the time to resolve them. Nothing you have done is cast in stone, and activities can be added to the mix at any time. Just be sure that any new activities you add are evaluated as rigorously as the earlier activities.

What's Next?

In this chapter you focused on evaluating current or new activities that support the goals in your strategic plan. In the next chapter, you will identify the current activities that support priorities that were not selected during the planning process. You will evaluate those activities and decide which to eliminate, which to modify, and which to leave unchanged. You will also be looking for ways to streamline library policies, procedures, and practices.

Key Points to Remember

The library's senior managers must develop—and agree to abide by—a set of criteria to be used to evaluate current and potential activities.

First evaluate the effectiveness of activities. Then consider efficiency.

Use three criteria to measure the effectiveness of an activity: number of people served, results produced, and audience reaction.

The *IFR* effectiveness measures are based on the assumption that an activity used by many people is more effective than an activity that is used by a few people.

Library board members should understand and support the criteria that will be used by the senior managers to evaluate the effectiveness of the current and new activities.

Senior managers should be responsible for evaluating the activities suggested by staff. Decisions about the future of library services must be made by those who have the authority to make those decisions and who will be held responsible for the consequences of them.

This evaluation process provides an opportunity for senior managers to consider the effectiveness of clusters of activities as well as the individual activities within the effective clusters.

If senior managers decide that a cluster of activities for a specific goal is ineffective, then all of the activities within that cluster are automatically ineffective. However, if the senior managers decide that a cluster of activities for a specific goal is effective, that doesn't automatically mean that each of the activities within the cluster is effective.

It will be important to keep the discussions about each activity focused and on target. It is easy to get bogged down in minutiae, and this may derail the entire process.

All effective activities are not *equally* effective. Divide the effective activities into three groups of priorities and focus first on implementing the activities with the highest priority.

The final list of activities with highest priority should include a mix of current and new activities. You cannot—and should not—change everything.

Revisit your communication plan at the beginning of each task to be sure that you are keeping all stakeholders informed.

Notes

1. Evan St. Lifer, "What Public Libraries Must Do to Survive," *Library Journal,* April 1, 2001, www.library journal.com/article/CA74712.html.
2. Child Trends Databank, www.childtrendsdatabank.org/figures/103-Figure-1.gif.
3. Sandra Nelson, *Strategic Planning for Results* (Chicago: American Library Association, 2008), 96.
4. Ibid., 235.

Chapter 4

Eliminate and Streamline

Status quo, you know, that is Latin for "the mess we're in."—Ronald Reagan

---

MILESTONES

By the time you finish this chapter you will be able to

- identify activities that support service responses that are not priorities in your library
- explain the difference between proactive and reactive activities
- define the term *sacred cow*
- provide all staff with the opportunity to identify the sacred cows in your library
- decide how to address current activities that support the library's goals but that have been determined to be ineffective
- decide how to address current activities that do not support library priorities or that are sacred cows

---

Vincent and Caitlin are two of the newest librarians at the Tree County Public Library. They are both recent library school graduates who were hired within the past year to replace retiring staff members. Although Vincent and Caitlin went to different universities, they both learned about many of the innovative programs and services that are being offered in public libraries across the country. They came to their new jobs hoping to be able to replicate some of the most exciting of the new programs they had read about. The planning process was initiated shortly after they were hired, and they were both looking forward to all the changes it would bring. They believed the process provided an opportunity to fundamentally redesign the Tree County Public Library's services.

However, the experiences that Vincent and Caitlin have had during their first year as "real librarians" have dimmed their optimism. So far, the *IFR* process has focused on identifying current and potential activities that support the goals in the new plan. Vincent and Caitlin are much more concerned about the current activities that do *not* support those goals and about the many unproductive operational practices they have observed. They both believe that an implementation process that only looks at activities that support the new goals is doomed to failure.

When Vincent and Caitlin talk about their jobs with their peers and supervisors, the focus is almost always on how to do something. Staff never seem to think about the bigger question of whether something should be done at all. This disconnect between business as usual and the emphasis on effectiveness in Tasks 3, 4, 5, and 6 makes it hard for Caitlin and Vincent to see those tasks as anything other than academic exercises. A comparison of current practices with some of the potential activities identified as effective in earlier tasks simply reinforces the disconnect.

For instance, a number of the activities with the highest priority identified in Step 6.2 relate to enhancing and expanding the library's website to create a more flexible and easily changed template and to add a variety of opportunities for social networking. These sounded like great ideas to Vincent and Caitlin—until they reminded one another of the current reality. The library's technology staff completely control the web page, and even minor changes can take months. In fact, if the technology staff don't like a suggested change, it never seems to get done. The branch managers are opposed to letting teens communicate with each other through blogs or forums on the library's website and have blocked every attempt to make that happen. Some staff feel threatened by the increasing number of people who use the library electronically and resist any effort to increase or enhance electronic access.

On the other hand, activities that support services that were not selected as priorities continue to flourish. Neither "Get Facts Fast" nor "Succeed in School" was selected as a priority in Tree County. However, the first thing that users see when they enter most of the library's facilities is an extensive print reference collection. The materials budget includes a significant allocation for standing orders, almost all of which are for reference items. Reference desks are staffed with two people in most facilities throughout the day, even though the number of reference questions being asked dwindles year by year. The children's staff make school visits to encourage children to come to the public library to do their homework. In Caitlin's branch, the children's librarian still maintains a vertical file of materials on topics that are frequently selected by students doing research papers. Caitlin has told her several times that it is a waste of time, but the staff member insists that teachers require students to have the "print" materials and this is the only way to meet that demand.

Both Vincent and Caitlin were pleased to see that the strategic plan included the organizational competency "The Tree County Public Library will utilize technologies and processes that improve access to information, enhance customer service, and maximize efficient service delivery." They're just afraid it won't address such long-standing practices as the additional processing that branch staff do when the books arrive from technical services. Before the books are shelved, the staff put genre labels on the spines. Some books also get colored dots: green dots for adult new books, orange for new teen books, yellow for award-winning books, and brown for high-interest, low-vocabulary books. Neither Vincent nor Caitlin can see any point in all of this extra processing, but they are not in a position to do anything to change the way the books are handled.

Vincent and Caitlin have learned what every new librarian learns: it is difficult to overestimate the power of the status quo. They have found that most of their colleagues believe that all of the work they are doing is relevant and important. Staff are proud of the services they offer, and they are uncomfortable when faced with the possibility that there might be other, more effective or efficient ways to deliver those services. Upon hearing that the library board had approved the goals and objectives in the new strategic plan, one of the staff members in Vincent's branch said: "Thank heaven that is finally over! Now we can get back to our real work." The "real work" she was referring to, of course, was the work she and others had been doing before the planning process began. She, like most of her colleagues, did not expect significant changes in her "real work" as a result of the new goals and objectives.

This is quite typical. While staff might worry that they will be assigned additional duties, surprisingly few staff expect to see any of their current activities streamlined, reduced, or eliminated. Nor do staff see the planning process as a framework for considering the efficiency of their activities. In many libraries, these staff assumptions are completely realistic based on the past practices of most libraries, when long-range planning had little effect on the day-to-day operations of the library.

However, no matter how accurate those assumptions once were, they are no longer valid. There simply isn't enough time available for staff to continue to do everything they have always done in the way that they have always done it *and* to implement the new activities needed to support the strategic plan. Furthermore, no realistic library administrator can expect to get the money needed to hire new staff to implement those new activities or to continue to support the current operational inefficiencies.

This leaves the library director with two possibilities. The first is to abandon this process and go back to business as usual, hoping that through a combination of good luck and better marketing the library will be able to make some progress toward the targets in the objectives in the strategic plan. (This scenario always includes the assumption that somehow the library's marketing, which has had little appreciable effect on library use for decades, will miraculously become as powerful as Wal-Mart's marketing in the future.) The second possibility is to put as much emphasis on identifying and evaluating the current activities that *do not* support the library's priorities as you have placed on identifying and evaluating the activities that *do* support the library's priorities, and to make a serious effort to streamline library policies, procedures, and practices. The first choice reinforces the status quo and puts the library's future in jeopardy. The second choice sets the stage for library services to continue to evolve to meet changing user needs and expectations.

Getting Started

The three tasks in this chapter require a different mind-set than the tasks in the preceding chapters. It is one thing to spend several hours in a fast-paced and creative process that allows you and your colleagues to think about the many new and exciting services that the library might offer, without having to worry about how those services will be delivered. And it is exhilarating to realize how many of the services that are offered now support the library's new priorities.

It is an entirely different thing to identify the many current library activities that do not support any of the library's priorities. Rather than challenging your imagination, this requires honest self-appraisal, clear-sighted pragmatism, and a willingness to set the stage for real change. This is harder for everyone involved because it moves the discussion from "what if?" to "how?" or—even more challenging—"why?" However, the difficulties that some may face with identifying activities that do not support the current priorities are often offset by the realization that it may be possible to finally do something about inefficient policies, procedures, or practices. Most staff members have at least one thing they want changed, and many have long lists of such things.

During Task 7, a representative team will review the service responses not selected as priorities during the planning process and will identify the current activities that support those service responses. In Task 8, all staff will be given the opportunity to identify the library's "sacred cows." In Task 9, the library's senior managers will decide how to address the ineffective activities that support the library's goals, the activities that don't support current priorities, and the inefficient policies, procedures, and practices identified during Tasks 5, 7, and 8.

TASK 7: IDENTIFY ACTIVITIES THAT DO NOT SUPPORT THE LIBRARY'S GOALS

Task 1:   Set the Stage
Task 2:   Communicate Effectively
Task 3:   Identify Activities
Task 4:   Organize Activities
Task 5:   Evaluate Activities
Task 6:   Establish the Priority of Effective Activities
Task 7:   Identify Activities That Do Not Support the Library's Goals
  Step 7.1:   Identify service responses that were not selected as priorities
  Step 7.2:   Identify current activities that support service responses that are not priorities
  Step 7.3:   Organize the current activities that support service responses that are not priorities
Task 8:   Identify Inefficient Activities and Steps
Task 9:   Decide How to Address Inefficient and Ineffective Activities
Task 10:   Identify Resources Available for Reallocation
Task 11:   Identify Needed Resources
Task 12:   Select and Implement Activities
Task 13:   Monitor Implementation
Task 14:   Make Change the Norm

This task is normally completed by a cross-functional team appointed by the library director. It can be started any time after the library priorities have been approved by the library board during the strategic planning process, but it is typically done after the review team has completed its work in Task 4.

Step 7.1
Identify Service Responses That Were Not Selected as Priorities

This may be the easiest step in the entire *IFR* process, but that hasn't always been the case. In the past, attempts to define services that were not priorities often became mired in semantic disagreements and philosophical debates and rarely produced useful information. One of the important benefits of the library service responses is that they provide a common vocabulary for describing library services. The service responses are detailed enough to make it clear to most staff, board members, and members of the public exactly what types of activities support each response.

Earlier in the planning process, the staff and the members of the community planning committee used the service responses as a framework for conceptualizing the library's services and identifying the library's service priorities. This makes it easy to identify services that are not priorities. They are those services described in the service responses that were *not* selected during the planning process.

Everyone involved in identifying the current library activities that support service responses that were not selected as priorities should receive a complete print copy of all of the service responses. Copy the pages that describe the service responses that were selected in one color and the pages that describe the service responses that were not selected in another color. This will make it very easy for staff to keep the two sets of service responses straight. The service responses that were selected as priorities have probably already been posted to the staff intranet. The service responses that were not selected should also be added to the intranet. Be sure that it is very clear which service responses were selected as priorities and which were not. The service responses are included in an appendix in *Strategic Planning for Results* and are available as an e-publication from the ALA.[1] A brief list of the service responses can also be found in figure 2.

Step 7.2
Identify Current Activities That Support Service Responses That Are Not Priorities

One way to think about the tasks in this chapter is to compare them to inventorying and weeding the library's collection. Most staff will agree that it is important to periodically check to be sure that the library's catalog accurately reflects the collection. They will also agree that most library materials have a finite shelf life. When the items were purchased, it was understood that they wouldn't be in the collection forever. There are any number of excellent reasons for removing an item from the collection: the information it contains is out-of-date or inaccurate, the item is damaged, the item hasn't been used within a specified time period, the library has too many copies of an item, and so on. None of these reasons in any way suggests that the item shouldn't have been purchased in the first place or that it wasn't an effective and meaningful part of the collection at one time.

The same is true for library activities. Everyone acknowledges that library users expect very different things from libraries today than they did a decade ago. Everyone also acknowledges that the tools that library staff have to do their jobs have changed significantly in that same time period. In the face of these changes, it would be unreasonable to assume that all of the activities that have been part of the library's services over the past five, or ten, or fifteen years (or longer) are still as relevant as they once were.

Who Should Be Responsible for This Step?

This is not a process that benefits from extensive staff involvement in the early stages. Staff are often too protective of the status quo to be able to look dispassionately at the library's current activities and identify those that do not support the library's priorities. However, once the initial lists of activities that do not support the library's priorities have been developed, those activities should be posted on the staff intranet and all staff should be encouraged to review them and suggest additions or modifications.

The library director should select a senior manager to facilitate the cross-functional team that will complete this step and should then work with other senior managers to identity staff from various classifications and units to serve as members of that team. The team should be large enough to be fully representative of the library staff and yet small enough to be manageable. In smaller libraries, the team could include six or nine members. In midsized libraries, the team may have nine, twelve, or fifteen members. In very large libraries, the team may have up to eighteen members. Notice that the recommended number of members is always divisible by three. This is because the team members will be working in small groups of three during their deliberations.

As always, keep things simple. In this case, that means keeping the team as small as possible, while still ensuring that all points of view are represented. Be sure to include

> Staff who serve children
>
> Staff who serve teens
>
> Staff who serve adults
>
> Staff with special areas of expertise (readers' advisory, reference, computer instruction, etc.)
>
> Professional staff
>
> Paraprofessional staff
>
> Support services staff
>
> Information technology staff
>
> Staff from small branches
>
> Staff from large branches
>
> Staff who provide special services (genealogy, local history, special needs, etc.)
>
> Staff who have worked in the library for a long time
>
> Staff who are relatively new employees

Obviously, these categories of staff are not mutually exclusive. You may appoint a new staff member with an MLS degree who serves teens. Another team member may be a longtime paraprofessional who has worked in several of the branch libraries. You will have to mix and match the needed characteristics with the available staff to find the right combination for your library.

How Much Time Will This Take?

Some processes are more likely than others to expand to fill the available time. This is such a process. The team members completing this step are only responsible for fact finding. Their only job is to identify the current activities that support service responses that are not a priority. They are not supposed to recommend how those activities should be handled, nor are they supposed to spend their time passionately defending one or more of those current activities. To continue with the earlier collection assessment analogy, the team will be completing an inventory of current activities. The decisions about what to do with those activities will be made later in Task 9. Therefore, teams in small or midsized libraries should be able to complete this step in one or two half-day meetings. Teams in large libraries may require more meetings because large libraries typically offer a more extensive list of programs and services.

How Should the Process Be Organized?

Most of the members of the team appointed to complete this task will have participated in the meetings held to identify the current activities that support the library's priorities in Step 3.2. They will remember how that process worked then and should be comfortable using the same general process again, which will make things simpler for the person facilitating the meeting.

One change in the process will be in the way that the small groups are formed. In the process described in Step 3.2, the participants divided themselves into small groups. In this process, the membership of the small groups should be predetermined before the meeting begins in order to be sure that each group includes staff with different experience and areas of expertise. The second change in the process affects the round-robin exercises. In Step 3.2, more people participated in the process and they were working with a relatively small number of goals. That allowed the review process to be done in a single round-robin exercise. In this process, a limited number of team members may be identifying current activities that support twelve or more service responses that were not selected as priorities. As a result, the round-robin process will have to be divided into segments.

If the team has been divided into three groups of three members each, the groups should work with three of the service responses that were not selected as priorities at a time (one group per service response). The facilitator will post signs with the names of those three service responses at intervals in the room, and ask each of the groups to identify current activities that support one of the three service responses. One person should record the activities on large sticky notes and write the name of the service response in the lower right corner of each sticky note (see Step 3.2 for more information on recording activities).

After ten or fifteen minutes, the facilitator will ask the groups to put their sticky notes on the wall under the appropriate service response sign and then move on to the next service response. The group that identified activities for the first service response will move on to the second service response, the group that identified activities for the second service response will move on to the third service response, and the people who identified activities for the third service response will move on to the first service response. Each group will read the current activities suggested by the preceding group and add any activities they think are missing. If the members of a group have questions about any of the activities posted by previous groups, the recorder should write each question on a sticky note and post it next to the activity. If possible, provide the recorders with sticky notes in a second color for questions. When the groups have finished making additions to the second service response, they will move on to the third and final service response in this round. Obviously, if the team is large enough to have four, five, or six groups, they can work with a corresponding number of service responses at a time.

When all of the groups have had a chance to identify current activities for all of the service responses under review in the first round-robin, the facilitator should take a few minutes to read aloud the list of activities that support one of the service responses. The focus of the review should be to answer these questions:

Does the list of current activities for this service response seem complete?

Are there activities that should be merged?

Are there activities that are too broadly defined to be accurately evaluated and, if so, should they be subdivided?

Are these activities clear enough so that people not in this meeting will understand them?

When the team members have finished reviewing each of the service responses in the first group, the facilitator will remove the sticky notes that list the current activities for each service response and put them into separate manila envelopes. As she removes the notes from the wall, she will check to make sure that the service response is written on each envelope. It is important not to mix the activities for the different service responses when they are filed. The team will then repeat the process for the next group of service responses. The process will be repeated until all groups have had a chance to identify current activities for all service responses that are not priorities and answer the questions listed above.

Will the Groups Find It Difficult to Identify Activities?

This will be a relatively easy and straightforward process for some service responses, but it may be a more difficult process for others. If "Succeed in School" is not a priority, the members of the team should have little trouble identifying the range of current activities which support that priority. The same is true for activities supporting "Build Successful Enterprises," "Create Young Readers," "Discover Your Roots," "Get Facts Fast," "Know Your Community," "Learn to Read and Write," "Make Informed Decisions," "Satisfy Curiosity," and "Stimulate Imagination." These are all traditional library services that most libraries have supported to a greater or lesser degree for years.

The groups may find it more difficult to identify activities that support "Visit a Comfortable Place" or "Connect to the Online World." These two service responses have more to do with the allocation of facility and technology resources than with staff activities. Besides, nobody thinks that the library should be an uncomfortable place or that the library will stop providing public access computers. If the groups start to have trouble identifying activities for these service responses, make a note of the problem and move on to other service responses.

Some members of the small groups also may find it difficult to identify activities that support service responses that the library has never seriously addressed. These might include "Be an Informed Citizen," "Celebrate Diversity," "Express Creativity," "Make Career Choices," "Understand How to Find, Evaluate, and Use Information," and "Welcome to the United States." If these have never been priorities for your library, there are probably few if any activities that support them. If this is the case, note it and continue the process. Remember, the key to this step—as it has been in every other step—is to keep things simple. It is impossible to identify activities that don't exist. Don't waste everyone's time trying to do so.

Step 7.3
Organize the Current Activities That Support Service Responses That Are Not Priorities

Before the activities identified in Step 7.2 can be shared with the staff and reviewed by the senior managers, they will have to be consolidated, sorted, and organized. The process used to do this will be similar to the process used to sort the current and new activities that support the goals in the strategic plan that was described in Step 4.1, with one exception. It will not be necessary to sort the activities into clusters before they are recorded.

Who Should Be Responsible for This Step?

Two or three people should be asked to manage this part of the process, and there are several ways to approach the selection of those people. You might decide to ask the same small group of staff members who were responsible for organizing the current and new activities in Step 4.1 to do the same for these activities. They understand the process, and they have agreed on a common vocabulary. However, they have already spent a lot of time on *IFR*-related tasks and may need to focus on their other duties. In addition, some of the team members who participated in the discussions in Step 7.2 may feel that one or more of the members of that team should have been asked to do this.

You could, of course, appoint two or three members of the cross-functional team that identified the activities in Step 7.2 to sort, merge, and organize those activities. These people will have participated in the discussions and will understand what was meant by each activity. However, they may not be familiar with the process used in Step 4.1, which means they may end up revisiting semantic issues that have already been resolved by the earlier group.

A third option is to appoint one member of the team that completed Step 4.1, one member of the team that completed Step 7.2, and one person who wasn't involved in either step. Such a team would not only address the drawbacks described in the first two options, but would provide an outside view of the activities that might help ensure that the final activities are described in language that will be easy for staff to understand. The downside of this choice is that it may take this group longer to complete the work because each member brings different experiences to the table.

How Should the Activities Be Organized?

Although you will be organizing activities that support twelve or more service responses, many of those service responses will only have a few activities. This means that there will be little point in trying to divide the activities into clusters. It will be much more useful to think about whether the activities are initiated by the staff or by the library's users. In other words, are they proactive or reactive?

PROACTIVE AND REACTIVE ACTIVITIES

In most libraries, when staff identify activities that support the library's goals, they focus on proactive activities. However, when staff identify activities that support service responses that are not priorities, those activities often include a mix of proactive and reactive activities. This will be an important distinction for the senior managers to consider when they are making the final determination about what to do with these activities.

> *Proactive activities.* Proactive activities are initiated and maintained by staff. Examples of proactive activities include all types of programming, in-depth collection development, pathfinders, staff-created electronic resources, exhibits or displays, instructional classes, digitizing projects, online and e-mail reference services, literacy tutoring, and class visits. Proactive activities may include

- Activities that do not support current priorities, but did support the library's previous priorities
- Activities that some staff or board members consider to be so basic that every library must offer them regardless of priorities
- Activities that were initiated by one or more enthusiastic staff members (or occasionally board members) but that have little to do with the library's priorities
- Activities that were initiated because of grant funding or donations

Reactive activities. These are activities that are initiated by the users, not a staff member. Examples of reactive activities include answering user questions, referring users to the place that has the answers they need, obtaining an item on interlibrary loan, and booking a tour.

SORT AND MERGE THE ACTIVITIES

Although the process used to organize the activities that support service responses that are not priorities will be similar to the process used to sort the activities that do support priorities in Step 4.1, there are noteworthy differences. In Step 4.1 the activities for each goal were grouped into clusters, and each cluster for each goal was recorded on a separate copy of Workform B. In this step, all of the activities for all of the service responses will be recorded on the same copy of Workform F, Identifying and Addressing Current Activities That Do Not Support Priorities.

The review team will work with the activities for one service response at a time, starting with the service response that has the most activities. They will post the sticky notes with the activities for that service response on the wall and sort them into two groups—proactive and reactive. As they post the activities, they should check to be sure that each includes the service response (or an intelligible abbreviation) and review the activities to be sure they are really activities and not steps. When all of the activities for the first service response have been organized, the team will move on to the next. When all of the activities have been reviewed, they should all have been moved into either the proactive group or the reactive group.

When the members of the review team have organized all of the activities for all of the service responses, a staff member who is skilled in working with spreadsheets should be asked to enter the results of their work into a single electronic copy of Workform F (available at http://e-learnlibraries.mrooms.net). As you can see in figure 16, the person entering the data will record the activity and the service response and indicate whether the activity is proactive or reactive. The "Decision" column (column D) will be completed by the library's senior managers in Task 9. After all of the activities for all of the service responses have been consolidated onto a single copy of Workform F, the activities should be sorted. First sort the information in column C into two groups: proactive and reactive. Then sort each of the two groups by column B ("Service Response"). As you can see, this sorting process will produce a list that begins with all of the proactive activities in order by service response, followed by a list of reactive activities in the same order.

How Can the Rest of the Staff Be Involved?

Although it would be difficult to involve all staff in the initial identification of activities that support services that are not priorities, everyone should be given an opportunity to

FIGURE 16
Workform F: Identifying and Addressing Current Activities That Do Not Support Priorities, Part I—Example

A. Activity	B. Service Response	C. Type		D. Decision	
		1. Proactive	*2. Reactive*	*1. Option*	*2. Notes*
1. Maintain a business reference desk in the largest branch	BUS	X			
2. Manage an oral history project	GEN	X			
3. Plan and present monthly genealogy classes	GEN	X			
4. Make school visits to ninth-grade classes to encourage students to use the library's resources for their homework	SCH	X			
5. Answer business reference questions	BUS		X		
6. Answer general reference questions	FACT		X		
7. Interlibrary loan items needed for research that we don't have	FACT		X		

review the organized lists of these activities. The best way to ensure that all staff who are interested have access to the lists is to post them on the staff intranet. If the full text of each of the service responses has not already been posted to the staff intranet, they should be made available as well. Consider creating blogs for each service response that was not selected as a priority in order to encourage discussion. In addition to the blogs, one staff member (either a member of the team that organized the activities or one of the senior managers) should be designated as the person to whom all suggested additions and revisions should be sent. Staff do not need to be given a long time to review the organized activities. Those who are interested will do it quickly. Those who are not interested won't do it no matter how much time you give them. A week or ten days should be more than enough time for staff review in most libraries.

At the end of the review period, the team that organized the activities should look at all of the suggested revisions and additions and modify the list of activities on Workform F as needed. They should also read through the blogs to identify questions or concerns that may need to be addressed. Perhaps some staff members found the descriptions of one or more activities to be unclear. Others may not have understood why a particular activity was included. Whenever possible, the activity descriptions should be revised to be made clearer. If that isn't possible, a note should be attached to the list so that the senior managers know there may be a problem. The revised copy of Workform F will be used in Step 9.1.

> **CAUTION**
>
> Make it clear to staff that the library's priorities have already been selected and that the service responses that were not selected as priorities will not be reconsidered.

TASK 8: IDENTIFY INEFFICIENT ACTIVITIES AND STEPS

In this task, the focus will shift from effectiveness to efficiency and productivity. The preceding task was completed by a select team of staff members. In Step 8.1, all staff members will be encouraged to think critically about the work that they do and to ask questions, identify problems, or suggest alternative methods. This will be done in unit meetings during which staff will have a chance to share their thoughts with one another. This informal process is likely to identify a wide variety of issues that may need to be addressed. In Step 8.2, a selected group of staff members will review and organize the information from the meetings held during Step 8.1.

The two steps in this task can be completed at the same time that the cross-functional team is completing Task 7.

Step 8.1
Identify Sacred Cows

Sacred cows are policies, procedures, and practices that have been immune from scrutiny or criticism, usually for no good reason. Every institution has its sacred cows, and libraries have their fair share. In fact, some people, including Karen Hyman, suggest that libraries have more than their fair share of sacred cows. Hyman's influential article "Customer Service and the Rule of 1965" appeared in the October 1999 issue of *American Libraries* and included the following sampling of sacred cows:

> Your reference staff refuses to fax responses, even when it's cheaper than reading the answer on the phone, because "it's not fair when everybody doesn't have a fax machine."
>
> Your library treats $20 videos like the Hope Diamond with user fees and special loss or damage agreements more restrictive than those for $75 books.
>
> You charge handling fees for "individual services" like interlibrary loans.
>
> You offer services that you don't publicize because too many people might want them.
>
> Your voice mail says you're busy serving library users and people should call back or come in if they want service.[2]

Reading this list of sacred cows today is depressing on a number of levels, not the least of which is that ten years after the publication of the article, all but the first are still true in many libraries. And even the first item on the list has not been resolved. It has simply been changed because of evolving technology—the issue is now e-mailing responses to reference questions instead of faxing them.

Many library sacred cows have been firmly entrenched for decades, although new ones are added regularly. In some cases, what is a sacred cow today was an efficient practice when it was initiated. When library circulation was manual, it made sense to write "copy 1" on the first copy of a title, "copy 2" on the second, and so on. This was the easiest way to maintain accurate circulation records. However, virtually every library today has an integrated library system, so there is no longer any reason to write the copy number in a book—and yet it is still done in some libraries.

If your library has abandoned this procedure, don't feel too superior too soon. There are literally dozens of other examples of policies, procedures, and practices that no longer make sense but continue. Most frontline staff are so busy doing things that they don't have a lot of time to think about why they are doing them. Does your library still have vertical files? Are they still being maintained? Does your library purchase print copies of the reference materials available to you online? Does your library still require three reviews of an item before it can be purchased? What do library users have to do to get a library card? Has anyone reviewed your technical services procedures recently?

A consultant was doing a technical services productivity review in a large public library several years ago. She was following the processing of a new DVD from the time it was unpacked until it was ready for circulation and was nearing the end of the line when she saw a staff member attach a "Be Kind—Rewind" sticker to the DVD case. She asked the staff member why she was attaching a rewind sticker to a medium that couldn't be rewound, and the staff member said "This is what they told me to do." The consultant then asked "them," in this case the processing supervisor, for an explanation. You can probably guess the answer. The library's media processing practices had been established when the library first started buying large quantities of mass-market videotapes. The stickers served a real need then—far too many users were returning videotapes that hadn't been rewound. When staff began buying DVDs, they were automatically processed using the media procedures, even though those procedures were no longer appropriate.

The procedures and practices described above made sense at one time. They had just outlived their usefulness. Some sacred cows never made any sense. Again there are dozens of examples. Both degreed librarians and paraprofessionals staff the library reference desks. Both provide the same services and answer the same types of questions. Yet in many libraries the degreed librarian is paid more and has a higher status than the paraprofessional. The public expects to have best sellers available as soon as possible, ideally at the same time they are available in bookstores. There are many ways that libraries can make this happen, including purchasing the items preprocessed and making arrangements for expedited in-house processing for high-demand items. Yet, in some libraries it can take two or even three weeks for high-demand items to be prepared to circulate.

Many sacred cows are allowed to continue because no one has asked "why?" Often the staff members who are actually responsible for doing the work have been doing it the same way since they were hired. Supervisors rarely spend much time telling new staff why they should do something. Instead they focus on helping the new employee learn how to do it. By the time the new employee is comfortable with the job, she has little reason and little incentive to wonder why. Furthermore, some supervisors actively discourage that kind of questioning.

Middle and senior managers, who are far enough removed from the pressures of day-to-day operations, may have the perspective needed to identify sacred cows, but they don't have any more time for reflection than the staff they supervise. As a result, too many library policies, procedures, and practices continue unexamined. It is in those unexamined areas that you will find time to reallocate to more effective activities.

Who Should Be Responsible for This Step?

This step has two purposes. The first, and most obvious, is to identify changes that can be made to free the staff time that will be required to implement the effective new activities to fully implement your strategic plan. Each staff member has a unique perspective on the library's current policies, procedures, and practices and all have something valuable to contribute to this part of the process.

The second purpose, while not as overt, is equally important. The entire *IFR* process is about change. It has been designed to help library managers and staff learn to respond proactively to external changes and to continually look for ways to improve services. For that to happen, all staff must be encouraged to work together to create a flexible and responsive library infrastructure. This step provides managers with an important opportunity to begin to engage the staff in this partnership.

What Process Should Be Used?

This step is intended to be relatively informal. The work typically takes place during one or more meetings at the unit level and it involves every unit in the library—both public service units and support units. The meetings will probably be facilitated by the unit managers. A second person should be designated as the recorder for each meeting. Managers in public service units may need to hold several meetings to provide all staff with opportunities to participate, but managers in support units should only need to have one meeting.

The unit manager should give each staff member a copy of the staff worksheet part of Workform G, Corralling Sacred Cows—Unit Information, to all staff a day or two before the meeting. As you can see in figure 17, the staff worksheet is a simple one-page handout with a cartoon sacred cow that includes just two questions:

> Have you ever wondered why you or your colleagues do certain things?
>
> Have you ever thought there must be a better way to accomplish some of the things that you do?

The worksheet is not at all official-looking, and the two questions are easily understood. Many staff will appreciate being given the opportunity to think about their responses to the questions for a while before having to share their perceptions with their colleagues.

The person facilitating the meeting (probably the unit manager) should begin the meeting with a very brief review of the *IFR* process to date and then go on to acknowledge what every staff member already knows: everyone is really, really busy. The facilitator will want to remind staff that they will soon be expected to assist in the implementation of new activities to support the goals in the strategic plan while continuing their work with the current activities that support those goals. Obviously there will have to be changes made somewhere to make that possible and, because staff will be affected by those changes, they are being given an opportunity to help shape the changes.

The facilitator should ask the meeting participants to move into small groups of two or three to share their preliminary answers to the first question on the sacred cow work-

SACRED COWS

Practices that have been immune from scrutiny or criticism, often for no good reason, are called *sacred cows*. Many library sacred cows have been firmly entrenched for decades, although new ones are added regularly. These practices continue because no one has asked "why?" Take a few minutes to think about the work that you and your colleagues do every day.

1. Have you ever wondered why you or your colleagues do certain things?

2. Have you ever thought there must be a better way to accomplish some of the things that you do?

---

sheet. Then she will ask the groups to report out in round-robin fashion: one sacred cow from each group until all of the groups have reported. The recorder will record the responses from each group. It will be easiest to record the discussion on a flip chart, but the recorder can also just take good notes.

During the open meetings to identify current and new activities to support the goals in the library's strategic plan (Step 3.2), staff were not encouraged to discuss their ideas. The purpose of that process was to identify a lot of possibilities quickly. In this meeting, staff *should* be encouraged to talk about each of the sacred cows as it is reported out. Often, staff will build on each other's ideas and come to a general agreement about what a sacred cow includes and how to describe it. Occasionally staff may disagree about the need to designate something as a sacred cow. One person's sacred cow may be another's cherished activity. In this exercise, everything that anyone thinks is a sacred cow is included in the report, even if not all staff members agree that it should be. The senior managers will be reviewing the lists and making the final determination about each sacred cow that is identified.

Although the primary purpose of this meeting is to identify sacred cows, staff may also want to describe the actions they think should be taken to resolve the situation. If the group reaches agreement relatively quickly, the suggested actions should be included in the notes. However, if the group is divided on the actions that should be taken, the recorder should note the options and the facilitator should encourage the members of the group to move on.

When the staff are through discussing their answers to the first question on the worksheet, the recorder should read her notes aloud to be sure that they are clear, accurate, and complete. The same process should be used to allow staff to share their responses to the second question on the worksheet. Unlike the first question, which focused on *why* things are done, the second question looks at *how* they are done. The responses to this question are likely to be more specific than the answers to the first question, and staff are

CAUTION
This is not the time to try to reach consensus on how to address sacred cows. Focus on identifying sacred cows that currently take a lot of staff time.

also more likely to have recommendations for streamlining practices or procedures they find inefficient.

When all of the staff have had an opportunity to attend one of the sacred cow meetings, the recorder and the unit manager should move on to Step 8.2.

Step 8.2
Organize the Sacred Cows

The organization process has two phases. In the first phase, each recorder and unit manager will complete the second part of Workform G for their unit. In the second phase, a small group of staff will review and consolidate all of the copies of Workform G onto Workform H, Consolidating and Sorting Sacred Cows, which will be reviewed and acted on by the library's senior managers in Task 9.

How Should the Sacred Cows from Each Unit Be Organized?

When all staff in a unit have had a chance to participate in a sacred cow meeting, the recorder and the facilitator should work together to consolidate and sort the sacred cows suggested by staff. In most cases, this shouldn't be difficult or time-consuming. In smaller units and units that provide support services, there may have been only one meeting to discuss sacred cows, and both the unit manager and the recorder attended that meeting. They will just have to transfer the minutes of that meeting onto a machine-readable copy of Workform G (available at http://e-learnlibraries.mrooms.net).

As the facilitator and the recorder transfer the minutes, they should merge related items. In the example in figure 18, the Elm Branch staff had identified several different problems associated with branch-level processing of materials. When the unit manager

---

FIGURE 18

Workform G: Corralling Sacred Cows—Unit Information—Example

I. Library Unit: Elm Branch

A. Unit Code	B. Sacred Cow (from the staff meetings)	C. Type of Sacred Cow	D. Recommended Action(s)
ELM	Storing the reserved books behind the desk so that staff have to pull them for the user	Procedure	Put the reserves on open shelves
ELM	Branch-level processing of materials. Staff members review every new book that comes to the branch and put new book labels on some and genre labels on others. Some books also get colored dots.	Practice	Discontinue the use of genre labels systemwide
ELM	It takes too long to circulate classroom collections	Procedure	
ELM	The procedure for issuing a new library card	Procedure	Stop filing paper copies of the user applications

and recorder completed Workform G for Elm Branch, they merged those problems in a single sacred cow. However, the facilitators and recorders will need to be very careful not to merge too many things together. If staff say that the procedures for issuing a new library card are too complicated, that the process used to circulate classroom collections takes too long, and that keeping holds behind the desk is inefficient, you should not merge all three of these sacred cows into the sacred cow "circulation procedures," which is so general that it means nothing. Facilitators and recorders in units that held two meetings will want to review the minutes from each meeting to identify common elements. Typically staff who work in the same unit identify similar sacred cows, which simplifies this process.

As you can see in the example in figure 18, Workform G includes columns for more information than the simple worksheet used during the staff meetings. Column A provides a place to record a unique code for the unit that identified the sacred cow. In most libraries, each unit already has such a code. If that is not the case in your library, assign each unit a unique three-letter code before the facilitators begin to enter data on to Workform G. When the sacred cows from each unit are merged into a single copy of Workform G, the data in this column will help the senior managers to know if the sacred cow is an isolated problem or a systemic issue. The sacred cows are recorded in column B of Workform G.

Column C of Workform G provides a place to indicate if the sacred cow is a policy, a procedure, or a practice. These three terms were defined in *Creating Policies for Results: From Chaos to Clarity:*

> *Policy Statement.* A brief, written statement that describes *why* the library
> does something. Policy statements are . . . approved by the library's
> governing authority.

> *Procedure.* Written step-by-step descriptions of *how* the staff will carry out
> the policy and regulations. . . . Procedures are developed by staff and
> approved by library managers. They are not reviewed by or approved
> by the library's governing authority.

> *Practice.* The way things are actually done in your library. Practice may
> or may not be supported by policy statements, regulations, and
> procedures. Practice is generally conveyed via oral tradition as part of a
> new staff member's orientation and it can become very subjective.[3]

These terms provide a useful rubric for organizing the sacred cows that come from unit meetings throughout the library and will be helpful when the senior managers meet to decide how to address the sacred cows. Column D of Workform G provides a place to record suggested ways for addressing each sacred cow. These suggestions may have come from the staff during the sacred cow meetings or they may simply reflect the unit manager's perceptions. Columns A, B, and C should be completed by every unit, but column D may be left blank.

Unit managers should transmit the completed electronic copies of Workform G for their units to their supervisors for review. The supervisors will review the forms, resolve any questions with the unit managers, and add to suggested actions in column D if they choose to. All of the electronic copies of Workform G will then be given to a small team for further review and organization.

How Should the Sacred Cows from All Library Units Be Organized?

Depending on the number of units in the library, there could be anywhere from five to fifty copies of Workform G. Before the members of the senior management team can use the information on the workforms to develop plans to streamline, reduce, or discontinue any of the sacred cows on the lists, the information will have to be put into a more manageable form using Workform H (available at http://e-learnlibraries.mrooms.net). This can probably be done by a team of two or three people, at least one of whom knows how to use a spreadsheet program.

When staff were organizing activities in Steps 4.1 and 7.3, they started with activities written on large sticky notes. In this step, the staff who are organizing the sacred cows will begin with machine-readable copies of Workform G. The process should start by consolidating all of the copies of Workform G into a single copy of Workform H (see figure 19). The data on Workform H can then be sorted by the data in column C ("Type of Sacred Cow"). This sorting process will produce a list that begins with all of the policy sacred cows and then lists all of the practice sacred cows and the procedural sacred cows.

POLICY SACRED COWS

The list of policy-related sacred cows will probably be brief. The reviewers should merge those that deal with the same policy into a single item in column B. They will include all of the unit codes from the units which identified that policy sacred cow in column A and all of the suggested actions for addressing that policy in column D.

FIGURE 19

Workform H: Consolidating and Sorting Sacred Cows—Example

A. Unit Codes	B. Sacred Cow	C. Type of Sacred Cow	D. Recommended Action(s)
CED, MAG, OAK	Issuing cards for nonresidents is too complicated	Policy	1. Clarify the policy concerning nonresident cards
ELM, PNE, CYP, OAK, CED, MAP, MAG	Branch-level processing of materials. Staff members review every new book that comes to the branch and put new book labels on some and genre labels on others. Some books also get colored dots.	Practice	1. Discontinue the use of genre labels systemwide or Have genre labels put on as part of the book's processing 2. Stop using dots
ELM, CYP, MAP	The procedure for issuing a new library card; particularly the registration process	Procedure	1. Stop filing paper copies of the user applications 2. Let users register electronically
ELM, OAK, CED, MAP	Storing the reserved books behind the circulation desk so that staff have to pull them for the user	Procedure	1. Put the reserves on open shelves 2. Eliminate reserves
OAK, MAP	It takes too long to circulate classroom collections	Procedure	1. Discontinue classroom collections

PRACTICE SACRED COWS

The second list of sacred cows will relate to library practices. The length of this list will depend on the quality, currency, and enforcement of the library's policy and procedures manual. In libraries with up-to-date written policies and procedures that are disseminated to staff and enforced by supervisors, there may be relatively few practice-related sacred cows. However, in libraries with weak and ineffectual policies and procedures or policies that are not enforced, this list may be longer than the list of procedural sacred cows.

Some of the sacred cows relating to practices will probably fall into several general categories, and the reviewers may want to list related practices sequentially. For instance, there may be a variety of sacred cows that deal with the ways that staff in different branches plan and present story programs, including registration restrictions, name tags for participants, age levels for various programs, maintaining a separate picture book story collection for staff use only, incorporating craft activities, and the classifications of the staff authorized to present story programs. While these are all clearly related, they are equally clearly separate sacred cows. If they are listed together separately but sequentially, the senior managers who will be making decisions about the sacred cows will be able to see that there are a number of related issues to address and will be able to make consistent decisions. Of course, if there are practice sacred cows that are *very* similar, they should be merged into a single item in column B. The reviewers will then include all of the unit codes from the units which identified that practice sacred cow in column A and all of the suggested actions for addressing that practice in column D.

PROCEDURAL SACRED COWS

The last list of sacred cows to consider will be those relating to procedures. There will probably be many more procedural sacred cows than policy sacred cows, but a quick review of the former will show that they too can be easily grouped into several broad categories such as circulation, processing, cataloging, and public access computing. For example, procedural sacred cows relating to circulation might include the new user registration process, storing DVDs behind the desk to reduce theft, and the way that users are notified that they have overdue items. As you can see, although these sacred cows are all related to circulation, each is a separate and distinct issue. The reviewers will want to list these items sequentially on the copy of Workform H that includes all of the procedural sacred cows, but they certainly should not be merged into a single entry.

When the people consolidating and organizing the sacred cows have completed their work, they will have one copy of Workform H sorted by policy sacred cows, sacred cows relating to library practice, and procedural sacred cows. Copies of the completed workform should be posted on the planning intranet site for staff review and discussion. You may also want to create a sacred cow blog to encourage discussion. As noted earlier, staff do not need to be given a long time to review the sacred cows. Those who are interested will do it quickly. Those who are not interested won't do it no matter how much time you give them. At the end of the review period, the people who organized the sacred cows should look at all of the suggested revisions and additions and make any needed changes on Workform H.

TASK 9: DECIDE HOW TO ADDRESS INEFFICIENT AND INEFFECTIVE ACTIVITIES

The three steps in this task will be completed by the library's senior managers. The current ineffective activities that support the library's goals were identified during Step 5.2. The current activities that do not support the library's priorities and the sacred cows were identified earlier in this chapter in Steps 7.2 and 8.1. The senior managers will want to address all of the ineffective, inefficient, and nonpriority activities at the same time. They will be making decisions that may lead to significant changes in the library, and they will want to keep the big picture in mind when making decisions about specific activities. Many library activities are interconnected, and changing one may affect others.

Under ideal circumstances, every library activity would be effective and every effective library activity would be managed in the most efficient manner possible. However, in the real world, you can only address so many problems at one time. It would be impossible—and undesirable—to simultaneously discontinue every ineffective activity that supports one of the library's goals, every activity that supports a service response not selected as a priority, and every sacred cow that exists. On the other hand, it would be just as unwise to approach this step with the assumption that only a few service tweaks and modest adjustments will be needed. That is virtually never the case.

After completing a planning process, the senior managers in one midsized library agreed that the discussion of sacred cows and the identification of ineffective activities and activities that did not support priorities had been very effective in their library. They decided that each month one of the five senior managers would be responsible for working with his or her staff to identify ineffective activities or activities that did not support one of the library's priorities or to identify a productivity issue and suggest a solution. They expected to run out of things to consider within a year. That was five years ago, and they are still finding issues to address. In this library, the process of looking for more effective and efficient ways to do things has morphed into a continuous improvement cycle. Staff are now constantly looking for better ways to do things. All of the staff have seen the benefits of the process, and they take great pride in identifying new issues to consider.

If the managers in the library described above had tried to identify and fix every issue in the library at the same time, chaos would have ensued. Public services would have been severely affected and any other projects—like this implementation process—would have been overshadowed. During Steps 9.1, 9.2, and 9.3 you will focus on identifying changes that will save significant staff time or will dramatically improve public services. You will not be trying to simultaneously solve every productivity problem in the library. You can integrate the processes described in Tasks 6, 7, and 8 into your ongoing management practices when you have completed all of the tasks and steps in *Implementing for Results*.

Step 9.1
Determine How to Address the Ineffective Activities That Support the Library's Goals

These activities have already been reviewed by the senior managers in Step 5.2. At that time, the senior managers agreed that these activities were ineffective. Therefore, these should be the easiest group of activities to address. You know that there are many more effective current or new activities that will support your priorities. You have carefully considered each of the activities once already. Now you have to decide what to do about these ineffective activities. You have eight choices for addressing each ineffective activity, which are listed in figure 20.

Based on your preliminary evaluation of these activities, the only logical action to take at this time is to eliminate or significantly reduce these activities in some or all units in order to free the resources needed for the more effective activities. However, if there are many ineffective activities that support the library's goals, you may have to decide which of them to deal with first. If that is the case, address the ineffective activities that require the most resources first and plan to deal with the other activities in the months ahead. Be sure to make a note describing why you postponed dealing with certain activities and when you intend to address them in column B of Workform E (see figure 21).

FIGURE 20

What You Can Do to Address Ineffective or Inefficient Activities or Activities That Do Not Support Your Priorities

---

A = Eliminate the activity in all units

B = Eliminate the activity in selected units

C = Continue the activity with reduced resources in all units

D = Continue the activity with reduced resources in selected units

E = Modify the activity to make it effective in all units

F = Modify the activity to make it effective in selected units

G = Continue the activity unchanged in all units

H = Continue the activity unchanged in selected units

FIGURE 21

Workform E: Addressing Current Ineffective Activities That Support Each Goal, Part II—Example

---

A. Current Ineffective Activity	B. Decision	
	1. Option	2. Notes
1. Create themed bulletin boards each month in the children's areas of all branches	D, B	Create a single generic bulletin board display in each children's area now. In next FY, remove all bulletin boards from children's areas and have the walls painted.
2. Plan and present monthly puppet shows using puppets hand-created by staff	E	Continue the puppet shows with purchased puppets that can be shared by all branches.

Step 9.2
Determine How to Address Activities
That Do Not Support Priorities

For the first time in this process, the library's senior managers will be reviewing activities that do not support the library's priorities. In other words, they already know that every activity they will be reviewing is less effective than *any* of the effective activities that support the library's priorities, including those in the C or supplemental group (Step 6.2). Therefore, the evaluation process in this step will not be a matter of deciding which of the activities that do not support priorities should be continued in some form. Instead, it will be predicated on the assumption that all of the activities that do not support priorities should be eliminated or changed from proactive activities to reactive activities, unless there is a compelling reason to continue to support them at some level.

At first glance this may seem like a small distinction, but a closer examination makes it clear how radically this differs from the current norm in most libraries. Any time a changing situation requires that staff assess current resources, the immediate reaction is to circle the wagons and protect as much as possible. Virtually everyone is more comfortable with across-the-board cuts that affect all activities equally than they are with cutting ineffective activities so that effective activities can be maintained or enhanced. The general feeling seems to be that it is better to do a lot of things adequately than to do a few things well. There are any number of problems with this feeling, but one of the most basic is that it ultimately results in providing minimal levels of support for an array of disconnected services that meet no one's needs very well. However, there is an illusion of a positive payoff from this approach for the managers who take it. By treating all activities "equally," no staff member has a reason to feel singled out or picked on. Staff won't be happy, but they will be able to take some satisfaction in knowing that everyone else is unhappy too. In other words, resource allocation decisions are made based on how staff will feel about the decisions rather than on the responsible use of public money. By contrast, when you start with the assumption that an activity that doesn't support a priority will be eliminated unless you find a reason to keep it, you will base your decisions on the merits of the activity rather than on the feelings of the staff.

What Is the Most Efficient Process to Use?

At the end of Step 7.3, the team responsible for sorting and organizing the activities that support service responses that are not priorities listed all of the activities on Workform F. The activities on that workform were sorted into two groups, proactive and reactive, and the activities in each group were sorted by the service response they supported. You have the same eight options for addressing these proactive and reactive activities that you had for addressing the ineffective activities in Step 9.1 (see figure 20).

Start by reviewing the reactive activities. This will be relatively simple and shouldn't take much time. The review of the proactive activities may require more discussion, and the final review may also take some time. It will depend on how many real changes you decided to make in the proactive activities.

EVALUATE REACTIVE ACTIVITIES

In Step 7.3, reactive activities were defined as activities that are initiated by the user, not the staff member. These activities will probably include maintaining a minimal level of

FIGURE 22

Workform F: Identifying and Addressing Current Activities That Do Not Support Priorities, Part II—Example

A. Activity	B. Service Response	C. Type		D. Decision	
		1. Proactive	2. Reactive	1. Option	2. Notes
1. Maintain a business reference desk in the largest branch	BUS	X		B	Eliminate this desk and answer business questions from the central information desk
2. Manage an oral history project	GEN	X		A	This was a grant-funded project. The grant money has been expended and the project will not be continued.
3. Plan and present monthly genealogy classes	GEN	X		D	The staff in the local history room will present quarterly genealogy classes
4. Make school visits to ninth-grade classes to encourage students to use the library's resources for their homework	SCH	X		E	Complete scheduled school visits and assess whether visits should be made to a different age group or at a different time of year. Change focus to booktalking and encouraging students to use the library to find things to read, listen to, or view for pleasure
5. Answer business reference questions	BUS		X	G	See #1
6. Answer general reference questions	FACT		X	G	No change
7. Interlibrary loan items needed for research that we don't have	FACT		X	G	No change

collection support in nonpriority subject areas and answering user questions or referring the users to a place that has the answers they need. You certainly are not going to stop answering user questions or making appropriate referrals. Unless staff are spending an inordinate amount of time on collection management in a nonpriority subject area, there is no reason to discontinue any of these reactive activities. You may be able to make minor modifications in these activities, but those modifications are unlikely to result in significant time savings, so you will probably decide to maintain them at their current levels. Make a note of your decision for each reactive activity in column D of Workform F (see figure 22).

EVALUATE PROACTIVE ACTIVITIES

Proactive activities are initiated and maintained by staff and will be more challenging to evaluate, both because most of them have at least a small audience and because some of them have strong advocates among the staff. The instructions for the review team in Step 7.3 included a list of the four main types of proactive activities. The review team was not asked to specifically cluster the proactive activities by these categories. They were simply intended to help the team members differentiate the proactive activities from the reactive

Eliminate and Streamline **99**

activities. As you review the activities that do not support the library priorities, you will want to think about these four types of activities as well. You may find that each type of proactive activity will have different challenges.

Activities that do not support current priorities, but did support the library's previous priorities. The list of proactive activities has been sorted by the service response that each activity supports, so it will be easy to identify the activities that support your previous service priorities. This may be the most difficult type of activity for you and your colleagues to evaluate. There are probably a lot of activities in this group, and those activities are likely to be so much a part of "the way we do business" that staff—including some senior managers—will find it hard to imagine that they could be eliminated, reduced, or streamlined.

However, if you are serious about finding time to implement the effective activities you have identified, you will eliminate or *significantly* reduce these activities for two reasons. First, these are going to be the activities that are currently consuming the most staff time. Second, and equally important, by eliminating or dramatically reducing these activities you are sending a clear message to staff that the library's senior managers are serious about reallocating resources to support the new strategic plan.

In some instances, the activities that you eliminate will have been superseded by activities that support the library's new priorities. For example, in Tree County the service response "Succeed in School" had been a priority, but it was not a priority in the new strategic plan. The children's librarians were still making regular school visits to encourage students to use the library's homework resources. Obviously, this is no longer an effective activity for the Tree County Public Library staff. That does not mean, however, that the children's librarians have to give up making school visits. Instead it means that the purpose and timing of the school visits will change. If one of the library's new priorities for children is "Stimulate Imagination," the school visits could focus on booktalking and encouraging children to use the library for recreational reasons. If the school visits were scheduled to be presented in the spring, they could be used to publicize the summer reading program as well.

The library may be providing some activities that support previous priorities in collaboration with other agencies or organizations. When you evaluate these activities, see if you can find a way to continue the collaboration while shifting the focus from activities that do not support your priorities to activities that do. If the Tree County Public Library had partnered with the Parent-Teacher Association to present programs on helping students use the Web to do their homework, they might continue the collaboration but shift the focus to a cosponsored family reading club that supports the service response "Stimulate Imagination."

Activities that some staff or board members consider to be so basic that every library must offer them regardless of priorities. Like the activities in the preceding group, these activities are considered by at least some staff or some board members to be "the way that we do business." The biggest difference is that these activities never supported any of the library priorities. They were initiated because someone—typically a manager or board member—believed that the activities should be an integral part of every library's services, including yours. You should always be wary of sentences that begin "Of course, every library must. . . ." There are, of course, general activities that take place in every library such as circulation, collection management, and the reactive activities described above. However, none of these general activities relates to a library's service priorities.

These activities will be easy to identify once you have addressed the activities that support the library's previous priorities. The remaining activities will be scattered among a variety of service responses. At first glance it may be difficult to see what they have in common, but closer examination often shows that some of the activities and the service responses they support reflect specific values. "Get Facts Fast" was a priority for many libraries in the past. However, some librarians and board members firmly believe that the public library should be a research center for the community. As a result, they initiated and supported activities that went well beyond the activities needed to support "Get Facts Fast." These activities have often had significant collection implications (a high percentage of the materials budget allocated to standing orders, subscriptions to esoteric periodicals, massive back files of periodicals, in-depth collections in very narrow subject areas, etc.), but they also have staffing and facility implications. Most managers would agree that very few public libraries need a librarian who specializes in nineteenth-century painting or who has spent her career building a comprehensive collection of first-person accounts of the Napoleonic Wars. However, those same managers may find it more difficult to reassign a librarian who is both interested in and knowledgeable about business resources to other duties, even though "Build Successful Enterprises" has never been a library priority. After all, shouldn't all libraries have a business specialist? The answer, of course, is *no*. The only public libraries that may need a business specialist are those in which providing services to the business community is a high priority.

Activities that support "Learn to Read and Write" and "Know Your Community" may fall into this category as well, because some people may consider them to be "basic library services." These people may believe that it is the library's responsibility to provide literacy support or to be the primary referral agency in the community regardless of the library's other priorities. For these people, the activities that support priorities that they believe have the most value will always be more important than any other activities, including the priorities in the library's strategic plan.

Although some people will have an emotional response to any changes in activities of this type, these activities cannot be considered to be immune from change. They take time and other resources away from the activities that you know are more effective. They should either be shifted from proactive to reactive or eliminated entirely.

Activities that were initiated by one or more enthusiastic staff members but that have little to do with the library's priorities. By the time you have addressed the activities in the first two groups, these activities will be easy to identify. They are often associated with a single staff member. The staff member attended a conference and returned to the library with a wonderful idea for a program. She was willing to do the work needed to initiate the activity. She may have taken it for granted that the activity would be acceptable and initiated it without formal approval, or she may have asked for and received permission. In either case, it is unlikely that anyone was thinking about the activity in the context of the library's priorities. Once the activity was initiated, it was integrated into the library's ongoing operations and never reviewed again.

This will sound familiar to managers in most public libraries, who will be all too aware of the emotional commitment the staff member has made to the activity she started. Activities of this type are so closely associated with the person who started them that any threat to the activity can be perceived as a threat to the staff member. Nevertheless, you cannot allow the wishes of a single staff member to take precedence over the responsible management of the library's resources.

Activities that were initiated because of grant funding or donations. These activities can be difficult to address. Obviously, if the activities are part of a current grant project you can't do anything about them. You might, however, take a few minutes to agree that in the future all grant applications must support one or more of the library's priorities. Activities that were initiated with grant funds but are being maintained with operational funding should be treated just like the activities in the preceding groups—they should be eliminated or dramatically reduced.

Activities supported by donations present a particular challenge. Making changes in these activities may have political implications. In most libraries, this will be a very small percentage of the activities that do not support priorities. If there are political reasons to continue these activities, you may choose to do so, but you might want to consider if the activities can be modified to support the library's current priorities.

Make a note of your decision for each proactive activity in column D of Workform F as you make the decision. See figure 22 for an example of a partially completed copy of Workform F.

REVIEW YOUR DECISIONS

When you have completed column D for every reactive and proactive activity on Workform F, ask someone to sort the list of activities one final time. This time sort the activities you plan by the code in column D.1 ("Option"). Activities with an A or B code will be eliminated in all or some units, respectively. Activities with a C or D code will be continued with reduced resources in all or some units. Activities with an E or F code will be modified to make them effective in all or some units. Activities with a G or H code will be continued unchanged in all or some units. (See the codes in figure 20.)

Compare the number of activities in each pair of codes. Which is the longest? Did your focus shift from eliminating activities to reducing or streamlining them somewhere in the process? It often does. The status quo exerts a powerful influence on everyone. When you look at all the activities you decided to reduce or modify, do the decisions you made seem logical? Consistent? Explicable? They often don't. Sometimes people get so involved in arguing about the merits of each individual activity that they lose sight of the big picture. If there are issues that remain to be addressed in the list of activities, you may want to revisit some of your decisions. How many activities do you plan to continue unchanged? Why? You *know* these activities do not support your priorities and you *know* they are using resources that you will need to implement the effective activities you identified earlier in this process.

> **CAUTION**
>
> Be prepared for negative reactions from some staff when they see the final copy of Workform F. Change is always hard, but even the people who are unhappy will appreciate being informed.

This is not the last time you will review these activities. Before you make your final decisions, you will estimate the resources that will be saved through the changes you are considering in Step 10.1. However, when you are finished with this step, you should post the copy of Workform F on the staff intranet for staff review and comment.

Step 9.3
Determine How to Address Sacred Cows

At the end of Step 8.2, all of the sacred cows that staff identified had been reviewed, merged as needed, and sorted into three groups: policies, procedures, and practices on Workform H. Before you can begin this step, a staff member who knows how to sort

FIGURE 23
Workform I: Addressing Sacred Cows—Example

I. Type of Sacred Cow: Procedures

A. Unit Codes	B. Sacred Cow	C. Recommended Action(s)	D. Decision	
			1. Option	2. Notes
ELM, CYP, MAP	The procedure for issuing a new library card; particularly the registration process	1. Stop filing paper copies of the user applications 2. Let users register electronically	A, E	1. Stop filing paper copies of the user applications immediately 2. Revise procedures to let users register electronically
ELM, OAK, CED, MAP	Storing the reserved books behind the circulation desk so that staff have to pull them for the user	1. Put the reserves on open shelves 2. Eliminate reserves	E	1. Revise procedures to put the reserves on open shelves while ensuring patron confidentiality
OAK, MAP	It takes too long to circulate classroom collections	1. Discontinue classroom collections	E	1. Gather more information from children's librarians and circulation attendants

and move data in an Excel worksheet should be asked to move the data for each of the three types of sacred cows to a separate copy of Workform I, Addressing Sacred Cows (see figure 23).

You will use different processes to resolve each of these types of sacred cows. Policies and procedures are both officially sanctioned by the library, and any modification of them will require formal action. The library board will have to be involved in addressing sacred cows that are policies. Procedural changes will be made by formally revising the written step-by-step descriptions that tell staff how to do something. Sacred cows that deal with practices, however, may not be as straightforward. These are often informal actions, and they will have to be addressed in different ways, depending on the sacred cow. The options range from "just say no" to codifying the practice into an approved and efficient procedure.

What Factors Should Be Considered during the Review?

Every library's sacred cows are a little different, and the solutions for addressing those sacred cows will be different as well. As you review the list of sacred cows, keep these things in mind.

Is it really a sacred cow? There is far from universal agreement on the library activities that should be considered sacred cows. Staff-generated lists of sacred cows often include such diverse activities as the summer reading program, overdue fines, allowing patron-placed reserves, and purchasing many copies of high-demand items. The senior managers in most libraries wouldn't consider any of these sacred cows. Just because someone on the staff thinks something is a sacred cow doesn't make it true.

Does this take a lot of staff time? This question applies to all three types of sacred cows, but it is often particularly applicable to procedures and practices. You can't change everything all at once, so you should focus first on addressing sacred cows that take significant amounts of staff time. Be careful not to fall into the trap of thinking that transactions that only take a few seconds or minutes are automatically less time-consuming than transactions that take an hour or more. Time is not measured by looking at the time of an individual transaction. It is measured by calculating the total time for all of those transactions within a period of time.

Start by considering how often something occurs. It clearly makes sense to give priority to addressing the sacred cows that require staff to do something many, many times in a given month. If a library that circulates 20,000 DVD items in a month can reduce the amount of time required for each transaction by just one minute, it will result in a savings of 333 hours per month. That is a *lot* of time. If the current library procedures require the DVDs to be stored in a room behind the circulation desk and retrieved by the circulation staff, the time that could be saved is significant.

In a library that purchases 20,000 new books per year, it may take 45 seconds to stamp the library's name in three or four places, including the "secret page." If the book is just stamped once, the amount of time required for each transaction could be reduced by at least 25 seconds, resulting in an annual savings of nearly 140 hours.

Consider how many staff are affected by the sacred cow. Staff may spend a total of an hour filling out paperwork to get approval to have something printed, but there are probably no more than four or five print requests a month and a limited number of staff are affected. On the other hand, it may take just two minutes to affix labels and dots to a new book in a branch, but it involves the staff in every branch. If each branch gets 500 new books a month, that is a total of nearly 17 hours per branch per month. In a library with eight branches, this activity takes 136 hours a month, or nearly one full-time equivalent (FTE).

Does this sacred cow affect the quality of the services the public receives? Some sacred cows require a lot of staff time behind the scenes, but don't affect the services the public receives. Others affect the public as much or more than the staff. The policies, procedures, and in some cases practices related to issuing library cards range from simple and straightforward in some libraries to overcomplicated and time-consuming in others. Think about the process a user goes through in your library to apply for a new card. How many pieces of ID are required? What types of ID are acceptable? Does the user have to have an ID that verifies both his identity and his address? What are the policies for youth cards? How long is the application form that must be completed by the user? Can the application form be completed electronically? How long does it take to get a new library card "approved"? Are there restrictions on the number of items that can be checked out on the day the application was made? What are the rules for nonresidents? What happens if the user lost his card and wants a replacement?

What Is the Most Efficient Process to Use?

You will use the same codes to indicate how you plan to address sacred cows that you used earlier when reviewing ineffective activities that support the library's goals and activities that support service responses that are not a priority (see figure 20). The recommended default choice for addressing the ineffective activities and those activities that don't support priorities was to eliminate or significantly reduce them. You may be able to eliminate or reduce a few practice sacred cows, but you are more likely to be streamlining policies and procedures rather than eliminating or reducing them. One of the procedural sacred cows in figure 23 deals with issuing new cards. The problem is that the process is manual and that staff are required to keep paper copies of the users' registration forms on file. The solution is to change the procedures for issuing new cards, not to stop issuing new cards or to try to issue fewer new cards.

POLICY SACRED COWS

You can't resolve policy sacred cows in this review process. All you can do is make a decision to review the policies in question and work with the members of the library board to make the necessary revisions. If the organizational competencies you identified earlier include reviewing and revising your policies, make a note to address the policies identified in the sacred cow process early in the review. If you didn't include addressing policies in your organizational competencies, you should do so now.

SACRED COWS RELATING TO LIBRARY PRACTICES

These sacred cows often offer the best opportunity for the senior managers to make an immediate impact. By definition, library practices are things that have not been officially sanctioned by a policy or procedure. Therefore, at least some of them should be able to be summarily stopped. The discussion earlier about the dots and labels that were affixed to books in the branches of the Tree County Library is an excellent example of a practice that can be discontinued.

However, you will need to be careful about making wholesale changes. There is a limit to how many changes can be made at once. Depending on how many practice-related sacred cows there are in your library, you may have to address some of them now and plan to address others later after the major changes resulting from the *IFR* process have been implemented.

There are at least three criteria to consider when deciding which practice sacred cows to address first. You will certainly want to discontinue every practice that is in direct contradiction to a current library policy or procedure. You will also want to streamline, reduce, or eliminate the practices that most staff dislike—and the more strongly the staff feel, the more quickly you should take action. Finally, you will want to address those practices that take the most time. You may find that some of these are the same practices that many staff dislike, but it is just as possible that these will be practices that staff like and support. While it is important to address practices that most staff dislike, you cannot let time-consuming and inefficient practices continue just because some staff support them.

PROCEDURAL SACRED COWS

Many procedural sacred cows are relatively complicated. The actual sacred cow may be a substep or even a substep of a substep of an activity. You can't just stop one part of a larger process without affecting the rest of the process. The procedural sacred cows were grouped by similarity on Workform I. Circulation sacred cows were listed sequentially, as were processing sacred cows, cataloging sacred cows, maintenance sacred cows, and so on. Some libraries ask a committee of circulation attendants to make recommendations for addressing the circulation sacred cows, a committee of processing staff to recommend ways to streamline the processing sacred cows, and so on. The important thing now is for the senior managers to agree that the procedures should be studied and to make plans to initiate the needed reviews.

When all of the sacred cows have been reviewed and the senior managers have made their preliminary decisions about how to address each one, those decisions should be recorded on the appropriate copies of Workform I and the completed workforms should be posted on the staff intranet.

What's Next?

In this chapter, you and your colleagues have taken the time to systematically review and identify activities that need to be eliminated, reduced, or streamlined in order to provide the resources needed to implement the activities that you agreed would be effective earlier in this process. In the next chapter, you will work with staff to estimate specifically how many resources will be made available as a result of the preliminary decisions you made during the tasks in this chapter. You will also estimate how many resources will be required to implement the most essential of your effective activities, and you will make the final selection of activities for this planning cycle.

Key Points to Remember

There is not enough time available for staff to continue to do everything they have always done in the way they have always done it *and* to implement the new activities needed to support the goals in the library's strategic plan.

Identifying the many library activities that do not support the library's priorities can be difficult for some staff. It requires honest self-appraisal, clear-sighted pragmatism, and a willingness to set the stage for change.

It is easy to identify library services that are not priorities—they are described in the library service responses that were not selected during the planning process.

In the face of all the changes that have affected libraries in the past decade, it would be unreasonable to assume that every activity that has been a part of the library's services for the past five, ten, or fifteen years is still as relevant as it once was.

There are two kinds of activities: reactive and proactive. Reactive activities are initiated by the user. Proactive activities are initiated by the staff. You can eliminate or reduce proactive activities, but most reactive activities will continue unchanged.

Sacred cows are policies, procedures, or practices that have been immune from scrutiny, usually for no good reason. Most sacred cows are allowed to continue because no one has asked "why?"

One person's sacred cow may be another's cherished activity.

The entire *IFR* process is about change. It has been designed to help library managers and staff learn to respond proactively to external changes and to continually look for ways to improve services. This means that all staff will have to work together to create a flexible and responsive library infrastructure.

It would be impossible—and undesirable—to simultaneously discontinue every ineffective activity that supports one of the library's goals, every activity that does not support a priority, and every sacred cow.

You cannot allow staff feelings to take precedence over the responsible management of the library's resources.

Revisit your communication plan at the beginning of each task to be sure that you are keeping all stakeholders informed.

Notes

1. Sandra Nelson and June Garcia, *Public Library Service Responses* (Chicago: American Library Association, 2007).
2. Karen Hyman, "Customer Service and the Rule of 1965," *American Libraries,* October 1999, 54–57.
3. Sandra Nelson and June Garcia, *Creating Policies for Results: From Chaos to Clarity* (Chicago: American Library Association, 2003), 4.

Chapter 5

Consider Time and Other Resources

It was a matter of reallocating resources to focus on high-priority projects.—Doyle Karr

MILESTONES

By the time you finish this chapter you will be able to

- determine how much staff time will be available for reallocation in each unit if an activity is eliminated, reduced, or streamlined
- identify the collection, facility, and technology resources that will be available for reallocation in each unit if an activity is eliminated, reduced, or streamlined
- revise the library's materials budget to support the goals in the strategic plan
- determine the resources that will be required in each unit to implement new or significantly expanded activities
- make use of the other books in the Results series to determine the resources required to implement complex activities
- organize and summarize the unit resource allocation information so that it can be used to make final decisions

Latisha is the children's services coordinator for the Tree County Public Library, and she has been actively engaged in the implementation process from the beginning. Initially, she was skeptical about having staff involved in the identification and review of activities, but as the process continued she became a true believer. Before meetings were held to identify the current and potential activities that supported the library's goals (Steps 3.2 and 3.3), Latisha and the youth services staff looked at the children's programs and services offered by dozens of other libraries as well as other agencies that serve children. Their research resulted in many new ideas which they shared during the meetings. A number of the youth services ideas met all three effectiveness criteria in Step 5.2, and the senior managers included some of the most exciting of those ideas on the list of essential activities with the highest priority (Step 6.2). Latisha felt that all of the hard work that she and the children's staff had done would pay big dividends, and she was looking forward to reviewing the high-priority activities with the staff during the next youth services meeting.

Before the youth services meeting, Latisha was helping Tanya, the children's librarian from Elm Branch, write a script for a new holiday puppet program. As they worked, Latisha started talking about how much she was looking forward to implementing some of the exciting new activities. Tanya agreed, but with less enthusiasm than Latisha had expected. Latisha thought that Tanya was just upset about some of the proposed changes, and that was certainly a part of the problem. The puppet show that Latisha and Tanya were developing would be the first puppet show to be presented with commercial puppets rather than the specially designed puppets that Tanya and a small group of children's librarians had been creating for many years. Tanya and her fellow puppet-makers loved making puppets and were firmly convinced that their handmade puppets were far superior to anything that could be purchased. The senior managers had decided in Step 9.1 that the time spent making the puppets should be reallocated to support essential activities, and they had agreed that there was no reason to wait to implement their decision. Tanya and her fellow puppeteers had already been informed that the library system would be purchasing puppets for future puppet shows, and Tanya was not happy to be giving up an activity she had found both meaningful and rewarding.

As they continued to talk, Latisha realized that although Tanya was upset about some of the activities that were scheduled to be eliminated, she was also excited about a number of the new children's activities that were being planned—excited and more than a little frightened. Tanya's biggest concern was how she was going to find the time to actually do any of the exciting new activities. She said that she was already way too busy. When Latisha reminded Tanya about the activities such as making puppets that were being eliminated, Tanya said she didn't think that the couple of hours a month she spent making puppets were going to make much difference in her workload. Tanya knew that some of the operational efficiencies that were going to be instituted systemwide would save her a little time, but she doubted that any of the changes would be enough to make a real difference in the time she had available for new things. Latisha knew that Tanya's feelings were shared by other staff. The grapevine had been in overdrive since the planning process began, and it was currently focused on all of the "worst-case scenarios" that might result from discontinuing or reducing some long-standing activities and adding new activities to a staff that already felt overburdened.

Latisha was still thinking about her conversation with Tanya when she went to lunch with two of her good friends, both of whom were branch librarians. Latisha hoped that her friends would be able to suggest some ways to address the staff's anxiety about change, but instead she discovered that they too had concerns. The branch managers said: "The senior managers don't know what it is like to serve the public day in and day out, and they can't make informed decisions about the amount of time that activities take. Furthermore, they have no idea how the public is going to react to the changes they are making. *We* are going to have to deal with all of the problems that result from their decisions." Latisha left her lunch feeling even more concerned about the next steps in the process than she had been when the lunch began.

The feelings that Tanya and the branch managers shared with Latisha are not unique to the Tree County Public Library. Similar conversations will be replicated in every library that goes through the *IFR* process. By this point in the process, even the most disengaged staff members will have realized that the senior managers are not just talking about change. They are already on the road to making changes. This can be frightening on several levels. Intellectually, staff will know that they may have to learn new skills and do new things. The comfortable routines of their jobs will be disrupted. Emotionally, staff may worry about their ability to learn new skills, about the level of support they will be given during the changes, and about the public's reactions to the changes. Some staff will be angry because activities that they have spent years providing are being eliminated, reduced, or streamlined. No matter how many times they are told that the decisions were based on the public's changing needs, for some staff it will still feel like a personal rejection.

This is a dangerous time in the process. The preparatory work has been done, but few decisions have been made. If there is any staff resistance to the process (and there will be), it will be getting stronger as information about possible changes becomes public. Some library directors might be tempted to try to placate the staff. They might decide to wait for a while before making any decisions in order to "give the staff more time to adjust." However, extending the time line will have the opposite effect. One of the biggest reasons for staff resistance is the fear of the unknown. Making people wait longer for final decisions will increase resistance, not reduce it. Furthermore, library directors who extend the time line often end up extending it to infinity. The decisions that need to be made aren't going to be any easier next week or next month or next year. By the time a library reaches this part of the *IFR* process, everyone will have invested a great deal of time, energy, and thought in the process. If the library director does not complete the process, all of that work will be wasted—and the director's credibility will be seriously damaged.

This is also a time in the process when the senior managers may start to feel a little overwhelmed. In many libraries, the implementation process started immediately after the planning process concluded, which means that the senior managers have now been working on these projects for five or six months. It would be one thing if this was the only thing that the senior managers had to do, but unfortunately all of their other responsibilities continued throughout the process. Everyone has been working very hard for a long time.

Although the process is reaching an end, the amount of work to be done in the tasks in this chapter can seem daunting. Unlike previous tasks, the tasks in this chapter focus on resource allocation and will require that the senior managers gather and analyze data about the time associated with performing specific activities. Many senior managers have had little experience with this kind of detailed time analysis. In the past, new activities were implemented with only a limited idea of the time that would be required. Staff were generally expected to perform the new activities *in addition to* their current activities, rather than *in place of* their regular activities. This practice, of course, resulted in staff being assigned to do far more work than they could ever accomplish. Most managers would agree that the previous practice doesn't work, particularly after completing the earlier tasks in the *IFR* process. However, some managers may be tempted to return to the "good old days" rather than spending the time and energy needed to gather and analyze cost data.

Fortunately, the actual work to be done in this chapter is far less time-consuming than it may appear to be initially. It is relatively easy to determine the resources that have been allocated to support current activities. Even the amount of time staff spend on those activities can be estimated quickly through sampling. It will not be much more difficult to estimate the resources required for the majority of the new activities than it will be to estimate the resources allocated to current activities. It can be more challenging to identify the resources that will be needed for complex new activities, but very few libraries will have more than five or six new activities that require serious data collection, and many libraries will have fewer. In fact, most libraries will be implementing fewer than twenty new or significantly expanded activities in total. So while the tasks in this chapter may seem to be intimidating, they will be considerably easier to manage than you might think.

Getting Started

During Task 10, senior managers will work with unit managers and frontline staff to estimate the resources that will be saved by reducing or discontinuing ineffective activities that support the library's goals and activities that don't support the library's priorities, and by streamlining or eliminating sacred cows. Then, in Task 11, the unit managers and frontline staff will estimate the resources that will be required to implement both the current and new activities that have the highest priority. Finally, they will summarize the information they have gathered so that the senior managers can use it to make the final decisions about activities.

Involving unit managers and frontline staff in the discussions of needed and available resources should make everyone more familiar with—and therefore more comfortable about—the final decisions when they are made. It is also an acknowledgment that the people who actually do the work are in the best position to estimate how much time that work takes.

TASK 10: IDENTIFY RESOURCES AVAILABLE FOR REALLOCATION

Step 10.1 will be managed by a data coordinator appointed by the library director and will involve staff throughout the library. Step 10.2 will be completed by the staff who allocate the library's materials budget.

Steps 10.1 and 10.2 should be started as soon as possible after the effective activities have been prioritized (Step 6.2) and decisions have been made about activities to reduce, streamline, or eliminate (Task 9). The two steps in this task can be completed at the same time.

Step 10.1
Identify Resources Available for Reallocation in Each Unit

Thus far, the *IFR* process has focused almost exclusively on evaluating the effectiveness of activities. The senior managers included a very general assessment of the resource implications of their decisions during Step 6.2, when they were prioritizing the effective activities, and again in Task 9, when they were deciding what activities to reduce, eliminate, or streamline. Those are the only two instances in which the resource implications of the activities under review have been considered. Obviously, you can't make final decisions about the library's activities without a more detailed understanding of the resources that are currently allocated to support effective activities and the resources that can be made available to be reallocated to new activities.

When you are considering the resource implications of adding, eliminating, or changing activities, you will be looking at four resources: staff, collections, facilities, and technology, which are described in figure 24. You will notice that money is not on the list of resources. In this context, money is *not* a library resource. Money provides the means for you to pay for staff with the knowledge, skills, and abilities needed to implement essential activities; to purchase and maintain collections; to build and maintain facilities and equipment; and to purchase and maintain computer hardware, software, and networks. The money, in and of itself, has no value to the library's users. It is the resources that are purchased with the money that provide the value.

Who Should Be Responsible for This Step?

The library director should appoint one manager as the data coordinator for this step. Much of the information on the workforms that will be used to estimate the resource implications of the activities that will be eliminated, reduced, or streamlined will be collected and recorded by the data coordinator. The data coordinator will need four skills. She will need to be organized, she will need to be analytical, she will need to be familiar with library operations, and she will need to be an effective communicator.

FIGURE 24

Types of Resources in Libraries

Staff (Knowledge, Skills, and Abilities)

Knowledge refers to the information and concepts acquired through formal education and job experience. *Skills* are the manual and mental capabilities acquired through training and work experience, the application of knowledge gained through education or training, and practical experience. *Abilities* are the natural talents, capacities, and aptitudes possessed by employees.

- Full-time/part-time
- Full-time equivalent (FTE)
- Classification

Collection (Print, Media, and Electronic Resources)

Staff in libraries in which a service response is a priority will develop collections in much greater depth or breadth than would be the case in libraries in which the service response is not a priority. Libraries will provide materials in the languages spoken by the people within the target audience and will purchase materials in the formats most appropriate for their community and their service priorities.

- Adult
- Teen
- Children

Facility (Space, Furniture, and Equipment)

Space describes an area of the library building that has a common usage or purpose. *Furniture and equipment* are the physical items within the structure. All library facilities should be in full compliance with the provisions of the Americans with Disabilities Act.

- Total space
- Space by function
- Lighting, HVAC, wiring, etc.
- Shelving
- Storage

Technology (Hardware, Software, Networks, and Telecommunications)

Hardware includes computer workstations, servers, and other technologies such as scanners, self-check machines, and printers. *Software* includes desktop operating systems and unique programs that support the service responses (for example, literacy tutoring programs for Learn to Read and Write). A *network* is a group of interconnected computers. *Telecommunications* refers to technology for the transmission of data. All libraries will provide public access to the Internet and have sufficient bandwidth to manage the online services provided. The library will have a web page. All library technology will be in full compliance with the provisions of the Americans with Disabilities Act.

The data coordinator will be responsible for gathering existing information and for managing the sampling process that will be done to determine the amount of time it takes to do something (more about this later). The data coordinator will have to be able to explain to the unit managers the source of each of the data elements recorded on the workforms. She will have to be able to explain what information the unit managers will be expected to report and how that information should be reported, which requires both communications skills and a clear understanding of the work that is done in the library's units. Finally, she will be responsible for reviewing the information that is reported on the workforms and identifying and resolving anomalies. The data coordinator may want to ask one or two people to work with her on this task. It would certainly be helpful to have someone with data entry and word processing skills participate in this process.

How Should the Unit Managers Be Brought into the Resource Allocation Process?

In Task 9, you decided to eliminate some activities entirely and to reduce or streamline others. You did this so that you could free staff time and other resources to implement the essential activities needed to reach the targets in the objectives of your strategic plan. The decisions in Task 9 were made by senior managers who may or may not have been familiar enough with the activities under review to make informed estimates about potential time savings. Even if the estimates the senior managers made were right on target, unit managers and frontline staff may be skeptical until they see actual data. Therefore, this step starts with a meeting of unit managers and ends with a second meeting of the same managers.

The unit managers and their staff will have seen the list of activities that senior managers agree should be eliminated, reduced, or streamlined, but they were not participants in the discussions that led to those decisions. The frontline staff will undoubtedly have questions about some of the decisions that were made, and the unit managers themselves may have concerns. Therefore, the work in this task should begin with a meeting of all unit managers. This meeting has two purposes. The first is to explain the decisions to eliminate, reduce, or streamline ineffective or inefficient activities. The second is to introduce the work that will be done in this step and to make sure that the unit managers understand the crucial role they will play in that work.

This meeting will probably be the first opportunity the library director has had to explain the reasons for the decisions made during Task 9 and the first time the unit managers have been given a chance to ask questions. The meeting should begin with a review of each of the activities that the senior managers decided to eliminate, reduce, or streamline. The director should briefly explain the rationale for each decision and answer any questions that the unit managers have.

When all of the activities that the senior managers decided to eliminate, reduce, or streamline have been discussed, the director can ask the unit managers if they have questions about other activities or sacred cows that are not scheduled to be changed. If there are questions that have to do with an activity that senior managers decided specifically not to change, the director can explain why. If there are questions that have to do with activities or sacred cows that were not considered by the senior managers, those activities or sacred cows can be noted and reviewed by the senior managers after the meeting.

When everyone has had a chance to discuss the activities that will be eliminated, reduced, or streamlined, the director will want to remind the unit managers that these changes are being made so that the resources currently used to support them can be reallocated to more effective activities. The director should acknowledge the concerns that staff have expressed about finding the time to implement the essential new activities, and she can use that as an introduction to a brief description of the process that will be used to collect information about the staff time that will be made available as a result of the planned changes.

Of course, most of the activities that will be eliminated, reduced, or streamlined use other resources as well, and the director will briefly discuss the collection, facility, and technology resource implications of the decisions to eliminate, reduce, or streamline some activities. The director will also want to point out that in some instances activities that are being reduced or streamlined are being automated. Those activities might require additional facility or technology resources, and so information about the additional resources that will be required if an activity is reduced or streamlined will also be collected. Finally, the director should tell the unit managers who will be coordinating the data collection process.

The data collection coordinator should distribute and briefly review each of the four workforms that will be used to record the information that is collected about activities

> **CAUTION**
>
> This is not the time for unit managers to protest decisions that were made or to lobby to continue activities that will be eliminated, reduced, or streamlined.

that are being eliminated, reduced, or streamlined (Workforms J, K, L, and M), the workform that will be used to estimate the resources required for new or expanded activities (Workform O), and the three workforms that will be used to summarize that information (Workforms N, P, and Q). All of these workforms are discussed in detail later in this chapter. The data collection coordinator should briefly explain the process that will be used to collect and record the data and be sure that the unit managers understand their roles in that process.

Staff time is the largest and most critical resource in most libraries, and each of the four workforms used to collect and record data starts by estimating the amount of time that will be available for reallocation if an activity is eliminated, reduced, or streamlined. The information about the time that will be available will be based on systemwide averages of the time required to complete each of the activities or certain steps within the activities. If the activity is always performed by staff in the same classification, the unit managers will not have to provide any information about staff resources. If the activity is performed by staff in different classifications, the unit managers will be asked to indicate the classifications of employees who perform the activity in their units.

What Data Will Be Needed to Determine the Amount of Time Saved?

Every library activity requires some staff time, and nothing gets done unless someone does it. By the end of Task 9, the senior managers had identified the activities to be eliminated, reduced, or streamlined in some way. You will consider each of the activities that you plan to eliminate, reduce, or streamline separately in order to determine the amount of staff time that will be made available as a result of the changes made in that activity.

This probably sounds like an enormous amount of work, but as you will see, it really isn't. In fact, in some cases you already have the information needed to estimate time savings. If one paraprofessional librarian has been assigned to staff a business reference desk eight hours a day and you decide to eliminate that desk, it is not hard to figure out that you will save eight hours of paraprofessional staff time a day. However, if the time that will be saved is not as obvious as that, you will need to know the answers to six questions about each activity that you plan to eliminate, reduce, or streamline in order to make an informed estimate:

1. Is this activity being modified or eliminated, and if it is being modified, what modifications are being made?
2. What level of staff is completing the activity or step?
3. Are all of the steps in this activity completed by the same level of staff?
4. What are the starting and ending points of an instance of this activity or step?
5. How long does it take to complete a single instance of the activity or step?
6. How many times is the activity or step repeated in a specified time period?

As you can see from these questions, it will not be as difficult to determine the amount of time you will save by eliminating, reducing, or streamlining activities as you might have thought it would be. You already know the answers to the first four questions for every activity that you plan to eliminate, reduce, or streamline, and you know the answer to the sixth question for many of those activities. You will only have to collect the information needed to answer the fifth question about each ineffective or inefficient activity and the sixth for those activities for which that information is not readily available. There is more information about each of these six questions in the following sections.

IS THIS ACTIVITY BEING ELIMINATED OR MODIFIED, AND IF IT IS BEING MODIFIED, WHAT MODIFICATIONS ARE BEING MADE?

This information comes from the decisions made by the end of Task 9. If you plan to eliminate an activity, all of the staff time spent on that activity will be available for reallocation. You will only have to collect information about the time it takes to complete the entire activity to determine how much time will be saved. In contrast, if you plan to modify an activity, you typically plan to eliminate or streamline some of the steps within that activity. You will save the time that had been spent on the steps you modify but will continue to spend time on the remaining steps. Therefore, when you collect time information for activities that will be modified, you will have to determine how much time will be saved in each step that will be reduced or eliminated.

WHAT LEVEL OF STAFF IS COMPLETING THE ACTIVITY OR STEP?

The next thing you need to know is which staff members are spending their time completing the activity being eliminated, reduced, or streamlined. You won't need to know their names, but you will need to know their classifications, and that information is easily obtainable from the managers in the units in which the activity occurs.

Staff members are not all interchangeable. Think about the current and new activities on your list of essential activities. Few of those activities can be completed by a generic staff person. The staff who are responsible for each activity or step within the activity will require different knowledge, skills, and abilities. Let's say that when the managers in Tree County complete the analysis of the time that will be saved by eliminating or reducing activities, they find that the Elm Branch will have thirty-five hours of staff time a month available for reallocation. Therefore, staff at the Elm Branch could spend additional time on some of the new high-priority activities. Perhaps the highest-priority activities in Tree County are youth-related, and so the managers decide that the Elm Branch staff should add thirty-five hours of youth services activities to their work plans. Then they discover that only five of the thirty hours of staff time that are available for reallocation in the Elm Branch are from the youth services staff. The other thirty hours come from a combination of adult services and circulation staff. The Elm Branch manager may be able to cross-train these staff to do some youth activities, but she can't turn them all into youth services providers, nor should she.

If the senior managers used the criteria described in Step 6.1 to select the activities with the highest priority, they should have selected activities that serve all of the target audiences. When the Elm Branch manager actually implements the activities with the highest priority, she will be reallocating the time of staff in the appropriate classifications and with the necessary skills to be able to do the work required to implement each of those high-priority activities.

ARE ALL OF THE STEPS IN THIS ACTIVITY COMPLETED BY THE SAME LEVEL OF STAFF?

While many activities are completed by staff with the same classification, some activities may have to be completed by different levels of staff. Planning and presenting a program on Civil War armaments may require the coordinated efforts of the librarian who organizes and presents the program, the marketing staff who publicize the program, the support staff who prepare the handouts used during the program, the pages who pull the books to be used in a display associated with the program, and the custodial staff who set up the meeting room for the program and clean up afterward. For activities such as this one, you will work with the unit managers or the staff members who are responsible for the activity to list the steps within the activity and to identify the classification of the staff completing each step.

WHAT ARE THE STARTING AND ENDING POINTS OF AN INSTANCE OF THIS ACTIVITY OR STEP?

One day during a Tree County Public Library branch managers' meeting, a manager asked her colleagues how long it took in their branches to get returned items back on the shelves. Although several managers could make guesstimates, no one knew for sure. The branch managers agreed to gather the information needed to determine the average time it took to reshelve items and report back at the next branch managers' meeting. When the branch managers reported their findings, they were amazed by the differences in each branch. They couldn't imagine why it would take over three times as long to shelve an item in the Cypress Branch as it would in the Pine Branch.

Gradually, as they talked it became clear that although they all thought they were gathering information about the same activity, each of them interpreted the activity differently. The Cypress Branch manager started timing the activity at the point that staff went out to empty the book drop. The Pine Branch manager started timing the activity when a page took a book truck of items that had been presorted to the shelves. Branch managers in several other branches started timing when items were placed on the book truck to be sorted. The Maple Branch manager left newly returned items on the book trucks near the circulation desk for twenty-four hours, and reported that over half were recirculated without ever being reshelved.

This story illustrates the biggest potential problem with the time data you collect: if the data to be collected are not clearly defined, they won't be consistent. Fortunately, this is one of those rare instances in which the biggest potential problem in a process has a very simple solution: someone will have to specifically identify the starting and ending points of the activity or step *before the data are collected*. If they don't, your data will be as useless as the shelving data gathered by the Tree County branch librarians.

HOW LONG DOES IT TAKE TO COMPLETE A SINGLE INSTANCE OF THE ACTIVITY OR STEP?

You will almost always have to collect data to answer this question, and that will take time. However, it shouldn't take a lot of time. You don't need absolutely statistically valid data for this process. You simply need reasonably accurate estimates. You obtain these estimates by collecting a sampling of data from several units about the time required to complete a single instance of an activity or step and averaging that data to determine the systemwide average time per instance that you will use as the basis for decision making. Senior managers in most libraries will have identified fewer than twenty activities to eliminate or streamline, and in many cases that number will be far fewer. It shouldn't take more than a week or two to collect the time data needed for that number of activities.

Sampling is a process by which a subset of information is used to represent the whole universe of that information. In this context, this means that instead of asking every single staff member to record exactly how much time it takes to perform an activity or step, you will ask a few staff members from different units to keep track of their time and use the average of their time as the system average. Time sampling will be relatively simple for activities that are performed by staff in the same classification and are being eliminated, and slightly more complex for activities that are being modified or are performed by staff from different classifications. The important thing to remember in each instance is to review the information gathered through sampling carefully and address any discrepancies. Each of these issues is discussed in the following sections.

Sampling to determine the time saved by eliminating an activity performed by one classification of staff. You will, of course, need to discuss the activities with the people who actually do them in order to determine the beginning and ending points of the activity being eliminated. To determine the time required for repetitive tasks completed by one classification of staff, ask two or three staff members from two or three different units to record the time they start the activity, the time they finish the activity, and the number of units of the activity that were completed in that time. Divide the time spent on the activity by the number of units of the activity that were produced by each person in your sample to determine the average time it took each staff member to complete one instance of the activity. If the time per instance figures are reasonably consistent, average them to determine the system time per instance.

For example, if you are trying to find out how much time branch staff in Tree County are spending putting dots and labels on books, you would ask two or three staff members in different branches to record the time they begin to put labels and dots on a stack of books and the time they finish adding the labels to the books in the stack. You would then divide the total times for each staff member by the total number of books she labeled in that time. Let's say that Nancy completed 15 books in 22 minutes, Julie completed 12 books in 17 minutes, and Jeanne completed 20 books in 31 minutes. Nancy's average time per book was 1.37 minutes, Julie's average was 1.41 minutes, and Jeanne's average was 1.55. If you average these three figures, you get a systemwide average time per instance of 1.44 minutes. Is this number statistically valid? No. Is this number accurate enough to be used to estimate the amount of time that will be saved by having staff stop putting extra dots and labels on books in the branches? Absolutely.

The time required for some activities may be spread over several days or even several weeks. In an earlier example, a librarian was planning and presenting an adult program. He won't do all the planning and presenting of the program in a single easily measurable block of time. The simplest way to determine how long each instance of activities like this takes is to ask two or three staff members who plan and present programs to record the starting and ending times whenever they work on the program. When they have completed the activity, compare the time logs. The times on the logs will probably be far more diverse than the times reported for putting labels and dots on books in the branches.

There are just too many variables in program planning. If the times reported are wildly inconsistent, you may have to repeat the data collection process. However, what you are looking for is a reasonable average that most staff will think is realistic. The data you collect will probably provide a framework for determining that average.

In a few instances, it isn't worth the time to try to collect any data to determine how much time will be saved by eliminating an activity for one classification of staff. In one library, managers decided to hire part-time student workers to provide computer assistance to users in order to free professional and paraprofessional time for other activities. The amount of time that the professional and paraprofessional spent providing computer assistance varied significantly hour by hour and day by day, and data would have been difficult and time-consuming to collect. Instead, everyone involved agreed to estimate the amount of professional and paraprofessional time that would be saved by the change. While the staff who provided the service tended to estimate high and the senior managers tended to estimate low, the agreed-upon compromise was one that everyone supported.

Sampling to determine the time saved by eliminating an activity performed by more than one classification of staff. You will use the process described above to determine the average time per instance for the activities that are completed by staff with different classifications. The only difference is that you will be sampling to determine the time that will be saved by eliminating each *step* within the activity that is completed by staff of a different classification.

Sampling to determine the time saved by reducing, streamlining, or eliminating a step within an activity. In the above examples, the activities in question were being eliminated, and the only possible ambiguity was the starting and ending points of each activity. The process will be a little more complex with activities that are going to be reduced or streamlined. You will first have to define exactly what steps within the activity are being eliminated, reduced, or streamlined. Then you can determine how much time each of those steps currently takes and how much time will be saved by changing or eliminating those steps.

Dealing with discrepancies. If the time per instance figures for an activity are significantly different, check to be sure that your instructions were clear and that everyone who participated in the test was starting and ending the activity or step at the same point. Then repeat the data collection process with two or three new staff members. A larger sample should make it clear which times are typical and which are outside the norm. If you are still having trouble determining an average time per instance, you may want to read more about collecting and using data to determine the amount of work done in a specific time in chapter 3 of *Staffing for Results: A Guide to Working Smarter.*[1] However, don't forget that all you really need for this step are reasonably close estimates. Keep things simple if you can.

> **CAUTION**
>
> Do not spend too much time collecting data. You only need to collect enough data to develop estimates of time savings that are realistic and believable.

HOW MANY TIMES IS THE ACTIVITY OR STEP REPEATED IN A SPECIFIED TIME PERIOD?

Some activities, such as circulation and readers' advisory support, are completed thousands of times a month in many libraries. Others, such as the One Book–One City program, are completed once or twice a year. Most libraries already collect systemwide and branch-level data about the number of times activities are completed frequently. If not, it is easy enough to determine the frequency of an activity through sampling, and it is certainly simple enough to count the number of times that infrequent activities occur.

What Data Will Be Needed to Determine the Effect on Collection, Facility, or Technology Resources?

This step started by describing how to determine the staff time that will be saved by eliminating, reducing, or streamlining an activity, because when you decide to eliminate, reduce, or streamline an activity you are often doing so to save staff time. You will also save other resources, but in some cases those savings are secondary. There are obvious exceptions to this statement, of course. If you decide to significantly reduce your print reference collection and move the remainder to a less visible place in the library to create space to merchandise your new and current materials, the major effects will be on your facility and collection resources. Certainly, when you implement your new effective activities, you will require a mix of staff, facility, collection, and technology resources. Therefore, you will need to carefully assess the effect that eliminating or reducing an activity will have on each of those resources. While that effect is typically to free resources for reallocation, occasionally you may actually need *more* technology and facility resources rather than less, particularly if you are automating a step that was previously completed manually. Therefore, when you are considering the effect that eliminating or streamlining an activity will have on collection, facility, and technology resources, you will be answering two questions:

1. What collection, facility, or technology resources, if any, will be available for reallocation in each unit when this activity is eliminated, reduced, or streamlined?
2. What additional collection, facility, or technology resources, if any, will be required in each unit when this activity is eliminated, reduced, or streamlined?

In the preceding discussion of staff time saved, you were encouraged to base your calculations of the time that would be saved by eliminating or reducing an activity on systemwide averages that will almost always be applied uniformly in every unit. When collecting data about the effect that eliminating or reducing an activity will have on collection, facility, and technology resources, you will probably find that the situation is quite different in every unit. This means that the unit managers will have to answer the following questions.

WHAT COLLECTION, FACILITY, OR TECHNOLOGY RESOURCES, IF ANY, WILL BE AVAILABLE FOR REALLOCATION IN EACH UNIT WHEN THIS ACTIVITY IS ELIMINATED, REDUCED, OR STREAMLINED?

To answer this question, unit managers will provide a general description of the resources that are currently being used to support an activity. If you have decided to modify the procedures for circulating DVDs by shelving the DVDs on open shelves rather than on closed stacks, the biggest savings will be in staff time, but the branch staff will also be able to reuse or remove the DVD shelving that was behind the circulation desk. The unit managers will be able to easily see how many units of shelving will be made available, how tall that shelving is, and approximately how much space will be freed if those shelves are moved. The process won't require complex measurement and calculations. A simple descriptive sentence or two will suffice.

WHAT ADDITIONAL COLLECTION, FACILITY, OR TECHNOLOGY RESOURCES, IF ANY, WILL BE REQUIRED IN EACH UNIT WHEN THIS ACTIVITY IS ELIMINATED, REDUCED, OR STREAMLINED?

When the senior managers were deciding which of the ineffective or inefficient activities to eliminate or streamline, their main concern was to free staff time for more effective activities. When activities are eliminated, the resources that were required to support them are almost always made available for reallocation. When resources are modified, those modifications may free staff time by utilizing other resources. To continue the example in the preceding paragraph, when you decided to house the DVD collection on open shelves rather than closed stacks, you freed the space on the closed stacks. However, you will need to find space on your open stacks to house the DVDs, and this will undoubtedly mean that some of the items currently on those open stacks will have to be moved or discarded.

How Will the Data Be Collected and Recorded?

There are four workforms that will be used to record the data in this step, and they are all available at http://e-learnlibraries.mrooms.net. Two of the workforms will be used to record data about activities performed by staff in a single classification, and two will be used to record data about activities that are performed by staff from more than one classification. Each of these workforms is explained in detail below, but before you begin reading about them, take a minute to look again at the list of activities that you are planning to eliminate, reduce, or streamline on Workforms E, F, and I. You are probably quite familiar with most of the activities listed on these workforms. You won't need to collect much data or do much research to determine how much time you will save by eliminating or streamlining these activities or to calculate the other resource implications of your changes. In most cases, you will simply be recording information you already have on the following workforms so that the information will be available in the same format for all units. This will certainly take some time, but it will be neither difficult nor labor-intensive.

WORKFORM J, ELIMINATING ACTIVITIES PERFORMED BY STAFF IN A SINGLE CLASSIFICATION—SYSTEM INFORMATION BY UNIT

Data about activities to be eliminated that are performed by staff in a single classification will be the easiest data to collect, record, and analyze. The data coordinator will use a single copy of Workform J to record data from all of the units in which the activity that is being eliminated is performed. This workform can also be used to record data about systemwide activities that involve staff of the same classification, such as juvenile book review meetings.

As you can see in figure 25, much of the data needed to complete the "Staff Resources" section of Workform J (section II) is already known. The data coordinator will have to use sampling (see above) to develop an estimate of the time it takes to complete one instance of the activity, but that estimate will be used to determine the time that will be saved in all units in which the activity is performed. The data coordinator will also have to determine the number of times the activity is performed annually in each unit, but those data are often already available as well.

FIGURE 25

Workform J: Eliminating Activities Performed by Staff in a Single Classification—System Information by Unit—Example

I. Activity Being Eliminated: Plan and moderate book discussion groups

II. Staff Resources

    A. What is the classification of staff who complete this activity? Librarian

    B. What are the starting and ending points of each instance of this activity to be eliminated?

        1. Starting point of an instance of the activity: Planning the book discussion meeting

        2. Ending point of an instance of the activity: The end of the book discussion meeting

    C. How long does it take to complete a single instance of the activity? 3 hours

    D. Calculate the staff time that will be available for reallocation if this activity is eliminated.

1. Unit	2. Number of Instances Each Year	3. Time per Instance (from II.C above)	4. Annual Time Saved (in hours)
a. Cypress	24	3 hours	72 hours
b. Elm	12	3 hours	36 hours
c. Pine	12	3 hours	36 hours

III. Other Resource Implications

    A. Identify the effect that eliminating the activity will have on collection resources, if any.

1. Unit	2. Collection Resources Available for Reallocation	3. Additional Collection Resources Required
a. Cypress	None	None
b. Elm	None	None
c. Pine	None	None

    B. Identify the effect that eliminating the activity will have on facility resources, if any.

1. Unit	2. Facility Resources Available for Reallocation	3. Additional Facility Resources Required
a. Cypress	Small meeting room will be available for four hours a month (two hours twice a month)	None
b. Elm	Small meeting room will be available for two hours once a month	None
c. Pine	Small meeting room will be available for two hours once a month	None

    C. Identify the effect that eliminating the activity will have on technology resources, if any.

1. Unit	2. Technology Resources Available for Reallocation	3. Additional Technology Resources Required
a. Cypress	None	None
b. Elm	None	None
c. Pine	None	None

The data about the effect that eliminating the activity will have on collection, facility, and technology resources in each unit will probably have to be provided by the unit managers in each unit in which the activity is performed. However, all that is required is a one- or two-sentence description, which should not be difficult to obtain.

The data coordinator will record the resource data from all of the units in which each activity occurs on a single copy of this workform. If there are fifteen inefficient or ineffective activities performed by staff in the same classification, there will be fifteen copies of Workform J, one for each activity. Each workform will include all of the resource implications for all units in which that activity occurs.

WORKFORM K, REDUCING OR STREAMLINING ACTIVITIES PERFORMED BY STAFF IN A SINGLE CLASSIFICATION—SYSTEM INFORMATION BY UNIT

You will use Workform K to record data about activities performed by a single classification of staff that will be reduced or streamlined by changing one or more steps of the activity. Workform K is very similar to Workform J. The data coordinator will use a single copy of the workform to record data from all of the units in which the activity that is being modified is performed. The only real difference is that the data coordinator will use sampling to gather data about each of the *steps within the activity* that are changed instead of collecting data about the entire activity. As you can see in figure 26, the data coordinator will only collect data about the steps of the activity that are being changed. She will not collect data about steps that will remain unchanged. The purpose of this workform is to calculate the time that will be saved as a result of the changes being made. If you don't change a step, you aren't going to save any time.

WORKFORM L, ELIMINATING ACTIVITIES PERFORMED BY MORE THAN ONE CLASSIFICATION OF STAFF—UNIT INFORMATION

It is slightly more complicated to determine the time that will be saved by eliminating activities that are performed by more than one classification of staff. Parts of Workform L will be completed centrally by the data coordinator, and the rest of the workform will be completed by the unit managers. The unit managers will have to be involved because the classification of the staff assigned to the various steps in activities often varies considerably among the library units. The only way to get a relatively accurate sense of the time that will saved by each classification within each unit is to have a separate copy of the workform completed for each unit in which the activity occurs. If you have eight branches and the activity occurs in all eight of them, you will complete eight copies of Workform L for that activity.

Although a separate copy of Workform L will be completed for each unit in which the activity is performed, the data coordinator will want to be sure that everyone is collecting comparable data. Therefore, before the copies of Workform L for an activity are sent to the units to be completed, the data information illustrated in figure 27 should be entered by the data coordinator. If necessary, the data coordinator can bring together a small team of unit managers to help determine the steps and starting and ending points of each step and the time that will be saved by eliminating, reducing, or streamlining that step. Figure 28 is an example of two copies of Workform L, after the Cypress and Elm Branch library managers have added information about the classifications of staff who complete the activity in their branches to the workforms.

FIGURE 26

Workform K: Reducing or Streamlining Activities Performed by Staff in a Single Classification—System Information by Unit—Example

I. Activity Being Modified: The procedure for issuing new cards will be modified. Users will complete an electronic application for a card. No paper files of registration forms will be maintained.

II. Staff Resources

   A. What is the classification of staff who complete this activity? Circulation staff

   B. Calculate the time required to complete one instance of each of the steps to be reduced or streamlined and the total time that will be saved.

1. Step That Will Be Changed	2. Time Saved as a Result of the Change
a. Users will complete an online registration form—staff will no longer have to enter the data	3 minutes
b. Paper application forms will no longer be filed	2 minutes

   C. Total time saved for all steps (total of column II.B.2): 5 minutes

   D. Calculate the time that will be available for reallocation if the activity is modified.

1. Unit	2. Number of Instances Each Year	3. Time per Instance (from II.C)	4. Annual Time Saved (in hours)
a. Cypress	925	5 minutes	77 hours
b. Elm	1,200	5 minutes	100 hours
c. Pine	830	5 minutes	69 hours

III. Other Resource Implications

   A. Identify the effect that modifying the activity will have on collection resources, if any.

1. Unit	2. Collection Resources Available for Reallocation	3. Additional Collection Resources Required
a. Cypress	None	None
b. Elm	None	None
c. Pine	None	None

   B. Identify the effect that modifying the activity will have on facility resources, if any.

1. Unit	2. Facility Resources Available for Reallocation	3. Additional Facility Resources Required
a. Cypress	Filing cabinet behind desk can be moved	Space for a public access computer on or adjacent to the circulation desk
b. Elm	Filing cabinet in the staff workroom can be used for other purposes	Space for a public access computer on or adjacent to the circulation desk
c. Pine	Filing cabinet next to circulation desk can be surplused	Space for a public access computer on or adjacent to the circulation desk

   C. Identify the effect that modifying the activity will have on technology resources, if any.

1. Unit	2. Technology Resources Available for Reallocation	3. Additional Technology Resources Required
a. Cypress	None	New computer for the public to use to register
b. Elm	None	Same
c. Pine	None	Same

FIGURE 27

Workform L: Eliminating Activities Performed by More Than One Classification of Staff—Unit Information, Part I—Example

> NOTE: All of the information in this example was recorded by the data coordinator before the workform was sent to the units.

I. Unit: Cypress

II. Activity Being Eliminated: Branch staff will stop adding labels and dots to books in branch libraries

III. Staff Resources

A. Calculate the time required to complete one instance of each of the steps to be eliminated.

1. Step That Will Be Eliminated	2. Starting Point	3. Ending Point	4. Classification of Staff Who Perform Step	5. Time Saved per Instance
a. Sorting books by type and genre	When the books arrive at the branch	When the books have been sorted		.25 minutes (15 seconds)
b. Adding genre labels and dots	With a stack of books	When the books have been labeled		1.44 minutes

B. Calculate the time that will be saved by staff in each classification if the activity is eliminated.

1. Classification of Staff	2. Number of Instances Each Year	3. Time per Instance (from III.A.5)	4. Annual Time Saved (in hours)
	3,500	.25 minutes (15 seconds)	14.6 hours
	3,500	1.44 minutes	84 hours

I. Unit: Elm

II. Activity Being Eliminated: Branch staff will stop adding labels and dots to books in branch libraries

III. Staff Resources

A. Calculate the time required to complete one instance of each of the steps to be eliminated.

1. Step That Will Be Eliminated	2. Starting Point	3. Ending Point	4. Classification of Staff Who Perform Step	5. Time Saved per Instance
a. Sorting books by type and genre	When the books arrive at the branch	When the books have been sorted		.25 minutes (15 seconds)
b. Adding genre labels and dots	With a stack of books	When the books have been labeled		1.44 minutes

B. Calculate the time that will be saved by staff in each classification if the activity is eliminated.

1. Classification of Staff	2. Number of Instances Each Year	3. Time per Instance (from III.A.5)	4. Annual Time Saved (in hours)
	2,800	.25 minutes (15 seconds)	11.7 hours
	2,800	1.44 minutes	67.2 hours

NOTE: The information recorded by managers from the Cypress Branch and the Elm Branch is printed in bold italics.

I. Unit: Cypress

II. Activity Being Eliminated: Branch staff will stop adding labels and dots to books in branch libraries

III. Staff Resources

A. Calculate the time required to complete one instance of each of the steps to be eliminated.

1. Step That Will Be Eliminated	2. Starting Point	3. Ending Point	4. Classification of Staff Who Perform Step	5. Time Saved per Instance
a. Sorting books by type and genre	When the books arrive at the branch	When the books have been sorted	*Circulation staff*	.25 minutes (15 seconds)
b. Adding genre labels and dots	With a stack of books	When the books have been labeled	*Paraprofessionals*	1.44 minutes

B. Calculate the time that will be saved by staff in each classification if the activity is eliminated.

1. Classification of Staff	2. Number of Instances Each Year	3. Time per Instance (from III.A.5)	4. Annual Time Saved (in hours)
a. *Circulation staff*	3,500	.25 minutes (15 seconds)	14.6 hours
b. *Paraprofessionals*	3,500	1.44 minutes	84 hours

I. Unit: Elm

II. Activity Being Eliminated: Branch staff will stop adding labels and dots to books in branch libraries

III. Staff Resources

A. Calculate the time required to complete one instance of each of the steps to be eliminated.

1. Step That Will Be Eliminated	2. Starting Point	3. Ending Point	4. Classification of Staff Who Perform Step	5. Time Saved per Instance
a. Sorting books by type and genre	When the books arrive at the branch	When the books have been sorted	*Clerical staff*	.25 minutes (15 seconds)
b. Adding genre labels and dots	With a stack of books	When the books have been labeled	*Librarians*	1.44 minutes

B. Calculate the time that will be saved by staff in each classification if the activity is eliminated.

1. Classification of Staff	2. Number of Instances Each Year	3. Time per Instance (from III.A.5)	4. Annual Time Saved (in hours)
a. *Clerical staff*	2,800	.25 minutes (15 seconds)	11.7 hours
b. *Librarians*	2,800	1.44 minutes	67.2 hours

NOTE: The information recorded by managers from the Cypress Branch and the Elm
Branch is printed in bold italics.

I. Unit: Cypress

II. Activity Being Modified: Cash handling procedures will be simplified. One staff member will count the cash each
morning and justify the totals with the cash register tape and receipts. If the cash count matches, the cash, the tape,
and the receipts will be put in a cash bag and sent to accounting, where the count will be verified. There will be no
need for the branch staff to complete a separate cash report; the cash register tape will serve as the report. There will
be no need for a librarian to verify the count if the tape and cash match.

III. Staff Resources

A. Calculate the time required to complete one instance of each of the steps to be changed.

1. Step That Will Be Changed	2. Starting Point	3. Ending Point	4. Classification of Staff Who Perform Step	5. Time Saved per Instance
a. Complete a cash report	When the cash count has been justified with the cash register tape	When the report has been completed	*Circulation staff*	5 minutes
b. Verify the cash report	When the cash report is completed	When the cash report has been verified	*Branch manager (in her absence the librarian in charge)*	20 minutes

B. Calculate the time that will be saved by staff in each classification if the activity is changed.

1. Classification of Staff	2. Number of Instances Each Year	3. Time per Instance (from III.A.5)	4. Annual Time Saved (in hours)
a. *Branch manager*	240	20 minutes	80 hours
b. *Librarian in charge*	113	20 minutes	37.7 hours
c. *Circulation staff*	353 (days the library is open)	5 minutes	29.4 hours

WORKFORM M, REDUCING OR STREAMLINING ACTIVITIES PERFORMED
BY MORE THAN ONE CLASSIFICATION OF STAFF—UNIT INFORMATION

You will use Workform M to record information about activities that are performed by
more than one classification of staff and that will be reduced or streamlined rather than
eliminated. As you can see in figure 29, the process will be very similar to the process
used to complete Workform L. A separate copy of Workform M will be completed for
each unit in which the activity to be reduced or streamlined is performed, and the data
coordinator will want to be sure that everyone is collecting comparable data. Therefore,
parts of Workform M will be completed centrally by the data coordinator and the rest of
the workform will be completed by the unit managers. It will be important for the data
coordinator to provide a clear description of the modifications that are being made in the
activity, so that all of the unit managers understand the modifications and report accurate
information.

How Should the Information Collected Be Presented to the Unit Managers?

When the data coordinator and the unit managers have completed all of the required copies of Workforms J, K, L, and M for all of the activities that are being eliminated, reduced, or streamlined, they will have a lot of information—and a lot of paper. All of this information was collected to help unit managers make decisions about reallocating resources at the unit level, and the unit managers will need to have that information in a format that is easy to use and understand.

WORKFORM N, ESTIMATING RESOURCES AVAILABLE FOR REALLOCATION—UNIT SUMMARY

Each unit manager can use Workform N (see figure 30; available at http://e-learnlibraries .mrooms.net) to summarize the resource implications of the changes that are being made for her unit. The data coordinator should send each unit manager a packet of these documents:

A copy of the completed Workform J for each activity that is performed in the unit

A copy of the completed Workform K for each activity that is performed in the unit

A copy of Workform L for each activity completed by the unit manager

A copy of Workform M for each activity completed by the unit manager

A blank copy of Workform N (with instructions) to be used to summarize the information from Workforms J, K, L, and M

The unit managers should be asked to number each of the copies of the workforms for each activity that is performed in their units sequentially. If five activities performed by staff of the same classification are being eliminated in the Elm Branch, the branch librarian would number the copies of Workform J for those activities 1–5. If three more activities performed by staff of the same classification are being modified in the branch, the manager would number the copies of Workform K for each of those activities 6–8. If the Elm Branch manager had completed four copies of Workform L and five copies of Workform M, she would number the copies of Workform L 9–12, and the copies of Workform M 13–17.

Once the unit managers have numbered each of the workforms that contains information about an activity that will be eliminated, reduced, or streamlined in their units, they will be ready to use Workform N to summarize the resource implications of all of those changes. When the Elm Branch manager totals all of the hours of librarian time that will be made available for reallocation from all of the activities recorded on Workforms J, K, L, and M, she will write the total hours in column B of Workform N. She will also record the numbers of all of the workforms for the activities that the librarians had been performing in column C. Then, when the branch manager needs to know exactly which activities will have to be eliminated, reduced, or streamlined to free the librarian time required to implement new activities, she will be able to quickly and easily find the detailed information she must have.

The unit managers should be given a week to review and summarize all of the information gathered during this step and to review the unit summaries with their supervisors.

I. Unit: _____

II. Summarize the staff resources that are available for reallocation as a result of eliminating, reducing, or streamlining activities.

A. Classification	B. Total Hours Available for Reallocation per Year	C. Notes
Branch manager		
Librarian		
Paraprofessional		
Circulation		
Page		
Custodial		

III. Summarize the other resources that will be made available for reallocation as a result of eliminating, reducing, or streamlining activities.

A. Resource	B. Describe	C. Notes
Collection	None	
Facility		
Technology		

IV. Summarize the other resources that will be required as a result of eliminating, reducing, or streamlining activities.

A. Resource	B. Describe	C. Notes
Collection		
Facility		
Technology		

The library director should then hold a second meeting with the unit managers to provide them with a chance to share the findings with one another, discuss staff reactions to the findings, and ask questions. During this meeting, the library director will also want to be able to discuss the changes that will be made in the materials budget to support the goals and objectives in the strategic plan (discussed next in Step 10.2).

Before adjourning this meeting, the director should make two things very clear. First, no final decisions have been made about the ineffective, inefficient, and nonpriority activities. Those that have already been identified are almost certainly going to be eliminated, reduced, or streamlined. However, if those changes don't result in enough resources to implement both the current and new essential activities identified in Step 6.2, more changes will be made. Second, the effect of all of the changes that are being made will be monitored. If a decision about one or more ineffective or inefficient activities turns out to have unintended consequences, the decision will be revisited. Very few management decisions are cast in stone.

Step 10.2
Revise the Materials Budget to Support the Library's Goals

Up to this point, the process has focused on unit-level resources. Most of the inefficient, ineffective, or nonpriority activities that will be eliminated, reduced, or streamlined are performed at the unit level, and in most cases the changes will affect unit resources. The inclusive term *unit* has been used rather than the more specific term *branch* throughout this book. Library units include the library director and her support staff, the web development staff, the technology support staff, the maintenance team, the accounting unit, and the marketing team, among others. Although staff in many of these units provide systemwide services, they can all use the workforms described in Step 10.1 to record the resource implications of the changes that are being made in the library that affect their units.

In most libraries, there is only one resource that is allocated and managed centrally and that is the materials budget. Of course, there are some unit-level implications for collections when some activities are changed or added. In an earlier example, the Tree County Public Library was planning to close the business reference desk in the largest branch. As a result, that branch would probably purchase fewer business books and data-bases, and that would make some of the materials budget for that branch available for reallocation. However, those changes would probably not be made by the branch man-ager. Instead, the person who allocates the library's materials budget would make the adjustments centrally.

What Process Should Be Used?

In earlier tasks, you and your colleagues identified and evaluated the current activities that support your goals (Step 3.2) and the current activities that support service responses that were not selected as priorities (Step 7.1). You will go through a similar process in this step. You will start by listing the objectives in the strategic plan that are collection-based. Once you have listed those objectives, you will know what targets you are working toward in each objective. Then you can identify the portions of the materials budget that are currently allocated in the areas addressed by those targets and determine what addi-tional collection resources will be required to meet the targets. Finally, you will reduce the amount of the materials budget allocated to support service responses that are not priori-ties so that you can allocate the money necessary to reach the targets in the objectives.

What Data Will Be Used to Determine the Material Resources Needed to Meet the Targets in the Objectives?

The first thing you need to know is what you are trying to accomplish and how you will measure your progress. If you used the *SPFR* process, each of your objectives includes a measure, a target, and a date by which the target will be met. You will find two types of collection-based measures in your objectives: measures of client satisfaction with the col-lection and measures of circulation or use of collections. The majority of your collection-based objectives will include circulation targets. One of the Tree County Public Library's objectives is "Each year, easy books and picture books will be checked out at least 125,000 times." The measure in this objective is the circulation of easy and picture books, the tar-get is 125,000 circulations, and the date by which the target will be met is each year.

The second piece of data you will need is the current circulation of the items that are included in the objective. In Tree County, easy and picture books were circulated 110,000 times in the previous fiscal year. Based on those data, the Tree County staff know that they will need to increase circulation by 15,000 (13.6 percent).

The third piece of data you will need is the current turnover rate for the items that are included in the objective. Turnover rate is the average number of times an item in a collection circulates each year. To calculate turnover rate, you divide the total annual circulation of a collection by the number of items in that collection. The Tree County Public Library has 22,000 easy and picture books, which means that each book is circulated an average of five times in a year.

The final thing to consider is the condition of the items in the collection. If many of the items are old or damaged, it is reasonable to assume that the turnover rate of new items will be higher than the turnover rate of the existing items. The Tree County Public Library's easy and picture books were in generally good condition, but the staff assumed that the turnover of the new books would be slightly higher than the turnover of the existing books, and they decided to use a turnover rate of six items per year to estimate the number of new easy and picture books that would be required to increase circulation by 15,000 items a year. The staff divided the desired increase in circulation (15,000) by the expected turnover rate of the new books (6) and found that they would need 2,500 new easy and picture books to meet the target in the objective. After some discussion, the Tree County senior managers decided that the new programming activities, the new Books to Go bags, and the increase in the number of items that could be checked out by a single user would also lead to more circulation, and they would need to purchase between 1,800 and 2,000 new items to meet their targets. If the average discounted cost for easy and picture books is $12.00 per book, the library would need to allocate between $21,600 and $24,000 in additional funds for easy and picture books. That money will have to be reallocated from other parts of the materials budget.

What Data Will Be Used to Determine Which Parts of the Materials Budget Can Be Reallocated?

The money needed to purchase materials to support the goals and objectives will come from reallocating monies currently being spent on materials that support service responses that were not selected as priorities during the planning process. This is similar to Steps 7.1 and 7.2, during which you identified the library's current activities that do not support any of the library's priorities.

In many libraries, the major decisions about the allocation of the materials budget are made centrally. One or more senior managers decide how much money will be allocated to each of the units of the library. They also determine how much of the materials budget money will be allocated for print materials, how much will be allocated for media, and how much will be allocated for electronic resources. Senior managers determine the proportions of the budget that will be spent on children's materials, teen materials, and adult materials, as well as the proportions of the print budget that will be spent on fiction, nonfiction, reference, and periodicals. In most cases, they decide what proportion of the collection budget is allocated for different subject areas as well. Therefore, any changes in these allocations will have to be made centrally as well.

There is no formula for this step. Instead there are a series of questions to consider:

What percentage of your materials budget is currently being allocated for materials that support service responses that were not selected as priorities?

What portion of your materials budget is allocated for reference? Is this congruent with your new service priorities?

What portion of your materials budget is being spent on standing orders? When were standing orders last reviewed to be sure that they reflected the library's priorities?

Do the databases that the library purchases support the new service priorities?

What percentages of your materials are allocated for print materials, media, and electronic resources? Do these percentages reflect the priorities in your goals and objectives?

What percentages of your materials budget are allocated for children's materials, teen materials, and adult materials? Do these percentages reflect the priorities in your goals and objectives?

These questions can be used as a starting point for a careful review of the existing materials budget in your library—and the answers to these questions will probably raise more questions that you need to address. Remember, the underlying philosophy of the entire Results series is that the majority of a library's resources should be allocated to support the priorities in the library's strategic plan. This philosophy provided the framework for the decisions you made when evaluating the current and new activities that will be performed by staff in the future, and this is the philosophy that must provide the framework for the decisions you make about your materials budget.

Some librarians find it more difficult to reallocate the materials budget than to reallocate staff time. They were taught that it was important to develop and maintain a "balanced" collection when they were in library school. A "balanced" collection was often defined as a collection that contained a broad range of materials in most subject areas, regardless of the use of those materials. In effect, this type of balanced collection is a "just in case" collection. Library staff purchase, catalog, shelve, and maintain a large number of items that are rarely used "just in case" someone wants them. The Results model encourages staff to develop "just in time" collections. These collections include enough copies of high-demand items and items that support the library's priorities to meet the needs of most of the library's users, and they take advantage of interlibrary loan to fill occasional requests for specialty items. "Just in time" collection development practices are what will allow you to meet the targets for client satisfaction in your collection-based objectives which use that as a measure.

It is important not to confuse the "balanced" collections described above with the basic library principle of providing materials with different perspectives on topics of public interest. This type of balance is embedded in the intellectual freedom statements of every public library and has nothing to do with service priorities selected by the library and the community. It is one thing to offer materials that reflect various points of view about the First or Second Amendments to the Constitution. It is an entirely different thing to have a standing order for books on literary criticism just in case someone might want them, particularly if "Succeed in School" is not a library priority.

TASK 11: IDENTIFY NEEDED RESOURCES

The first step in this task will be coordinated by the data coordinator appointed by the library director and will be completed by unit managers. Other staff with special skills may be involved in identifying the resources needed for the new activities. Step 11.2 will be completed by the unit managers.

The work on Step 11.1 can and should begin as soon as the senior managers have determined the priority of the effective activities in Step 6.2. Step 11.2 can begin as soon as Steps 10.1, 10.2, and 11.1 have been completed.

Step 11.1
Identify the Resources Needed for Essential Activities

Every library manager knows that resources are finite. Each library has a certain number of FTEs, an existing collection and a defined materials budget, existing facilities and a limited maintenance and improvement budget, and a current technological infrastructure and a budget for upgrades and replacements. Managers may have the option of moving some of the money allocated for nonpersonnel resources from one category to another, but no manager can create resources when none exist. Your success in implementing the essential activities in your plan will be based on two factors: your ability to use the existing resources that have been made available by eliminating, reducing, or streamlining ineffective or inefficient activities to support the new or expanded activities, and your ability to continue to provide the same levels of resources to your current essential activities that you have in the past. The last thing you want to do is cannibalize your current effective activities to support new activities.

It is at this point that the planning and implementation processes come full circle. When the community planning committee, the staff, and the board worked together to identify the library's priorities, they used *Public Library Service Responses* as the framework for their decision making. You started the *IFR* process by identifying current and new activities that support your priorities in Steps 3.2 and 3.3. You used the service responses that were *not* selected in Task 7, when you identified the activities that supported those service responses, and again in Step 10.2 to identify needed changes in the way your collection resources are allocated. In this task, you will start by reviewing each of the service responses that *were* selected as priorities once again.

Each of those service responses includes a list of critical resources, which were defined as "the types of resources that libraries that select the service response will need in order to provide the service effectively."[2] The lists are illustrative rather than prescriptive, and the specific resources each library will require will depend on the activities that will be implemented in that library. However, the lists of resources in each service response will provide a starting point for identifying what will be required to implement activities which support that service response, as you can see in figure 31.

FIGURE 31

Create Young Readers Critical Resources

Staff (Knowledge, Skills, and Abilities)

- Staff are knowledgeable about early childhood development
- Staff are knowledgeable about early literacy
- Staff are knowledgeable about materials for preschool children
- Staff can design and deliver effective programs for preschool children
- Staff can teach parents and caregivers the skills needed to support early literacy
- Staff can develop or assist in the development of a website appropriate for preschool children
- Staff can establish partnerships with parents, child care providers, and others who serve children ages birth to five
- Staff can record podcasts or digital videocasts and make them available to download

Collection (Print, Media, and Electronic Resources)

- Board books
- Book/media kits
- Books and media on early literacy for parents and caregivers
- Concept books
- DVDs and CDs
- E-books for children
- Educational software to encourage vocabulary development and motor skills
- I Can Read books
- Picture books

Facilities (Space, Furniture, and Equipment)

- Dedicated area for children ages newborn to five that is comfortable, safe, and appropriate for this age group as well as the adults with them
- Dedicated space for family use
- Space to provide preschool programs
- Family restrooms
- Family computer areas that support shared use of digital resources
- Appropriate shelving for preschool materials
- Child-friendly furniture and computer desks
- Listening and viewing stations
- Appropriate seating at computer workstations to encourage adults and young children to use computer programs together

Technology (Hardware, Software, Networks, and Telecommunication)

- Child-friendly computers

Source: Sandra Nelson and June Garcia, *Public Library Service Responses* (Chicago: American Library Association, 2007).

Who Should Be Responsible for This Step?

The library director will want to appoint a coordinator for this step. Ideally, the same person who served as data coordinator for Step 10.1 will be asked to coordinate this step. The skills required to coordinate both steps are the same, and the data coordinator will be the person most familiar with the resources available for reallocation. That will be critical information in this step.

In this step, and in the remaining steps and tasks in this book, final decisions will be made and those decisions will have an effect on all four types of library resources (staff, collections, facilities, and technology). These are management decisions and should be made by the managers who will be responsible for implementing them. Therefore, the unit managers will be working with their supervisors throughout this step.

What Process Should Be Used?

Once you have a general idea of the types of resources needed to support the new activities related to a service response, you will be ready to move on to a more detailed analysis of the required resources. The process of identifying the resources you will need to implement new essential activities will be similar to the process used to determine what resources could be made available for reallocation in Task 10. You will consider each activity individually for each unit in which it will be performed and you will identify all of the staffing, collection, facility, and technology resources that will be required to perform the activity in that unit.

DEFINE THE SCOPE OF EACH NEW OR EXPANDED ACTIVITY

Before you can determine the actual resource requirements for new activities, someone will have to clearly define the scope of each new activity. One of the goals in the Tree County Public Library is "Adults will have timely access to new and popular materials and programs that stimulate their imaginations, respond to their current interests, and provide pleasurable reading, viewing, and listening experiences." The senior managers decided that providing a download station in each branch was an essential activity to support this goal. This description provided enough information for the senior managers to evaluate the activity and decide that it was effective. It does not provide enough information for unit managers to make informed resource-allocation decisions. The activity description was expanded to read "Provide each branch with a dedicated computer to serve as a download station for digital content" before it was sent to the branch managers.

ESTIMATE THE RESOURCES THAT WILL BE REQUIRED FOR EACH ACTIVITY

Once someone or some group has clarified the scope of each of your new activities, you are ready to identify the types of resources that will be required to support each activity (staff, collection, facility, and technology) and estimate the amount of each type of resource that will be required to implement the activities in each unit. Because you are now considering new activities, you won't be able to use actual measures. Instead, you will have to make informed estimates of the resources that will be needed.

Every activity requires some staff resources, so you will start by estimating the amount of staff time that will be required to implement an activity. Although the process will be similar to the one you used in Step 10.1, there are several significant differences. The most obvious difference is that you can't use sampling to estimate the time it will take to perform one instance of an activity because the activity isn't currently being performed. However, few of your new activities are going to be wildly different than anything you have ever done before. You should be able to extrapolate reasonable estimates from the work you did in Step 10.1 for many new activities. If not, you can call libraries that currently perform the activity and ask for an estimate of the time required, or you can use your common sense and make an informed guess.

For many of your new activities, this will be a very straightforward process. One of the Tree County Public Library's new activities was "Present story programs in day care centers." Once the decision has been made about how many story programs will be presented in day care centers each month by the staff in each unit, there should be no difficulty in estimating the time each instance of the activity will take and how much total time will be required in each unit. Staff already plan and present story programs in the library, so they know how much time that requires. All they will need to do is estimate the amount of time needed to schedule the programs in the day care centers and the amount of travel time that will be required for each program. If, after six months, it appears that the timing estimates were wrong, they can use the process described in Step 10.1 to determine the actual time per instance and make the necessary adjustments.

You will also have to consider both the time required to start a new activity and the time required to maintain that activity. You may find that you will have to allocate more staff time during the first six months of an activity, while staff are planning the activity and learning the new skills they will need to perform it. After the activity has been fully implemented and staff are comfortable with their new responsibilities, the time required to perform the activity may decrease. This is one reason why you will want to consider staggering the implementation of new activities that will require significant training, rather than trying to implement them all simultaneously.

At least a few of your new activities will be more complex and require more analysis than the preceding example. If the managers of the Tree County Public Library had decided to create a public video-editing lab to support the service response "Express Creativity," they will need to do some research to determine the types and amounts of staffing, facility, technology, and collection resources that will be required.

Fortunately, there are a number of books in the Results series that were written specifically to help them—and you—collect and analyze the information you need to make informed estimates about the resources that will be required to implement complex new activities. Even better, the workforms and instructions from all of the books are available in electronic form at http://e-learnlibraries.mrooms.net. *Managing for Results: Effective Resource Allocation for Public Libraries* was one of the first books written in the series.[3] It is basically a compendium of workforms designed to help you gather the data you need to make informed resource-allocation decisions about all four types of library data. There are four additional Results books that address specific resources. Two of those books were written to help you determine the staffing resources that will be required to implement a new activity: *Staffing for Results: A Guide to Working Smarter*[4] and *Human Resources for Results: The Right Person for the Right Job.*[5] The other two books, *Managing Facilities for Results: Optimizing Space for Services*[6] and *Technology for Results: Developing Service-Based Plans,*[7] complete the list of resource-specific Results titles that are currently available.

You will notice that there is no Results book on managing collections. Such a book is in the works and will be available in the future. In the meantime, the "Collections" workforms in *Managing for Results* provide the framework needed to gather and analyze data about your current collections and the collections that will be needed to support your new activities. Those workforms, used in conjunction with the suggested collection resources in each of the service responses, and the information in Step 10.2, should provide the information you need to make informed estimates about the collections that will be needed to implement your activities.

WORKFORM O, ESTIMATING RESOURCES REQUIRED TO IMPLEMENT A NEW OR EXPANDED ACTIVITY—UNIT INFORMATION

You will use Workform O (see figure 32; available at http://e-learnlibraries.mrooms.net) to organize and record the data you collect about the resources needed for each activity in each unit. The data about the resources required to implement an activity (column A) will be recorded centrally by the data coordinator before the workforms are sent to the units. However, the data coordinator will not be responsible for making the actual resource estimates for each new activity. That will be done by staff with expertise in the areas supported by the new activity. Youth services staff might be asked to estimate the resources required to present story programs in day care centers. Staff who work with teens might be asked to work with technology support staff to estimate the resources required for a public video-editing lab. The data coordinator will coordinate their efforts, and the senior managers will review the final estimates before they are recorded on Workform O.

Although you will use Workform O to record all of the resources that will be needed for each new activity in each unit, you will not need to collect all of the data in every row for every activity for most of your new activities. Figure 33 is an example of Workform O that staff in the Elm Branch completed for the activity "Provide each branch with a dedicated computer to serve as a download station for digital content." The unit manager only completed the rows that related to that activity. Remember the basic rule that has been reiterated throughout the *IFR* process: Keep it simple!

If you need to collect more data about a complex activity, you will be using the workforms in the other books in the Results series (see the appendix). Each of the four types of library resources has been subdivided into categories on Workform O, and those categories are the same categories that are described in the Results book about that resource. The two Results books dealing with staffing provide detailed guidance on collecting data about hours by classification and knowledge, skills, and abilities. The collection workforms in *Managing for Results* collect data on print material, media, and electronic resources. The workforms in *Managing Facilities for Results* are divided into five categories on the workform: equipment and furniture; square footage; shelving; physical plant; and access, spatial relationships, and signage. Finally, the workforms in *Technology for Results* focus on helping you to identify needed servers, workstations and other equipment, software, and bandwidth.

FIGURE 32

Workform O: Estimating Resources Required to Implement a New or Expanded Activity—Unit Information

I. Unit: _____

II. Activity: _____

	A. Resources Required to Implement the Activity in the Unit	B. Resources Available through Reallocation in the Unit	C. Additional Resources Required and Suggested Source
1. Staff Resources			
a. Hours			
1) Manager			
2) Librarian			
3) Paraprofessional			
4) Clerical			
5) Page			
6) Maintenance			
7) Other			
b. Knowledge, Skills, and Abilities			
2. Collection Resources			
a. Print Materials			
b. Media			
c. Electronic Resources			
3. Facility Resources			
a. Furniture and Equipment			
b. Square Footage			
c. Shelving			
d. Physical Plant (electrical, lighting, etc.)			
e. Access, Spatial Relationships, Signage			
4. Technology Resources			
a. Servers			
b. Workstations and Other Equipment (printers, etc.)			
c. Software			
d. Bandwidth			

WORKFORM P, ESTIMATING RESOURCES REQUIRED FOR NEW OR EXPANDED ACTIVITIES—UNIT SUMMARY

Each unit manager can use Workform P (see figure 34; available at http://e-learnlibraries .mrooms.net) to summarize the resources that will be required to implement the new essential activities in her unit. When the unit managers have completed all of the copies of Workform O for all of the new activities that will be performed in their units, they should number the workforms sequentially. Then they will be ready to use Workform P

I. Unit: Elm Branch

II. Activity: Provide each branch with a dedicated computer to serve as a download station for digital content

	A. Resources Required to Implement the Activity in the Unit	**B.** Resources Available through Reallocation in the Unit	**C.** Additional Resources Required and Suggested Source
1. Staff Resources			
a. Hours			
1) Manager			
2) Librarian	8 hours per month	Yes	None
3) Paraprofessional	8 hours per month	Yes	None
4) Clerical			
5) Page			
6) Maintenance			
7) Other			
b. Knowledge, Skills, and Abilities	How to use the download site	No	Training provided tech staff
3. Facility Resources			
a. Furniture and Equipment	Workstation for the computer station	Yes	None
b. Square Footage			
c. Shelving			
d. Physical Plant (electrical, lighting, etc.)	Electrical outlets for computer	Yes	None
4. Technology Resources			
a. Servers			
b. Workstations and Other Equipment (printers, etc.)	New computer	No	Purchased for all units from technology funds

to summarize the resource implications of all of the new activities. When the Elm Branch manager totals all of the hours of librarian time that will be required for all of the new essential activities recorded on Workform O, she will write the total hours in column II.B of Workform P. She will also record the numbers of all of the workforms for the activities that the librarians will be performing in column II.C. Then when the branch manager needs to know exactly which activities the librarians will be performing, she will be able to quickly and easily find the detailed information she must have.

I. Unit: _____

II. Summarize the staff resources that will be required to implement the new or expanded essential activities in your unit.

A. Classification	B. Total Hours Required per Year	C. Notes

III. Summarize the collection resources that will be required to implement the new or expanded essential activities in your unit.

A. Format	B. Total Required Each Year	C. Notes

IV. Summarize the facility resources that will be required to implement the new or expanded essential activities in your unit.

A. Resource	B. Amount Required	C. Notes

V. Summarize the technology resources that will be required to implement the new or expanded essential activities in your unit.

A. Resource	B. Amount Required	C. Notes

Step 11.2
Summarize Unit Data

When the unit managers completed Step 10.1, they used Workform N to summarize the resource implications of the activities that will be eliminated, reduced, or streamlined in their units. At the end of Step 11.1, they used Workform P to summarize the resources that would be needed in their units to implement the new essential activities that will support the library's strategic plan. Now they just have one thing left to do, and that is to compare the information on Workforms N and P. It is only by comparing the informa-

FIGURE 35

Workform Q: Summarizing Unit Resources

I. Unit: _____

II. Staff Summary

A. Classification	B. Total Hours Required per Year for All New Activities	C. Total Hours Available per Year from Reallocation	D. Difference (+ or −)	E. Notes

III. Summary of Other Resources

	A. Significant Surplus	B. Significant Shortfall	C. Notes
1. Collection			
2. Facility			
3. Technology			

tion on the two forms that they can get a full picture of the resource implications of the changes that are being considered.

WORKFORM Q, SUMMARIZING UNIT RESOURCES

The unit managers will use the information on Workforms N and P to complete Workform Q (available at http://e-learnlibraries.mrooms.net). As you can see in figure 35, the workform provides an easy way to compare the resources that are needed with the resources that are available. If there are significant shortfalls, the unit managers will have a chance to revisit the data they recorded earlier to see if they might be able to find the additional resources that are needed. If they are unable to resolve the disparity, the unit managers should be prepared to suggest how to address the shortfall when they meet with their supervisors. In the event that there are surpluses in some types of resources, the unit managers should also be ready to suggest how those surpluses might be allocated.

When the unit managers have completed Workform Q and done what they could to make needed adjustments in the detailed workforms, they should send copies of all the workforms completed in both tasks in this chapter to their supervisors. All of the copies of Workforms J, K, L, and M will be collected together in a single packet, and Workform N will be the cover sheet for that packet. All of the copies of Workform O will be grouped in one packet, with Workform P as a cover sheet. Workform Q will stand alone.

After reviewing the unit workforms, the supervisor will schedule meetings with each unit manager to review the information on the workforms. The supervisor will want to discuss any unit shortfalls or surpluses with the unit manager and consider the unit manager's suggestions for addressing those issues. The supervisor may ask the unit manager to make additional changes on Workforms J, K, L, M, or O to balance the available resources with the resources that will be required.

When the supervisor has approved the workforms for a unit, copies of those workforms should be sent to the data coordinator. The data coordinator will send the completed copies of Workforms N, O, and Q for all of the units to the senior managers and make copies of the detailed workforms available for review if necessary.

What's Next?

To complete the steps in this chapter, unit managers had to look carefully at the activities that their staff were currently performing. They also had to think about what effect the coming changes would have on their staff and on the other resources in their units. It is probable that you and all the other library managers will end this step with a much clearer picture of how the library's resources are being used than you have ever had before. In the next chapter, you will begin implementing the activities you have spent so long identifying and evaluating and you will consider how you will monitor your progress toward reaching the targets in your objectives. You will also think about how to integrate the changes you have made into the library's infrastructure.

Key Points to Remember

Change is hard and there will be some staff resistance to this process, particularly during the tasks in this chapter. Don't be tempted to slow the process to "give staff more time to adjust." Making people wait longer for final decisions will increase resistance, not reduce it.

The library director and the library's senior managers have too much invested in this process to quit at this point.

Review the communication plan and update it as needed. There may be some misinformation about this process throughout the library. You will also want to be sure that the board is informed about the process.

Staff members make up the library's largest and most important resource, and the reallocation of staff time will be a critical part of this process.

An activity or step that takes 30 seconds may seem inconsequential, until you realize that if that activity is completed 600 times a day, the staff member spends 300 minutes or five hours performing that activity. If you can reduce the time required for each instance by ten seconds, you will save 1.66 hours per day.

Staff members are not all interchangeable. Few activities can be completed by a generic staff person.

You will support new or expanded activities by reallocating existing resources that are currently being used to perform ineffective, inefficient, or nonpriority activities.

You don't need absolutely statistically valid data for the tasks in this chapter. You simply need reasonably accurate estimates, which you can obtain by collecting a sampling of data from several units.

You are collecting data in this chapter so that you and the other library managers can make informed decisions about the activities that will be implemented and the activities that will be eliminated, reduced, or streamlined. The detailed data must be summarized before it can be used to make decisions.

Ultimately, you will have to balance the resources required for new activities with the resources that can be made available through reallocation. Unit managers should be expected to suggest ways to address any disparities between them.

Notes

1. Diane Mayo and Jeanne Goodrich, *Staffing for Results: A Guide to Working Smarter* (Chicago: American Library Association, 2002), 42–60.
2. Sandra Nelson, *Strategic Planning for Results* (Chicago: American Library Association, 2008), 145.
3. Sandra Nelson, Ellen Altman, and Diane Mayo, *Managing for Results: Effective Resource Allocation for Public Libraries* (Chicago: American Library Association, 2000).
4. Mayo and Goodrich, *Staffing for Results*.
5. Jeanne Goodrich and Paula M. Singer, *Human Resources for Results: The Right Person for the Right Job* (Chicago: American Library Association, 2007).
6. Cheryl Bryan, *Managing Facilities for Results: Optimizing Space for Services* (Chicago: American Library Association, 2007).
7. Diane Mayo, *Technology for Results: Developing Service-Based Plans* (Chicago: American Library Association, 2005).

Chapter 6

Make It Work

*Continuity gives us roots; change gives us branches,
letting us stretch and grow and reach new heights.*
—Pauline R. Kezer

MILESTONES

By the time you finish this chapter you will be able to

- select the final activities to be implemented during the current planning cycle
- select the final activities to be eliminated, reduced, or streamlined to provide the resources needed to implement essential new activities
- reallocate resources to fully implement your selected activities
- identify and collect the data you will need to monitor the progress being made toward reaching the targets in the objectives in your strategic plan
- report on your progress to your board, your staff, and the community
- integrate the changes you have made into the ongoing operations of the library

It has been almost seven months since the Tree County Public Library started the *Strategic Planning for Results* process and a little over three months since it began the tasks in *Implementing for Results.* When Mary and her staff look back, they are amazed at how much they have accomplished in a relatively short time. They are also delighted that the time for planning is almost over. Soon they will all be able to turn their attention to performing the essential activities that they have so carefully selected.

Mary, the library director, has scheduled several meetings with Greg, the head of public services, Latisha, the youth services coordinator, and other senior managers to review the resource allocation summaries prepared by each unit manager and make the final decisions about the activities to be implemented and the activities to be eliminated, reduced, or streamlined. While they were reviewing the branch summaries and making their final decisions, Greg mentioned that the branch managers, who had not been particularly enthusiastic about collecting resource allocation data initially, now think that all of the time they spent was an excellent investment. The other senior managers said that they have seen the same positive reactions from the unit managers they supervise. The senior managers agree that one of the serendipitous effects of the *IFR* process has been to fully engage middle managers in the discussion of the resources that would be needed to implement the essential activities that would support the library's strategic plan. Even more important, the library's middle managers now have a clear understanding of how the resources needed to implement those new activities would be found. For the first time, all of the library's managers, from the most senior to the most junior, are working with the same resource information and have a clear understanding of how allocation decisions are being made. The senior managers are confident that this shared understanding will make it easier for everyone to implement the decisions that they have made.

Suddenly it is three months later. All of the staff in the library are fully engaged in putting into practice the decisions that were made during the *IFR* process. The unit managers have eliminated a number of ineffective, inefficient, and nonpriority activities and reduced or streamlined others. They have used the resources that had been supporting those activities to initiate many of their essential new or expanded activities. They have also been placing more emphasis on maintaining the current activities that were deemed to be essential. Other essential new activities are still in the planning stages and are scheduled to begin over the next several months. The library's senior managers have been making progress toward achieving the organizational competencies identified during the planning and implementation process. The staff had been looking forward to *doing* instead of *planning to do* and their wishes have been granted. It has been a very eventful three months.

Mary has been including a brief description of all the changes that are being made in her monthly reports to the board. The board members have all been interested in the implementation process and supportive of the decisions that the senior managers have made. Mrs. Johnson, the chairperson of the library board, recently suggested that Mary report on the progress being made toward reaching the targets in the objectives in the strategic plan at the next board meeting. Mary thought that was a great idea. She was confident that the changes that had been made were effective, and she was sure that the board members would be impressed by the progress that was being made.

Mary asked Greg to work with her to develop the report to the board. They had worked closely together throughout the *IFR* process and they had been focusing on starting, changing, or stopping activities for several months. In fact, on some days they felt as if *all* they had done in the past several months was to monitor the implementation of the plan. They knew that new activities were being initiated on schedule and that ineffective, inefficient, or nonpriority activities were being addressed in every unit. However, when they began to write the report that Mrs. Johnson requested, they realized that there is a big difference between monitoring the *implementation* of a change and monitoring the *effect* of that change. When you monitor the implementation of a change, you are checking to make sure that deadlines are met and the expected actions are taken by the appropriate people. When you monitor the effect of a change, you are checking to see if the change produced the results you expected. These are two different processes that require two different sets of data.

Mary and Greg weren't even sure that the data they would need to assess the progress toward reaching the targets in the strategic plan were available. They developed a list of the targets in the objectives in the plan and were relieved to find that most of the data that were needed were being collected. Although none of the data had been gathered into a single report and the data had not yet been used to evaluate the progress the library was making toward reaching the targets in the objectives in the strategic plan, the data did provide a starting point for the report they were preparing for the board. Mary made arrangements to receive all of the data that were being collected, and she and Greg scheduled a second meeting to review and discuss the data.

During their second meeting, Mary and Greg discovered that the progress being made toward reaching the targets in the objectives was very uneven. In one case, the library had met the annual target in just three months. Progress toward reaching other targets was more in line with expectations, but there were several instances in which little or no progress at all had been made. In one case, the data from this quarter actually reflected a decline when compared to data from the same quarter in the previous year. They also discovered that they were not yet collecting the data needed to measure progress toward reaching any of the objectives in the strategic plan that measure how well the activity meets the needs of the users. Mary and Greg realized that they would need to have more information about the implementation process before Mary could prepare and present a report to the board. The members of the board were going to want to know why progress was being made in some areas and not others—and so did Mary and Greg.

Mary and Greg's situation is not uncommon. In most libraries, the first several months of actually implementing new activities and eliminating or streamlining others are so intense that there is little time for reflection and assessment. In far too many libraries, even after the first rush of changes has been implemented, no one takes the time to evaluate the effect of those changes. This is not surprising, when you consider that staff in many libraries have never formally evaluated any programs or services, with the possible exception of a few programs that were grant funded. It is to be hoped that managers in libraries with no history of evaluation would have identified an organizational competency and initiative dealing with evaluation during the *SPFR* process or earlier in the *IFR* process. However, even if they did, they may have set the deadline for completing the initiative for the end of the first year of the planning cycle. Too many managers still think of evaluation as something done at the end of a project rather than as an ongoing management tool.

Managers in some libraries may believe that they already have the needed evaluation competencies in place because they collect a variety of data which are entered on a monthly report form, or sent to the state library agency, or simply filed with similar data. However, these managers have confused measurement with evaluation.

> Measurement is the collection, analysis, and organization of objective, quantitative data. Measurement is no-fault. It does not in itself indicate whether a library is "good" or "bad," it simply describes what is. . . . Evaluation is the feedback loop of the planning process. It provides the information needed to keep the library headed in its chosen direction. Evaluation consists of comparing "what is" with "what should be."[1]

In the past it would have been very difficult for managers in some libraries to use the data they collected to evaluate a program or service, because no one in their libraries had defined "what should be." One of the most valuable things about the *SPFR* process is that the goals and objectives provide a clear picture of "what should be" and set the stage for managers to use the measurements they collect to formally evaluate their activities. However, it does little good to know "what is" and "what should be" if no one compares the two.

Sometimes managers don't think about evaluating the changes that have been made because they are confident that the decisions that were reached during the *IFR* process were absolutely right. These managers often get a rude awakening after eight or nine months when someone actually compares the data about what is happening with the targets in the objectives. What these overconfident managers forget is that every decision in the *IFR* process was based on a series of assumptions about the library's users and what those users want, about the staff's ability to implement the activities that were selected, about the amount of resources that would need to be reallocated, about the degree of buy-in to this process that they would get from staff, and about the types of tools and materials that would be available. It is very unlikely that every assumption they made was accurate. Things are changing too fast for that to be true. Inevitably, some activities will prove to be more effective than others and some reallocation decisions will have to be revisited.

In the end, it doesn't matter what reasons managers have for not evaluating the progress that is being made toward reaching the targets in their objectives. If they do not evaluate their progress and take corrective action as necessary, much of the work they have done through both the planning process and the *IFR* process will have been wasted. The tasks in this chapter are designed to give you the information and the tools you need to make final decisions, monitor the effect of those decisions, make needed adjustments, and fully integrate the changes you have made into the library's infrastructure.

Getting Started

The library's managers have been involved in completing the tasks and steps in the *IFR* process for several months, and they are probably beginning to feel like the process will never end. Fortunately, the end of the first part of the process is at hand. In Task 12 the library's senior managers will use all of the data that has been collected to select the activities that will be implemented and those that will be eliminated, reduced, or streamlined. These decisions will provide all staff members with a clear direction for the future.

However, once the decisions have been made, another set of issues will have to be addressed. The changes that have taken so long to plan will have to be implemented and the effect of those changes will have to be monitored. In Task 13, staff will begin to monitor the progress being made toward reaching the targets in the objectives in the strategic plan and report on that progress to the board, the staff, and the members of the community. Managers will also prepare to make the adjustments that will inevitably be needed as the changes move from theory to practice. In Task 14, the final task in this chapter, the library's managers will work together to define what remains to be done to fully incorporate the changes that are being made into the library's ongoing operations and to create an environment in which change is the norm rather than the exception.

TASK 12: SELECT AND IMPLEMENT ACTIVITIES

In Step 12.1, the library's senior managers will be responsible for making the final decisions about the activities to implement and those to eliminate or modify. In Step 12.2, every staff member in the library will have some responsibility for implementing the final decisions that are made.

The senior managers can make their final decisions as soon as the unit managers have completed their assessments of the resources available for reallocation and the resources that will be needed to implement the new or expanded essential activities.

Implementation begins as soon as the final activities are selected and continues throughout the entire planning cycle.

Step 12.1
Select Final Activities to Implement and to Eliminate, Reduce, or Streamline

In the mid-1990s a group of library directors and consultants came together to review the data from a survey of librarians who had used the Public Library Association's *Planning and Role Setting for Public Libraries* to develop strategic plans between 1987 and 1995. The survey produced two major findings. The first finding was that the PLA planning process was being used to develop strategic plans in libraries across the country. The second finding was that well over half the librarians who reported they had completed a plan indicated that little had been done to actually implement that plan. When the survey respondents were asked why they had made so little progress on implementation, the answer was almost always some variation of the phrase "We didn't have the resources we needed."

Based on the survey results, this group began developing tools to help library managers to identify the types and levels of resources that would be required to implement new or expanded activities and to identify how existing resources could be reallocated to support those activities. Their work ultimately led to the publication of *Managing for Results: Effective Resource Allocation for Public Libraries,* which includes over fifty workforms with detailed instructions for gathering and analyzing all sorts of library data. Toward the end of one long meeting that had been spent reviewing instructions for over a dozen workforms, one very experienced library director said with some exasperation: "At some point library managers are just going to have to *think!*" That will certainly be true in this step.

By the time you reach this step, you have all of the data you need to make informed decisions. You have identified the new or expanded activities that are essential for implementing the goals and objectives in your plan (Workform D). You have identified the activities you intend to eliminate, reduce, or streamline (Workforms E, F, and I). You know approximately what resources will be available for reallocation if you eliminate, reduce, or streamline the ineffective, inefficient, and nonpriority activities you have identified in each unit and approximately what resources will be required to implement the new or expanded activities in those units—and you know where there are disparities (Workform Q). You have also decided how you will reallocate your materials budget to support your priorities (Step 10.2). Now you need to act on the information you have collected.

What Information Do the Senior Managers Need to Make Their Decisions?

When Workforms D–Q have been completed, a staff member should be designated to record all of the essential (priority A) new or modified activities from Workform D in column A of Workform R, Planning to Implement New or Expanded Activities—System Information. The same staff member should record all of the activities that will be eliminated, reduced, or streamlined from Workforms E, F, and I in column A of Workform S, Planning to Eliminate, Reduce, or Streamline Activities—System Information (both are available at http://e-learnlibraries.mrooms.net). See figures 36 and 37 for samples of these two workforms.

The senior managers will receive a packet containing three workforms from each unit before meeting to make their final decisions. Each unit packet will include Workforms Q, N, and P.

In most cases, Workform Q will include all of the information the senior managers will need. The other two workforms in the packet have been included in case the senior managers decide they need more specific information about an activity. The data coordinator will also have copies of all of the supporting workforms (D–M and O) for each unit available if they are needed. The senior managers will also receive the partially completed copies of Workforms R and S (with the information recorded in column A of each workform) prior to the meeting.

FIGURE 36

Workform R: Planning to Implement New or Expanded Activities—System Information—Example

A. Activity	B. Units in Which the Activity Will Be Offered	C. Person Responsible for Initiating or Coordinating the Activity	D. Date the Activity Will Begin	E. Notes
Books to Go bags for preschool materials	All branches	Youth services coordinator and Books to Go committee	9/15/XX	Reallocate materials budget to purchase additional preschool materials for the bags
Present story programs in day care centers	All branches	Youth services coordinator and children's librarians	1/15/XX	Begin meeting with day care providers this fall to introduce the activity and schedule visits beginning in January

A. Activity	B. Units in Which the Activity Will Be Eliminated, Reduced, or Streamlined	C. Person Responsible for Initiating or Coordinating the Change	D. Date the Change Will Begin	E. Date of Completion	F. Notes
Stop creating handmade puppets for puppet shows	Systemwide	Youth services coordinator	Immediately	NA	Purchase puppets for systemwide use
Stop creating themed bulletin boards in youth services areas each month	All youth services areas	Youth services coordinator and the branch managers	For the remainder of this fiscal year, each children's area will have a single bulletin board display. Next FY, the bulletin boards will be removed.	August 15, 2XXX	Schedule removal of the bulletin board with the maintenance department

MATCH THE REQUIRED RESOURCES AND THE RESOURCES AVAILABLE FOR REALLOCATION

When the senior managers meet to review the information on the workforms and make their final decisions, they will start by considering this question: are there enough resources available for reallocation to implement the essential new or expanded activities? They will be able to quickly answer that question by reviewing the completed copies of Workform Q, which compare the available and needed resources for each unit, and they will answer the question in one of three ways.

Yes, there are enough resources available for reallocation in each unit to implement the essential new or expanded activities. If this is the answer, the senior managers can complete columns B–E on Workform R.

Yes, there are enough resources available for reallocation in each unit to implement the essential new or expanded activities, and there are additional resources that can be used to implement desirable activities. If this is the answer, the senior managers will complete a second copy of Workform R, with the desirable activities (priority B) from Workform D listed in column A.

No, there are not enough resources available for reallocation in each unit to implement all of the essential new or expanded activities. If this is the answer, the senior managers will have to go back and revisit the decisions made on Workforms D, E, F, and I.

They should start by looking at the current activities that they decided were effective on Workform D near the beginning of the *IFR* process. Are those decisions still valid? Now that they have spent more time exploring the current and new activities, is it possible that some current activities are less effective than the new activities on the list? Given the power of the status quo, the answer is probably yes. Do some of the current activities require more resources than can be justified by the results they will produce?

When the senior managers review the current activities that support the goals that will be eliminated, reduced, or streamlined on Workform E, they should pay particular attention to the activities they decided to reduce or streamline. Can these activities be further modified or eliminated entirely? Why are the activities being modified rather than eliminated?

The senior managers will want to reconsider the activities that support service responses that are not priorities on Workform F. Are there additional activities that can be moved from proactive to reactive? Are there activities that can be eliminated entirely?

Finally, they should look at the sacred cows on Workform I. Are there additional sacred cows that can be addressed? Can the sacred cows on the list be further streamlined? Can some of the sacred cows that were scheduled to be streamlined be eliminated instead?

This is another point at which the senior managers face a very clear-cut choice. They can either reduce, streamline, or eliminate additional ineffective, inefficient, or nonpriority activities so that they have the resources needed to implement essential activities, or they can continue ineffective, inefficient, or nonpriority activities instead of implementing essential activities.

The *IFR* process has focused on making data-based decisions for several good reasons. Data-based decisions are grounded in reality, they can be explained and justified, they provide a framework for making coordinated changes, and they provide a context for evaluating progress and making adjustments as needed.

However, there can be a danger in putting so much emphasis on making decisions based on data. Some library managers, particularly those who were once reference librarians, still believe that there is one right answer to every question and that every answer can be documented. They think that if they just collect enough data, they will find what they need to guarantee that the decisions they are making are the right decisions. The truth, of course, is that there is never enough data to make completely safe decisions about which activities to implement and which to eliminate, reduce, or streamline. You are making decisions based on your projections of future conditions. The data you have collected will help you to make accurate projections and will significantly improve the chances that the decisions you make will be successful, but you must be prepared to adapt your decisions to meet current conditions as you move forward.

MAKE FINAL DECISIONS ABOUT ACTIVITIES TO IMPLEMENT

When the senior managers have agreed that the needed resources are available for reallocation or have decided what they will do to address any shortfalls, they will be ready to complete the remainder of Workform R. As you can see in figure 36, the senior managers will decide who will be responsible for implementing the new or expanded activities and the date by which the activities will be implemented. These are two critical decisions. Nothing gets done unless someone is assigned to do it—and surprisingly little gets done if there is no deadline for completion.

MAKE FINAL DECISIONS ABOUT ACTIVITIES TO ELIMINATE OR MODIFY

The senior managers will not have finished their work until they have officially made plans to eliminate, reduce, or streamline the activities listed on Workform S (see figure 37). It is probable that a number of these activities have already been modified or eliminated, but there are undoubtedly some that still need to be addressed. You will note that this workform includes two date columns. You will record both the date the changes are scheduled to begin *and* the date the changes are scheduled to be completed. Some of the changes listed in column A of this workform will be challenging to implement, and some managers may be tempted to let the process linger too long. Assigning a completion date will make it clear to everyone that the changes are to be made in a timely manner.

Workforms R and S are the last workforms in the *IFR* process. When the senior managers complete those workforms, they will have done all of the preparation work necessary to meet the goals and objectives in the library's strategic plan. They will be ready to move on to the culmination of the process: implementation.

Step 12.2
Implement Your Decisions

The final step in this task could be called "Just do it!" You and your colleagues collected all of the data you need and used that data to make all of the decisions that need to be made. All that remains is to implement those decisions.

Does each unit have the right number of staff in the needed classifications to implement the essential activities? Have all staff received the training they need? Is there a clear time line for the facility work that is needed? Do staff have all of the equipment they need? Does each facility have the furniture needed to support the essential activities? If space in one or more units needed to be reconfigured, has that been completed? Scheduled? Has the collection budget been reallocated to reflect current priorities? Have the standing orders been reviewed and revised as needed? Are the collections in each unit being weeded as needed? Have the changes needed to ensure that the technological infrastructure is robust enough to support the essential activities been made? Scheduled? Have all of the new hardware and software that will be needed been ordered? Installed? Has the library's website been redesigned to support the essential activities? Have the organizational competencies been addressed? Are the initiatives that support those competencies being completed on schedule?

Managers have four primary responsibilities: they lead, they allocate resources, they organize work, and they monitor the work that is being done by those they manage. Asking these questions and others like them is an integral part of the first three of these responsibilities. You lead by making data-based decisions, you allocate resources based on the library's priorities, and you organize work based on the activities that support your strategic plan. The fourth managerial responsibility will be addressed in the next task.

TASK 13: MONITOR IMPLEMENTATION

The two steps in this task will begin as soon as the senior managers have selected the new or expanded activities that are being initiated and have identified the ineffective, inefficient, and nonpriority activities that are being eliminated, reduced, or streamlined. The senior managers will develop procedures to monitor each of the changes being made, and the unit managers will be responsible for the actual monitoring. When problems are identified, the people involved will work together to recommend solutions, which will be presented to the senior managers for action.

The members of the board will be kept informed about the progress being made through monthly reports from the library director.

Step 13.1
Collect Data and Monitor Progress Monthly

The term *monitor* means to check something at regular intervals in order to find out how it is progressing or developing. The key words in the definition are *regular intervals*. If you wait until the end of the year to check on the progress being made toward reaching the target in an objective and find that there has been no progress, you are stuck. You can't change the past and you will have no opportunity to make the adjustments needed to meet the target during that year.

> **CAUTION**
>
> The targets are just indicators. Don't lose track of the big picture. Are you making the differences in your community that you hoped to when you completed your strategic plan?

There is a lot of emphasis on meeting the targets in your strategic plan in this step, but it is important that you remember how and why those targets were established. The targets provide the library's managers and board members with the means to measure the progress being made toward the goals in the strategic plan, and the goals in the plan describe the difference the library will make for the people in the community. You didn't go through all of the work of creating a strategic plan and developing an implementation strategy just to put check marks on a list of targets. You and your colleagues have done all of this hard work so that you can provide excellent services that will meet the unique needs of the people you serve. The monitoring in this step is designed to provide you with the information you need to continually refine and enhance your activities to reflect the changing needs and interests of your community.

What Data Do You Need to Collect?

The monitoring process starts by identifying the data that will be needed to track the progress being made toward the targets in the objectives in your strategic plan and deciding how you are going to collect the needed data. This will not be difficult. Each objective includes a measure, a target, and the date by which the target should be reached. In the objective "Each year at least 5,000 preschool children will attend programs presented or sponsored by the library in nonlibrary locations," the measure is the number of preschool children who attend programs in nonlibrary locations, the target is 5,000, and the target is to be reached each year.

While it is easy to see that you will have to count the number of preschool children who attend programs presented or sponsored by the library in nonlibrary locations, it will be more challenging to determine how you will collect those attendance numbers. "Count the number of preschool children who attend programs" raises more questions than it answers. Who will be responsible for counting? How will the attendees be counted? Will they be asked to sign in or will someone manually count the people in the room? How will whoever is counting determine that a child is a preschooler? How should the number of attendees be recorded? Is there a standardized form? How often should the attendance numbers be tabulated? Who should receive the data after they have been tabulated? These questions and others like them will have to be resolved for the target in every objective in your strategic plan before you can begin monitoring your progress.

Your targets will probably include both qualitative and quantitative data, and the data collection processes will be different for each. *Quantitative data* are numerical and measure *how much* of something there is or *how often* something happens. Most library data are quantitative (circulation figures, number of reference questions, number of users who log on to the Internet, number of online searches, program attendance, etc.). This information is normally gathered two ways: electronically (the library's integrated library system, the library's web server) and manually (check marks to tally the number of questions asked at reference desks or attendance counts at programs).

Qualitative data come from surveys or interviews and provide information about *how people feel* about an activity (the percentage of users who think an activity meets their needs, etc.). This information is normally collected through surveys or focus groups. The measure in the objective "By 2XXX, at least 75 percent of the parents or caregivers who bring their children to the library will say that the library helps preschoolers to prepare to enter school" is a qualitative measure.

It is obvious from reading these two descriptions that it is almost always easier to collect quantitative data than qualitative data. This is particularly true for quantitative data that is collected electronically. After the report structure is established, these data take little time to collect and are normally reported monthly. Quantitative data that are collected manually can be more challenging. These data can be gathered in two ways: every instance can be counted, or a sampling of instances can be counted and used to extrapolate the total.

When Mary and Greg were reviewing the data needed to monitor the targets in the objectives in the Tree County Public Library's strategic plan, they agreed that they would count every preschool child who attended a program presented or sponsored by the library in nonlibrary locations rather than using sampling to determine the average number of children who attended programs. The audience for each program would be different, and it would be difficult to get an accurate picture of total program attendance using sampling. Sampling would also make it impossible to determine the number of preschool children who attended each program, and program attendance is often one of the success indicators for programs. Mary and Greg knew that at some point they were going to want to compare the attendance to see if programs presented in some venues were more effective than programs presented in other locations.

However, Mary and Greg decided to continue to use sampling to collect data about the repetitive activities that occur throughout the year that cannot be tracked electronically, as well as to collect the data needed for new repetitive activities. The staff in every public library collect data about the number of reference questions that are asked each year, because that is a data element that is required to be reported to all state library agencies. The managers in a few public libraries ask staff to keep a manual tally of every question. However, most managers (including those in Tree County) ask staff to tally the questions asked during two or three representative weeks during the year and then they use that sample to estimate the annual total, which is more efficient and often more accurate. Mary and Greg decided to ask the staff to use sampling to collect data about the number of people who receive readers' advisory assistance, a data element they had not previously counted.

Qualitative data is usually collected through a sampling process. It would be impossible—and undesirable—to survey each library user every time he or she visits the library. For most objectives, staff should survey selected users twice a year and use that sample as the basis for their annual measure. Of course, there are some objectives that include qualitative measures that will be collected more often. For instance, if one of your objectives is "At least 85 percent of the people who attend programs on local, state, and national issues will say that those programs were very good or excellent," you will probably ask each program attendee to complete a brief evaluation form at the end of each program.

In addition to a measure and a target, each objective includes a time by which that target should be met. In some objectives the time frame is "each year." In other objectives the time frame might be "by year 2XXX." The time frames may be different, but they will all be expressed in years and not months. This can create problems when you are trying to monitor your progress toward reaching that target on a monthly basis. You know that you won't be making exactly the same progress each month. There are too many variables—holidays, vacations, weather, the school calendar, and so on. The only way to get a true sense of what is happening each month is to use baseline data from the months in the preceding year as a benchmark against which you can compare the progress being made to see if you are improving, staying the same, or falling behind.

Of course, the library may not have baseline data for all the targets in all of the objectives. For example, one of the objectives in the Tree County strategic plan is "At least 25,000 adults will receive readers' advisory assistance each year." The library has never collected this data, so the data collected during the first year will provide the baseline for future years. The managers reviewing the data don't have to work completely in the dark. They can look at the previous year's benchmarks for similar targets to get a sense of the seasonal flow. Although answering reference questions and providing readers' advisory assistance are different activities, it is reasonable to assume that if the number of reference questions asked dips during December each year, you may see a similar dip in the number of people requesting readers' advisory assistance. You will have to be careful not to carry these comparisons too far, however. The number of reference questions probably increases in the spring when students are doing research papers, but that won't necessarily mean that requests for readers' advisory assistance will increase.

If you would like to learn more about collecting and evaluating library data, read *The Tell It! Manual: The Complete Program for Evaluating Library Performance.*[2] It includes information on a variety of data collection processes.

What Process Should Be Used to Collect Data?

The staff in virtually every public library in the country are currently collecting a wide variety of data. They are collecting data for the annual statistical report that is sent to the state library agency. They are collecting data to report on current grant projects—and some staff have never stopped collecting data about grant projects that were finished long ago. They have set their integrated library systems and their websites to collect and report on a wide variety of data elements. In view of all this data collection, one might think that library managers would have an easy time establishing a process for collecting the data needed to track each of the targets in the objectives in the library's strategic plan. Unfortunately, this is not the case. The data that are currently collected may not be valid, and the measures in the objectives in your plan will undoubtedly include data elements that you do not currently collect. It is one thing to collect a wide variety of data. It is another thing to collect data that are both pertinent and valid.

The problems with library data collection are well known to every manager. In many libraries, managers aren't even sure exactly what data are being collected in the various units. Even managers who think they know what data elements are being collected are often unclear about how the staff is defining each element. Although the state library agency has provided specific definitions for the data elements included in the state report, staff often use their own definitions instead. There are often no formal definitions for the data elements that are collected for local use only. Staff who collect data receive little or no training. The data that are collected are not checked for validity—or even logic. The list of problems goes on and on. For all of the reasons described earlier in this step, you will need current, valid data about the progress that is being made toward reaching your objectives.

To do that you will need to assign the oversight for all data collection to one of the library's managers. That manager should be responsible for collecting and verifying the data needed for the report to the state library agency, the Public Library Data Service, and the data needed to monitor progress toward reaching the targets in the objectives in the strategic plan. This job is too important to be assigned to a clerical support person from the director's office, which is where the responsibility rests in many libraries now.

The data coordinator should define each data element to be collected, determine how often it should be collected, develop and field-test surveys and other data collection instruments, decide how the data that is collected should be recorded, and identify the appropriate people to collect each data element. The data coordinator should also work with the library director to develop the forms to be used to report the data about the progress being made toward reaching the objectives in the strategic plan.

The actual data collection should be officially assigned to the appropriate staff members throughout the library. Information technology staff should be assigned to produce specified data from the integrated system. Web support staff should be assigned to produce specified data from the web server. Children's services staff should be told specifically what data to collect about program attendance, the number of off-site programs presented, and so on. Adult services staff will need to have specific instructions about the types of data they are to collect. All staff who are expected to collect data should be trained to collect the data in the same way and at the same times.

When the data have been collected and submitted to the data coordinator, someone should be asked to review the raw data to be sure it was collected and reported correctly

FIGURE 38

Common Sense Guidelines for Collecting Data

1. Develop and maintain a comprehensive list of the data elements that are included in the objectives in your strategic plan.

2. Develop and maintain a comprehensive list of the data elements that are reported to your state library agency and submitted to the Public Library Data Service.

3. Define all data elements clearly. Use the definitions from the state library agency, when these are available.

4. Determine when and how often each data element should be collected.

5. Review data that are available from your integrated library system to be sure that you have what you need to track your progress toward reaching the targets in your objectives, and make any needed modifications.

6. Determine an accurate sample size for your library. There are a number of resources on the Web that will help you determine the sample size.

7. Develop and field-test surveys and other data collection instruments.

8. Decide how the data that are collected should be recorded.

9. Decide how the data that are collected should be tabulated and reported.

10. Prepare written instructions for collecting and reporting each data element.

11. Determine who will be responsible for collecting each data element.

12. Bring the people who will be responsible for collecting the data together before you start data collection to be sure that they all understand the instructions and know how frequently they are expected to collect the data.

13. Assign someone to monitor the data collection to be sure that it is happening when it should.

14. Assign someone to review the raw data to be sure they were collected and reported correctly.

and then to tabulate the data and prepare the needed reports. The data coordinator will probably need to develop a formal data-collection plan to be sure that staff are collecting and reporting the right data at the right times. Figure 38 lists the steps needed to develop such a plan.

How Should the Monitoring Data Be Reported?

All of the stakeholder groups identified in Workform A will need to be kept informed about the progress the library is making toward reaching the targets in the objectives in the strategic plan. As you may remember, those stakeholder groups included the members of your board, the senior managers, unit managers, supervisors, and frontline staff. There are other groups that you will want to inform as well, including the members of the Friends of the Library, the library's regular users, and the members of the public. It will be important to make a special effort to keep the library's funders informed about the progress being made toward implementing your strategic plan.

It is clear when you read through this list of stakeholder groups that you can't just distribute a single progress report every month to everyone you want to keep informed. You will have to develop specific messages for each group. The most effective way to develop these messages is to use the questions from Workform A as a guide.

> Why do the members of the stakeholder group need to know about progress being made toward reaching the targets? What do you expect them to do with the information?

What do they know now about the progress being made toward the targets?

What will they need to know about the progress being made in order to do what you want them to do?

When do they need to know it?

How will they be informed?

Who will be responsible for telling them?

Several things become clear as you review these questions. The first is that the actions you expect from each stakeholder group are quite different. The senior managers will have to be ready to identify problems and decide how to resolve them. Unit managers and supervisors will be expected to work closely with the staff in their units to identify unintended consequences and unexpected public reactions. You are keeping frontline staff informed so that they know how the work they are doing is contributing to the library's overall success and they will continue to be fully engaged in providing quality services. Board members will be evaluating the broader implications of the shifts in resources. You want the members of the Friends of the Library and the library foundation to continue to provide financial support to help implement the essential activities. You want the library's users and the general public to support the library and encourage local funders to do the same. Last, but certainly not least, you want local funders to know that the library is spending public dollars effectively and that the expenditures are providing services that the community residents want and need.

> **CAUTION**
>
> Every stakeholder group will need different information about the progress you are making on implementing your plan. One size does *not* fit all.

When you look at what you want the stakeholder groups to do, it is obvious that some groups will need detailed statistical information and others will only be interested in brief success stories. The senior managers will need to have specific information about the monthly progress being made toward every target in the plan. The unit managers will also need specific information, but only for the targets for which they have some responsibility. The managers in the technical services department do not need to know the number of visits to day care centers being made every month—and they might not be very interested if you told them. The supervisors and staff will also be interested in the progress being made toward the targets they have some responsibility for meeting. The members of the library board will need to have an overview of the progress being made each month toward reaching the goals, and they will need to be informed about any significant problems or successes. The members of the Friends and the library foundation will be particularly interested in hearing about activities that they have funded. The library's users and the general public want to hear about the library's most successful activities. The library's funders will also be interested in success stories and should be quite responsive to data about the progress being made toward targets that measure public use and public satisfaction.

Once you decide what you want each stakeholder group to do and what they will need to know in order to take the actions you want them to take, you can tailor the information that each group will receive. Mary and Greg decided to start by creating a detailed monthly report template that they could use to track the progress toward reaching every target in every objective for each goal in the plan. See figure 39 for an example of the report for one of the Tree County goals. The targets in the Tree County Public Library's strategic plan are yearly, but Mary and Greg recorded all of the available baseline data for the targets in their objectives for each goal before they began monitoring the progress being made.

FIGURE 39
Tree County Public Library Monitoring Report Form

Goal: Preschool children in Tree County will enter school ready to learn.

1. Each year, at least 5,000 preschool children will attend programs presented or sponsored by the library in nonlibrary locations.

	FY XX		FY XX		FY XX	
	Month Last FY	*YTD*	*Month Last FY*	*YTD*	*Month Last FY*	*YTD*
July	230					
August	225					
September	420					
October	440					
November	370					
December	310					
January	460					
February	440					
March	425					
April	460					
May	320					
June	200					
TOTAL	4,300					
TARGET	5,000		5,000		5,000	

2. Each year, easy books and picture books will be checked out at least 125,000 times.

	FY XX		FY XX		FY XX	
	Month	*YTD*	*Month*	*YTD*	*Month*	*YTD*
July	13,500					
August	9,500					
September	8,000					
October	8,500					
November	7,200					
December	6,500					
January	8,300					
February	8,800					
March	8,400					
April	8,500					
May	8,800					
June	14,000					
TOTAL	110,000					
TARGET	125,000		125,000		125,000	

3. By 2XXX, at least 75 percent of the parents or caregivers who bring their children to the library will say that the library helps preschoolers to prepare to enter school.

	FY XX	FY XX	FY XX
October Survey	48%		
TARGET	60%	70%	75%

The Tree County Public Library's strategic plan has seven goals, and Mary and Greg will complete the monitoring report for each goal each month. They will post all of the monitoring reports on the staff intranet and send print copies of the appropriate reports to each unit manager. Unit managers have been told they will be expected to share the progress being made toward reaching targets with the staff responsible for performing the activities that support those targets.

Mary decided that the monitoring form in figure 39 provided considerably more information than the library board members would want or need, so she developed the abbreviated version of the report form illustrated in figure 40. Each month Mary uses the form in figure 40 to report on the objectives that support each of the seven goals in the strategic plan. She can normally fit the objectives and data for two goals onto one page, so the report is typically three or four pages long. This format makes it easy for board members to find the salient points, and the board's review and discussion of the report rarely take more than ten minutes. Mary focuses the discussion on how the staff have addressed any problems that occurred and on particularly effective activities.

FIGURE 40

Tree County Public Library Strategic Plan—Monthly Board Report Form

---

Monthly Update for _____

Goal: Preschool children in Tree County will enter school ready to learn.

1. Each year, at least 5,000 preschool children will attend programs presented or sponsored by the library in nonlibrary locations.

	This Month	Total YTD	On Target (Y/N)
Program Attendance			

Comments:

2. Each year, easy books and picture books will be checked out at least 125,000 times.

	This Month	Total YTD	On Target (Y/N)
Circulation of Easy and Picture Books			

Comments:

3. By 2XXX, 75 percent of the parents or caregivers who bring their children to the library will say that the library helps preschoolers to prepare to enter school.

	FY XX	FY XX	FY XX
October Survey			
TARGET	55%	70%	75%

Comments:

Mary worked with the staff member who manages the library's marketing to develop messages about the library's successes to the other target audiences they identified. They used the same workforms that they had used in *Strategic Planning for Results* as a framework for writing and delivering the messages: Workform L, Communicate the Results, and Workform M, Message Elements. These workforms have not been reprinted in this book, but they are available at http://e-learnlibraries.mrooms.net.

Step 13.2
Adjust as Needed

The senior managers in every library *must* review the monitoring data for every target in every objective every month. That is the only way they can identify issues and resolve problems in a timely manner—and there will be issues to be addressed in every library. The whole purpose of monitoring the plan monthly is to identify the targets that are not being met and decide what needs to be done to meet those targets. Remember the quotation by Colin Powell: "There are no secrets to success. It is the result of preparation, hard work, and learning from failure." You have prepared, and you have worked hard. Now you need to decide what you will do when your expectations aren't met.

Why Do Libraries Have Trouble Meeting Some Targets?

There are at least four possible reasons for not making the progress expected toward reaching targets in your strategic plan: you didn't provide the resources necessary to fully implement the activities that support the objective; the activities that were selected to support the objective were not as effective as you hoped they would be; you didn't implement enough activities to reach the target; or you set the targets too high initially.

INSUFFICIENT RESOURCES

The first—and most common—reason for not meeting targets is that the resources required to implement the essential activities were not made available. The resource that is most difficult to reallocate is staff time. Staff can't perform new activities if they are fully occupied with current activities. In chapter 5 you and your colleagues put a lot of effort into estimating both the amount of time that could be made available for reallocation if activities were eliminated, reduced, or streamlined and the amount of time that new or expanded activities would require. The library's senior managers worked hard to match the required resources with the resources available for reallocation in Task 12 when they were selecting final activities. Even so, in many libraries the time that staff expected to get by eliminating, reducing, or streamlining activities doesn't materialize and the time required to implement a new or expanded activity is greater than expected.

There are several reasons why this happens, and you will have to understand the cause of the problem before you can resolve it. Sometimes the problem rests with the decisions made by the library's senior managers. Perhaps they did not eliminate, reduce, or streamline enough activities to free the time needed for the new or expanded activities. These senior managers may have been overly optimistic about the time that would be saved by making minor changes, and they may have hoped to be able to avoid the risks involved in making more significant changes.

On the other hand, sometimes staff don't want to give up their familiar activities to do new things, and their unit managers allow them to continue to do things that were supposed to be eliminated, reduced, or streamlined. Again the underlying problem is resistance to real change. The status quo is comfortable and familiar. It takes a lot of time and energy to stop doing one set of activities and begin to do another set of activities. It may also take training. Frontline staff can't be expected to perform new activities without the appropriate training—and if they don't get the training they need, they will feel perfectly justified in not performing the activity.

Staff issues are not the only resource problems that library managers may have to address. Most library strategic plans include a number of objectives relating to the use of and satisfaction with the library's collections. To meet the targets in these objectives, managers will probably have to make significant shifts in the allocation of the library's materials budget (Step 10.2). It may take between six and nine months to see the first effects of these changes. The new materials will have to be selected, ordered, processed, and shelved before they can be used and even if you expedite each of these steps, they will all still take time. This will make assessing the progress being made toward your collection targets a little challenging during the first year of the planning cycle. However, as the new materials start to become available, you should begin to see some progress. If you don't, you may have to revisit the decisions you made in Step 10.2. In some libraries, there is more resistance to changing the materials budget than there is to reassigning staff time. In these libraries, managers have a tendency to make token changes in the materials budget and put their faith in displays and better marketing—and neither is likely to result in increased circulation or higher user satisfaction.

There may also be problems with the facility resources that have been allocated to support one or more activities. It will be virtually impossible to meet any targets that relate to services to teens if the only "teen" space in the library consists of a table, four chairs, and two 72-inch stacks of hardback books adjacent to the children's room. Facility resources can present a special challenge in older libraries that have become increasingly crowded. Staff have had to find ways to work around the facility's shortcomings, and they can become so used to "making do" that they never think about trying to make significant changes in the spaces in which they work. The situation is often further complicated by the territorial divisions in libraries. The children's area is separate from the adult area. The reference section is separate from the periodicals area. The circulation desk is separate from the public service desk. Public and staff spaces are clearly delineated. Stack spaces and computer spaces are clearly defined. Each of these territories is staffed by people who tend to want to protect their own territorial borders—or expand into someone else's territory. Often the only way to ensure that the library's facility resources fully support the library's essential activities is to look holistically at how all of the spaces in the building are being used. This can be a daunting prospect, particularly for managers who are fully engaged in the *IFR* process.

Technology resources present a special challenge as well, particularly in libraries in which the service response "Connect to the Online World: Public Internet Access" is a priority. In *Public Libraries and the Internet 2008,* John Bertot and Charles McClure reported that "the average number of public access Internet workstations in each public library outlet is another category that has reached a plateau with [an average of] 10.7 [units in each outlet]. This number is essentially unchanged since 2002."[3] Managers in libraries that have selected activities that require significant technology support will have to purchase additional computers, make arrangements for additional bandwidth, and provide wireless access. The money to purchase and maintain this hardware, software, and bandwidth often has to come from other parts of the library's budget, and that can trigger turf wars similar to the battles of territory that may occur when reallocating facility resources.

INEFFECTIVE ACTIVITIES

No matter how much time and energy you and your colleagues spent evaluating activities or how careful you were when selecting your essential activities, you will probably find that some of the activities you selected turn out to be less effective than you hoped they would be. While there are a variety of reasons for this, one of the most common problems is captured in the phrase "than you hoped they would be."

The decisions that were made when you were evaluating the effectiveness of current and potential activities in Step 5.2 were based on three criteria: the number of people that would use the activity, the effect the activity would have on reaching the targets for the objectives in the goal, and the probable audience reaction to the activity. In the case of current activities, you may have had some data about past use, effect, and response to use as a guide, but when assessing potential activities you had to use a combination of judgment and experience to make your projections. However, the past is not an infallible guide to the future, and neither are your judgment and experience.

The demographics in most communities will continue to change over the next decade. Businesses will open and businesses will close. New people will move into your community; others will move away. The average age and education levels will shift as the population evolves. The community's priorities may shift for reasons as diverse as a natural disaster, a significant change in available public revenue, or a change in local leadership. Any or all of these changes may affect the success of the library's activities.

While external forces will certainly influence the effectiveness of the activities that were selected as essential, such forces are not the only issue. In some cases, the library's senior managers may have selected activities based on what they *believed* should be effective rather than on what they *knew* would be effective. Every person's beliefs exert a powerful influence over that person's behavior. A library manager who truly believes that providing reference services is the most important function for any public library may have trouble evaluating reference-related activities in an unbiased manner and may be equally hard-pressed to evaluate activities that support services she has always thought of as peripheral.

These feelings have little to do with the service priorities selected during the planning process and everything to do with personal beliefs and values. In libraries in which the senior managers have a variety of beliefs and values, open discussions typically help everyone focus on the library's priorities. In libraries in which the senior managers have similar beliefs and values, those feelings often exert a strong influence on the activities that are considered to be essential. There is a third permutation of this discussion of belief and value. In some libraries, the director feels very strongly about some services or programs and imposes her beliefs on the remainder of the staff.

Of course, sometimes the problem isn't that the community is changing or that the library managers made decisions based on beliefs and values. Sometimes the problem is the activity itself. This is more often true for new activities than for current activities. Most new activities were described in just enough detail to give staff a general idea of what the activity included. These descriptions may not have included all of the information that would be needed to fully evaluate the potential challenges that would have to be addressed to successfully implement the activity.

One of the new activities suggested during the Tree County Public Library planning process was "Give the parents of each new child born in Tree County hospitals a library card for the child, a free book, and an invitation to attend monthly Born to Read programs." If this activity was selected to be implemented, staff would have had to describe it in more detail in order to estimate the resources that would be required to support it. The expanded description would probably have included the number of hospitals in the county, the number of children born in each hospital each year, and the average cost of the book that would be given to the child. It might also have included an estimate of the number of parents who might attend each Born to Read program.

When the staff actually start to implement this complex activity, they will discover that the effectiveness of the activity depends on a number of external factors that may not have been considered when the activity was selected. Will all of the hospitals agree to participate? Will local pediatricians cooperate? Will the library be able to use public money to purchase books to be given away? Can the money for books be raised from external sources? How will new parents be tracked so they can be reminded of the Born to Read programs? The wrong answers to any of these questions might make this activity less effective than expected.

INSUFFICIENT ACTIVITIES

It often takes a variety of different activities to reach the targets in an objective, and this may not become apparent until after the initial activities have been implemented. This is most often true for goals and objectives that are new priorities for a library. If "Be an Informed Citizen" was identified as a priority for your library and it had not been a priority in the past, you have little context for selecting activities in this area. The measures in your objectives might include the number of people who access a web page with links to information on local issues, the number of people who attend public affairs programs sponsored or cosponsored by the library, and the percentage of people who think that the library is an excellent place to find information on local, state, or national issues.

Perhaps your initial activities included developing and maintaining a "Be an Informed Citizen" web page, asking the League of Women Voters to present bimonthly programs at the library, providing transcripts of the meetings of the county commission, and creating a monthly display of books and other resources that highlight an issue of local, state, or national interest. When you review the progress you are making toward the targets in your objectives, you may find that you are not making the progress you expected to make. In this case, the issue probably isn't the activities that you are implementing. Each of those may be quite effective, but collectively they may not be able to produce the results you need. The real issue may be that you are doing too few activities. You will need to revisit the current and new or expanded activities that were identified for this goal on Workform C to see if there are additional activities there that you might want to try. If not, you will have to explore other options. You will almost certainly have to involve additional partners and consider different programming venues. For example, the monthly displays of books are passive and will only be seen by library users. You will also need to identify additional activities that will allow you to proactively reach people who don't use the library.

UNREALISTIC TARGETS

Many of the targets that were set for the objectives during the strategic planning process were based on data from previous years. Others were based on what the senior managers or members of the board considered to be realistic expectations. Many of the targets include an expected increase in use or perceived value, although some are based on maintaining the status quo.

There are staff who are uncomfortable with the emphasis on increasing use or value, and they will be inclined to assume that anytime a target is not being met it is because the target was set too high. This is rarely the problem. Targets should only be lowered if there is firm evidence that they were set too high. For instance, if you based your use projections on current population estimates from the state and the population estimates next year are significantly different, you should revisit your targets. If there is a natural disaster that affects your community, you may have to revise your targets for a year or two. Depending on the magnitude of the disaster, you may have to completely revise your plan. The needs of the residents in coastal cities in Louisiana, Mississippi, and Alabama were very different after Hurricane Katrina than before the storm, and those changing needs had a profound effect on the libraries in those cities.

Fortunately, natural disasters are rare, and significant shifts in population are not common either. In most libraries, the real issue with unrealistic targets will be that the targets were set too low, not that the targets were set too high. It will be easy to tell if this is the case in your library. If you are meeting or exceeding all of the targets in all of your objectives, it is probably not because you are perfect every day in every way. It is far more likely that you set your expectations too low.

Even managers in these libraries will find that they have issues to address when they begin to monitor the progress they are making toward reaching their targets. The most obvious issue is that the members of the board and anyone else who is paying attention may want to know why the library's managers are exceeding the targets in all of their objectives. Once it becomes clear that the original targets were set too low, the members of most boards will expect managers to establish more realistic targets for the next year of the planning cycle. A second issue is less obvious but potentially more damaging for the library. One of the purposes of the library's strategic plan is to "make it clear that the library's services and programs make a difference to the people in the service area."[4] If the targets in your plan are very low, it will be hard for the public to think of the library as a place that is trying to make a real difference in their lives.

How Should Problems Be Addressed?

The facile answer to the question of how to address problems is "It depends on the problem." Like most facile answers, this one is both true and overly simplistic. Yes, you will have to address each problem separately depending on the problem. If the problem is that enough resources weren't allocated to adequately implement the activity, allocate more resources. If the problem is that the activity itself wasn't as effective as expected, modify the activity to make it more effective or replace it with a more effective activity. If you need more activities to reach your targets, add them. In the unlikely event that your targets were too high, modify them to reflect current conditions. In the more likely event that your targets were too low, raise them to more realistic levels.

While all of the answers in the preceding paragraph are true, they focus on *what* to do and not *how* to do it. It is one thing to somewhat cavalierly say "allocate the needed resources." As you have learned, it is an entirely different thing to find the resources needed. The same thing holds true with the other facile answers. It will take resources to modify ineffective activities or add new activities, and modifying the targets in your objectives will also have resource implications.

The more complete answer to the question of how to resolve problems is "Base all of your resource allocation decisions on the priorities in your strategic plan." Unlike the first answer, which was narrow and simplistic, this answer is broad and holistic. If you take this approach to resource allocation, you will be ready to address implementation problems as they arise and you will have the tools you need to identify resources that can be reallocated.

You and your colleagues have just spent six or eight months identifying priorities, developing goals and objectives, brainstorming and evaluating activities, determining resource requirements, making data-based decisions, and establishing processes to monitor the results of your decisions. Although you have done these tasks in the context of developing and implementing a new strategic plan, they have a broader application. In fact, these tasks are the fundamental managerial functions in any organization—public, private, or not-for-profit. The library's managers and frontline staff and the members of the library board have participated in the process and they understand it. All you have to do is integrate what you have learned into the ongoing operations of the library. When you have done that, you will be in a position to quickly and effectively make the adjustments needed to reach the targets in the objectives in your plan.

> **CAUTION**
>
> You can't resolve each implementation problem separately. All of your operations are interconnected. You will have to deal with implementation issues holistically.

TASK 14: MAKE CHANGE THE NORM

Both of the steps in this task will be managed by the library director and her team of senior managers. However, every staff member will be responsible for seeing to it that these steps are completed. The work in these steps begins as soon as the senior managers make their final decisions in Step 12.1, and it continues throughout this planning cycle—and throughout the planning cycles to come.

Step 14.1
Integrate Changes into Library Operations

When you finish the *IFR* process, you may feel as if just completing the process has fundamentally changed the library's management and operations. After all, every staff member in the library has been given a voice in the process. Managers have more data about the resources required to implement activities than they have ever had before. The board, the members of the management team, and the frontline staff are all on the same page and working toward the same goals. You are right. All of these things are true right now. However, unless you take formal action to incorporate these practices and others into your ongoing operations, they won't be true for long.

Remember the comment that Vincent's colleague made earlier: "Thank heaven that is finally over! Now we can get back to our real work." Far too many staff in the library still consider the planning and implementing that you have been doing as a project rather than a process. That gives these staff members a skewed perspective about the future.

A project has a finite time line with a beginning and an end. Staff members know that the planning and implementation process started six or eight months ago, and unless they are told differently, they are going to assume that it was over when the senior managers made their final decisions in Step 12.1. In contrast, a process has a starting point but is open-ended. A project produces a product, typically a report. Some staff will see the completion and publication of the strategic plan and the decisions about the activities as the end product of this project. Processes do not result in reports. Instead they change the way things are done. Projects are often narrowly defined; they deal with a single issue or activity. Processes are normally broader in scope and focus. A project is typically completed by a small team who then present their product to a larger group. A process often involves everyone who will be affected by the process from the beginning.

How Can You Integrate What You Have Learned into Your Ongoing Operations?

You start by publicly linking every decision you make to the strategic plan. Do this even if the decision was made during the *IFR* process. What is important is to constantly and consistently send the message that the plan is the framework within which every library decision is being made. This is not only the right message to send the staff; it is the right message for library decision makers to hear as well. If you say it often enough it will become a self-fulfilling prophecy, and once that happens you are well on your way to becoming an organization that uses the Results principles as a management framework.

Earlier in the process, you and your colleagues identified some of the organizational competencies that would be required to support the goals and objectives in your plan. As you may remember, an organizational competency is "the institutional capacity or efficiency that is necessary to enable the library to achieve the goals and objectives in its strategic plan." Organizational competencies were introduced in Step 1.1 and discussed in detail in Task 8, Identify Organizational Competencies, in *SPFR*.

Many of the organizational competencies that are required to achieve your goals and objectives will also be required to change your library's management practices. Now would be a good time to review the organizational competencies you identified earlier to be sure that they include everything that is needed. As you review your organizational competencies, consider some of the following actions that must be taken to institutionalize the decision-making processes you and your colleagues have been using.

Staff allocations (both by classification and by unit, department, or agency) may need to be reallocated.

Performance appraisal documents will have to be revised to reflect the new activities that staff are expected to perform.

Job descriptions may need to be revised to reflect current duties and assignments.

The staff development plan will have to include the training needed to perform all new activities.

The current allocation of shelving may have to be modified to reflect the changes in the materials budget.

The collection development policies and guidelines will need to be revised to support the new priorities.

The collection will need to be evaluated and weeded.

The library's policies will have to be reviewed and updated to support the current priorities.

Procedures will have to be written or revised to reflect all of the decisions that were made to streamline sacred cows.

The library's website will need to be reviewed and updated to reflect new priorities.

These changes, and the others that will be needed, do not have to happen immediately nor do they have to happen simultaneously. Some of them will be more important in your library than others, and those are the ones you will address first. A process doesn't have an end date. Instead, it is a continual progression in which each change builds on the last and sets the stage for the next. It is in the act of making these changes that you integrate the Results principles into your operations.

Step 14.2
Stay Ahead of the Curve

Libraries that thrive in today's environment must be led by managers who are change-adept and able to create environments that support change. The characteristics of change-adept libraries and library managers were described in Step 1.2. "It isn't enough to make a commitment to change. A library must have the capacity in place to support the change process. The public libraries that are thriving in today's rapidly changing environment share a number of characteristics. Most important, they have strong leaders and excellent library boards. They have management teams and library boards that understand the difference between effectiveness and efficiency. Decisions are made based on data and not emotion. These libraries are market-driven in the true sense of marketing; they develop products that the people they serve want and they provide those products at the most convenient times and in the most convenient places. Libraries that manage change well are 'early adapters.' They experiment with new technologies and new service models before others. They create and support an environment that encourages taking risks, and they reward risk-takers. Finally, successful libraries have an effective group of managers and supervisors who have the skills needed to implement the changes and the responsibility and authority to do so."

Every task and step in this book has been designed to help you and your colleagues develop the characteristics needed to succeed now and in the future. You have learned the difference between efficiency and effectiveness, and you have developed the criteria you will use in your library to measure the effectiveness of current and potential activities in the future. You clearly understand that you must provide the products that people want in the places they want them, and this understanding is reflected in the criteria you will use to measure the effectiveness of your current activities and any new activities you initiate in years to come. You and every other manager in your library know how to collect the data needed to determine the resources that are required to support an activity, and you all know how to use that data to make decisions. Because every manager has been involved throughout this process, they have become more effective managers who have the skills they need to implement changes in their units.

The twin characteristics of being an early adapter and developing a risk-tolerant environment were not specifically addressed in any one task or step. Instead they permeated every task and step. The staff who were engaged in identifying potential activities were encouraged to get ideas from other libraries and from other organizations with similar missions. As a result, they were given an opportunity to explore cutting-edge services. By using the same set of external criteria to evaluate both current and new activities, senior managers were able to overcome the power of the status quo and seriously consider exciting new services. The focus on meeting the targets in the objectives in the strategic plan also encourages staff to adapt to new technologies quickly, particularly if the targets include measures of user satisfaction.

Finally, there is risk tolerance, a critical characteristic for those who want to stay ahead of the curve. You have just completed a challenging process during which you have redefined your library's services and programs. By now you know that there are no guarantees that every decision you have made will be equally effective. In fact, there is a very strong probability that some will far exceed your expectations and others will be a disappointment. This will not stop you from going forward with the plans you have made. You plan to monitor your progress regularly and to make changes as needed. You understand that all change entails risk. You have learned the truth of the famous Peter Drucker quotation: "It is not necessary to change. Survival is not mandatory." Libraries that are afraid to take the risk of making substantial changes are missing the point. The real risk that libraries face today is that they will be unable or unwilling to make the changes needed to continue to be relevant.

What's Next?

You, your colleagues, and the members of your board will work together to create a library that is an integral part of your community. You will provide services that are needed, used, and valued by all residents and you will adjust those services as conditions change. You will have the data you need to make sure that everyone knows that the library is spending public monies wisely and that the services you provide make a real difference to the people you serve. The members of your community will become library advocates. The members of your funding authority will consider the library to be a priority service that is as important to the quality of life in the community as the police, the fire department, and the schools. You will ensure that library services in your community continue to grow and thrive for the next generation.

Key Points to Remember

Senior managers will have to formally approve the implementation of every new or expanded activity and they will have to formally approve eliminating, reducing, or streamlining every ineffective, inefficient, or nonpriority activity.

Don't get so involved in collecting data that you lose track of the reason for collecting the data—and don't fall into the trap of thinking that there is one more piece of data somewhere that will help you decide.

Nothing gets done unless someone is assigned to do it—and surprisingly little gets done if there is no deadline for completion.

Planning for implementation is important. Acting to implement is critical.

Managers have four primary responsibilities: they lead, they allocate resources, they organize work, and they monitor the work that is being done by those they manage.

You must monitor the progress you are making toward reaching the targets in your objectives monthly. If you wait until the end of the year to check your progress and find that there are problems, it will be too late to make any needed adjustments.

Keep the data collection process as simple as possible. Use electronically produced data whenever possible. When you collect quantitative data manually, use a sampling methodology rather than counting every instance. Qualitative data is almost always collected through a sampling process.

You will need current, valid data about the progress that is being made toward reaching your objectives.

There are a variety of groups that need to be informed about the progress you are making toward implementing your strategic plan, and the members of each group will need different information.

The senior managers in every library must review the monitoring data for every target in every objective every month.

There are staff who are uncomfortable with the emphasis on increasing use or value, and they will be inclined to assume that anytime a target is not being met it is because the target was set too high. This is rarely the problem. Targets should only be lowered if there is firm evidence that they were set too high.

You have all of the skills you need to integrate the Results principles into the ongoing operations of the library.

Notes

1. Nancy Van House and others, *Output Measures for Public Libraries,* 2nd ed. (Chicago: American Library Association, 1987), xviii.
2. Douglas Zweizig and others, *The Tell It! Manual: The Complete Program for Evaluating Library Performance* (Chicago: American Library Association, 1996).
3. John Bertot, Charles R. McClure, and others, *Public Libraries and the Internet 2008: Study Results and Findings,* www.ii.fsu.edu/plinternet_reports.cfm.
4. Sandra Nelson, *Strategic Planning for Results* (Chicago: American Library Association, 2008), 100.

Appendix

Results Resource Allocation Workforms Available in Electronic Format

Electronic copies of these workforms are available at http://e-learnlibraries.mrooms.net.

STAFF RESOURCES

Managing for Results Staffing Workforms Summary

Workform	Title	Purpose
Overview		
Workform S1	Staff Functions Related to Service Priorities	To determine the staff functions that will be affected by the library's service priorities
Activities and Abilities		
Workform S2	Activities Involved in a Service Priority	To determine the characteristics of the specific activities necessary to provide one service priority
Workform S3	Staff Abilities Required for an Activity	To pinpoint the specific staff abilities needed for one activity related to a service priority
Workform S4	Checklist of Abilities for Activities	To clarify when, where, and how abilities for a service priority are to be utilized
Workform S5	Analyzing Training Needs and Costs for a Service Priority	To help assess the real costs of training staff to acquire desired abilities
Capacity, Utilization, and Productivity		
Workform S6	Estimating Hours Available for Full-Time Staff	To calculate the hours of expected work by staff category
Workform S7	Public Service Indicators	To compare activity levels among public service units/teams
Workform S8	Analysis of an Activity	To analyze the sequence of tasks involved in performing an activity
Observations and Time		
Workform S9	Daily Direct-Observation Log	To collect data on staff activities by structured observations
Workform S10	Unit/Team/Library Observation Summary	To show the number and variety of activities performed by various staff categories during one day

Workform	Title	Purpose
Workform S11	Staff-Activity Analysis	To illustrate the congruence of how a staff member spends time and the tasks important to the job assignment
Workform S12	Daily Time/Activity Log	To collect information about staff activities during one day
Workform S13	Activity Log Summary	To categorize and summarize activities performed by one employee in one day
Workform S14	Unit/Team/Library Activity Summary	To summarize time spent on many activities

Estimating the Costs/Value of Activities

Workform S15	Converting Capacity to Cost	To calculate compensation costs for different time periods
Workform S16	Estimating the Cost/Value of Individual Staff Activities	To analyze time and money spent for individual activities
Workform S17	Estimating the Cost/Value of Unit/Team Activities	To analyze time and money spent for unit activities
Workform S18	Estimating the Cost/Value of a Service	To calculate the anticipated or actual costs of activities related to a particular service priority

Staffing for Results Workforms Summary

Workform	Title	Purpose
Workform 1	Workload Analysis Project Overview	To organize your workload analysis project
Workform 2	Estimate of Productive Work Hours Available	To calculate the total number of hours available annually for any one category of staff
Workform 3	Determining Who Does What	To collect information about who does what activities and tasks in a work location or unit
Workform 4	Standard Terms in Our Library for Tasks and Steps	To provide staff with a standard set of terms they can use to complete the workload data-gathering workforms
Workform 5	Analysis of Staff Time: Work Unit Estimate of Time Spent on Activities	To estimate the percentage of time your staff members spend on each of their assigned activities
Workform 6	Analysis of Staff Time: Individual Estimate of Time Spent on Activities	To estimate the percentage of time you spend on each of your assigned activities
Workform 7	Recording Staff Tasks: Self-Report Log	To identify the tasks you perform during a workday through self-reporting
Workform 8	Recording Staff Tasks: Direct Observation Log	To identify the tasks a staff member performs during a workday through observation
Workform 9	Analysis of a Task: Observation Self-Report	To identify all of the steps involved in performing a task or to standardize the steps in a task
Workform 10	Time Spent on Input-Driven Tasks	To identify the relationship of outputs to the time spent during the performance of the steps of an input-driven task
Workform 11	Time Spent on Demand-Driven Tasks	To identify the average amount of time spent on each step in a demand-driven task

Workform	Title	Purpose
Workform 12	Time Spent on Public Desks	To identify the amount of time spent on tasks at public desks
Workform 13	Workflow Chart	To chart the time required for operations, transportation, approval, and/or storage when completing an activity

Human Resources for Results Workforms Summary

Workform	Title	Purpose
Workform 1	Committee Charge	To define the purpose of a project committee
Workform 2	Gap Analysis	To determine what staff resources will be required to accomplish specific activities
Workform 3	Position Description Questionnaire	To gather information about an employee's job
Workform 4	Job Description Template	To use to create a job description
Workform 5	Recruitment Process	To plan and manage your recruitment process
Workform 6	Developing Interview Questions	To develop questions to use during candidate interviews
Workform 7	Reference Check Form	To thoroughly check references
Workform 8	Individual Performance Plan	To plan individual activities for a performance period
Workform 9	Performance Evaluation Tool	To evaluate an employee's performance for the entire performance period
Workform 10	Self-Evaluation	To allow employees to provide feedback on their own performance
Workform 11	New Employee Orientation	To develop or revamp an employee orientation program and plan for the success of new hires
Workform 12	Exit Interview Questionnaire	To interview employees who have resigned their positions, in order to broaden your understanding of how employees see your library

COLLECTION RESOURCES

Managing for Results Collection Workforms Summary

Workform	Title	Purpose
Overview		
Workform C1	What's Important	To determine the data needed to complete the gap analysis process
Size		
Workform C2	Volumes—Print and Media	To record information about the number of volumes in the collections that support a specific activity
Workform C3	Titles—Print and Media	To record information about the number of titles in the collections that support a specific activity
Workform C4	Titles—Electronic	To record information about the number of electronic titles in the collections that support a specific activity

Workform	Title	Purpose
Utilization		
Workform C5	Circulation—Print and Media	To record information about the circulation of print and media items that support a specific activity
Workform C6	In-Library Use—Print and Media	To record information about the in-library use of print and media materials that support a specific activity
Workform C7	In-Library Use—Electronic	To record information about the in-library use of electronic resources that support a specific activity
Workform C8	Off-Site Use—Electronic	To record information about the off-site use of electronic resources that support a specific activity
Access		
Workform C9	Document Delivery	To record information about the number of days it takes users to get materials that support specific activities when those materials are not available at the time the user visits the library
Workform C10	Materials Availability	To record information about the success users have in obtaining materials that support a specific activity when they come to the library
Workform C11	Electronic Text Availability	To record information about the level of access provided to electronic resources that support a specific activity
Age		
Workform C12	Copyright—Print	To record information about the age of the print titles in the collections that support a specific activity
Workform C13	Copyright—Media	To record information about the age of the media titles in the collections that support a specific activity
Workform C14	Periodicals—Print and Microform	To record information about the coverage of the print and microform periodical titles that support a specific activity
Workform C15	Periodicals—Electronic	To record information about the coverage and the timeliness of the electronic periodical titles that support a specific activity
Condition		
Workform C16	Worn or Damaged—Print	To record information about the condition of print items in the collections that support a specific activity
Workform C17	Worn or Damaged—Media	To record information about the condition of media items in the collections that support a specific activity

FACILITY RESOURCES

Managing for Results Facilities Workforms Summary

Workform	Title	Purpose
Overview		
Workform F1	What's Important?	To determine what data is needed to complete the gap analysis process

Workform	Title	Purpose
Capacity		
Workform F2	Materials Storage	To assess the storage space available to house materials to support intended activities
Workform F3	Equipment and Furniture	To inventory the equipment and furniture the library has to support intended activities and to indicate the condition of the furniture and equipment
Workform F4	Space	To assess the capacity of the spaces in the library that support specific activities
Utilization		
Workform F5	Space	To assess the utilization of spaces in the library that support specific activities
Technology		
Workform F6	Facility Requirement	To assess the impact of technology on the library's facilities used to support an activity

Managing Facilities for Results Workforms Summary

Workform	Title	Purpose
Workform 1	Facility Projects	To review activities that support a goal to determine if they will require facility resources
Workform 2	Project Priorities	To write a brief project description, record decisions about the priority of each project, and identify projects that have been selected for the current year
Workform 3	Preliminary Task List and Time Line	To provide direction to a project manager or the facility reallocation committee about the major tasks and time frames for a facilities review and space allocation project
Workform 4	Need for Outside Experts	To record information and decisions about experts that will be used for a facility review and space allocation project
Workform 5	Facility Resources—Data Elements	To guide discussion of facility-related data elements and to provide a place for committee members to take notes during the discussion
Workform 6	Project Description—General	To record the project committee's expanded description of the project
Workform 7	Description—Physical Plan, Space, and Spatial Relationship	To describe the physical plant and space requirements of the activity under review
Workform 8	Need—Furniture and Equipment	To identify the types and capacity of the furniture and equipment that the public and the staff will need to support the activity and to estimate the amount of square footage each will need
Workform 9	Have—Furniture and Equipment	To describe the furniture and equipment items that are currently allocated for public and staff use to support the activity and to estimate the amount of square footage that each requires

Workform	Title	Purpose
Workform 10	Need—Shelving	To determine the number of regular and special shelving units needed for materials that support the activity and to estimate the total square footage required for that shelving
Workform 11	Have—Shelving	To describe the number of regular and special shelving units that are currently being used for materials that support the activity and to estimate the total square footage allocated for that shelving
Workform 12	Need—Physical Plant and Technology Support	To identify physical plant and technology support that will be needed to support the activity under review
Workform 13	Have—Physical Plant and Technology Support	To identify physical plant and technology support currently allocated to support the activity under review
Workform 14	Need—Access, Spatial Relationships, and Signage	To identify access, spatial relationships, and signage needs for the activity or service
Workform 15	Have—Access, Spatial Relationships, and Signage	To describe the current spatial relationships of the area that houses the activity
Workform 16	Square Footage—Needed and Current	To summarize the square footage needed to support the activity and to record the square footage currently supporting the activity, if any
Workform 17	Gaps and Options	To record gaps and, in the next step, options that the committee develops to fill the gaps that must be met to implement the project
Workform 18	Considerations for Placements of the Activity	To identify needed elements in multipurpose areas that could be used to support the activity under review; if the activity will require a walled or single-purpose space, use the workform to determine spatial relationships that would be appropriate
Workform 19	Expense Estimates for Options	To record cost estimates that the committee collects in order to evaluate and compare options to fill the gaps that must be met to implement the project
Workform 20	Preliminary Project Time Estimates	To record information about the projected time frames for the steps involved in purchasing or allocating the resources for the project; use this workform only to record information on options that might delay the project
Workform 21	Option Evaluation	To prioritize options developed to fill the gaps that must be met to implement the project
Workform 22	Furniture and Equipment List	To compile the information about all of the furniture and equipment that will be needed for the project and how it will be allocated
Workform 23	Cost Compilations	To list the cost estimates necessary for funding approvals

TECHNOLOGY RESOURCES

Managing for Results Technology Workforms Summary

Workform	Title	Purpose
Needs Estimates		
Workform T1	Equipment, Software, and Dial Capacity	To estimate the technological capacity needed to support a planned activity
Workform T2	Printers	To estimate how many and what types of printers are needed
Workform T3	Summary of Equipment, Printers, Software, and Dial Capacity	To summarize the capacity of technology needed to support a specific activity in each library unit
Workform T4	Leased Lines	To determine the leased line capacity needed to support a specific activity
Workform T5	Summary of Needs Estimates: Leased Lines	To summarize the leased-line capacity needed in each library unit to support a specific activity
Capacity		
Workform T6	Workstation and Terminal Functions	To record information on the number of single and multi-function workstations and terminals in each library unit
Workform T7	Workstation and Terminal Condition	To record information on the condition of the workstations and terminals in each library unit
Workform T8	Equipment, Software, and Telecommunications	To record information about the equipment, software, and telecommunications capacity in each library unit
Utilization		
Workform T9	Utilization: Observation	To collect utilization data through observation
Workform T10	Utilization: Public Services Sign-Up Analysis	To analyze utilization data obtained from sign-up sheets in library units that allow users to reserve a specific time to use equipment or to sign up on a first-come, first-serve basis
Workform T11	Utilization: Summary	To summarize the utilization data gathered using workforms T9 or T10
Comparison of Capacity Required to Unused Capacity		
Workform T12	Comparison of Capacity Required to Unused Capacity Available	To compare the capacity needed with the capacity available in each library unit
Additional Equipment and Lines Needed		
Workform T13	Technology Needed	To determine the number of additional devices to be purchased to reach needed capacity in each library unit
Workform T14	Leased-Line Capacity Needed	To determine the additional leased-line capacity to be acquired to reach needed capacity in each library unit
Workform T15	Costs of Needed Technology	To translate the number and types of devices needed and the dial and leased line telecommunications capacity required into estimated costs

Technology for Results Workforms Summary

Workform	Title	Purpose
Workform 1	Audiences and Planning Results	To clarify what the audiences who will review, approve, or use the technology plan need to know
Workform 2	Services Inventory	To develop an inventory of the technology-supported services in your library
Workform 3	Strategic Plan Links: Sustain, Expand, or Phase Out	To summarize the technology-supported public services in your library and link them to the library's strategic plan. To record the committee's recommendations on the future of the technology-supported public services.
Workform 4	Administrative Tools: Sustain, Expand, or Phase Out	To summarize the technology-supported administrative services in your library. To record the committee's recommendations on the future of the technology-supported administrative services.
Workform 5	New Public Services Support Projects	To evaluate potential new public service support projects
Workform 6	Evaluating Efficiency Projects: Staff Savings	To collect data needed to evaluate potential new efficiency projects
Workform 7	Infrastructure Assessment	To record the baseline of the library's technology and the possible upgrade and enhancement requirements of that technology
Workform 8	Technical Skills Assessment	To gather information on the technical skill level of each staff member of the library
Workform 9	Costs to Sustain Services	To record the estimated costs of investments needed to sustain the library's current technology-based services
Workform 10	Requirements of New or Expanded Services	To record the data gathered on products and services that can be used to expand current technology-based services or introduce new services
Workform 11	Technical Skills Needed	To compare the technical skills that proposed new or expanded projects require with the technical skills available on the library's staff
Workform 12	Project Time Estimates	To record the estimated time that will be required to implement a project
Workform 13	Summary of Projects	To summarize key information about the projects you are considering
Workform 14	Trigger Point Assumptions	To record the assumptions about available technology or costs that lead the planning committee or project manager to make decisions about specific technologies to use in the future
Workform 15	Technology Suggestion Form	To provide a way for staff to suggest technologies for the library to consider adding to the technology plan
Workform 16	Technical Inventory	To develop an inventory of your current technical infrastructure if your library does not already have an inventory

Workforms

WORKFORM A Developing a Communication Plan

Instructions

Purpose of Workform A

Use this workform to develop a plan to communicate before, during, and after each task in the *IFR* process.

Note about the Electronic Version

Use the Microsoft Word (with an embedded Excel worksheet) version of this workform (available at http://e-learnlibraries.mrooms.net) to add rows and expand the size of columns.

Sources of Data for Workform A

This workform is used to record decisions made by senior managers.

Who Should Complete Workform A

This workform should be completed by the manager who is assigned the responsibility of developing and monitoring communications relating to the *IFR* process.

Factors to Consider When Completing Workform A

1. Complete one copy of the workform for each of the 14 *IFR* tasks.
2. Some target audiences may not need to be informed about the work completed in some tasks.
3. Review and revise the communication plans for each task before you begin the steps in the task.
4. Use an electronic version of this workform. You will be reviewing and revising the information on the workforms throughout the process, and that will be easier if the information is in a machine-readable format.

To Complete Workform A

1. Line I: List the task.
2. Line II.A: List the date the task will begin.
3. Line II.B: List the date the task will end. If the task is open-ended, make that note on this line.

4. Column A: For each target audience, record the reason this target audience needs to be informed about this task. Will they have to take some action? Will they be affected by actions that others take? If there is no reason for the target audience to know anything about this task, note that in column A and leave columns B–F blank.
5. Column B: Briefly note what the members of the target audience currently know about the task. Include information that has been available formally and information that is being transmitted informally through the grapevine.
6. Column C: Describe what the target audience will need to know to take the action you identified in column A.
7. Column D: Many communications are time-sensitive. Indicate when the target audience will need to have the information described in column C.
8. Column E: There are a variety of media that can be used to transmit messages. Indicate the types of media that will be used to transmit the message in column C.
9. Column F: Record the name of the person who will be responsible for developing and transmitting the communication.

Factors to Consider When Reviewing Workform A

1. Review the target audiences listed in column A to be sure that they include all appropriate groups.
2. Review column C carefully to be sure that it includes all of the information needed for the target audience to take the action identified in column A.
3. After messages have been transmitted, check to be sure that they were received by the intended audiences and included the necessary information. Resend messages if necessary.
4. Review and revise this workform before each task begins and modify as needed.
5. Review this workform at the end of each task to be sure that the actions that you identified in column C have taken place. If they have not, modify the plan and resend the messages.

WORKFORM A **Developing a Communication Plan**

I. Task: _____

II. A. Start Date: _____ B. End Date: _____

	A. Why do they need to know about this task?	B. What do they know now?	C. What will they need to know?	D. When will they need to know it?	E. How will they be informed?	F. Who will be responsible for informing them?
1. Board/ Governing Authority						
2. Senior Managers						
3. Unit Managers						
4. Supervisors						
5. Staff						
6. Other						

Notes:

Completed by _____ Date completed _____

Source of data _____ Library _____

183

Instructions

WORKFORM B Identifying and Evaluating Activities by Goal and Cluster

Purpose of Workform B

Use a separate copy of the workform to record clusters of similar activities that support one of the goals in the library strategic plan. For example, all of the activities related to presenting programs that support one goal would be recorded together on one copy of Workform B. Activities that don't comfortably fit into any of the clusters should be grouped together as a "miscellaneous" cluster.

Note about the Electronic Version

Use the Microsoft Word (with an embedded Excel worksheet) version of this workform (available at http://e-learnlibraries.mrooms.net) to add rows and expand the size of columns.

Sources of Data for Workform B

The data for this workform will come from the sticky notes that were produced during the staff meetings that were held to identify current and potential activities (Steps 3.2 and 3.3).

Who Should Complete Workform B

1. A small team of two or three members who are appointed by the library director will complete lines I, II, III and columns A–C.

2. The library's senior managers will complete columns D.1–4.

Factors to Consider When Completing Workform B

1. Use a separate copy of the workform to record the activities for each cluster under each goal.

2. If there are activities that don't fit comfortably in any cluster, set them aside. When you have finished clustering all of the activities for a goal, go back and review the unclustered activities again. If there are several activities that are related, create a new cluster. Otherwise, consider them to be part of a "miscellaneous" cluster.

3. Clip the sticky notes for each activity and the sticky notes containing any supporting information for that activity together.

4. There is no particular order to the lists within each cluster.

5. You must use an electronic version of this workform. The information on this workform will be used again, and it will be easier to transfer if it is in a machine-readable format.

To Complete Workform B

1. Line I: Record the goal.

2. Line II: Record all of the objectives for the goal.

3. Line III: Record the cluster of activity.

4. Column A.1: Record the first activity on line A.1 and write "1" on the sticky note(s) with that activity. Record the second activity on line A.2 and write "2" on the sticky note(s) with that activity. Continue until all of the activities in the cluster have been recorded

5. Column B: Place a check mark in this box if there are sticky notes with additional information (steps, activities that were merged, or questions) attached to the main activity.

6. Columns C.1–2: Indicate whether the activity is current or new. Current activities are being performed now. New activities include both activities that have never been performed in the library and significant modifications of current activities.

7. Columns D.1–4: These columns will be left blank when the original data is entered by the review team in Step 4.1. The senior managers will record their effectiveness ratings in these columns in Step 5.2. The effectiveness criteria are explained in detail in Step 5.1.

Factors to Consider When Reviewing Workform B

1. Is the information complete and accurate?

2. Have all of the sticky notes been numbered to correspond with their numbers in column A?

3. There is additional information about factors to consider after the effectiveness scores have been determined in Step 5.2.

WORKFORM B Identifying and Evaluating Activities by Goal and Cluster

I. Goal: _____

II. Objectives: _____

III. Cluster: _____

A. Activity	B. Other Information	C. Type		D. Effectiveness			
		1. Current	2. New	1. Audience	2. Results	3. Reaction	4. Total
1.							
2.							
3.							
4.							
5.							
6.							
7.							
8.							
9.							
10.							

Completed by _____ Date completed _____

Source of data _____ Library _____

Instructions

Purpose of Workform C

Use this workform to consolidate and sort the clusters of activities for each goal.

Note about the Electronic Version

Use the Microsoft Word (with an embedded Excel worksheet) version of this workform (available at http://e-learnlibraries.mrooms.net) to add rows and expand the size of columns.

Sources of Data for Workform C

The data in this workform come from the completed copies of Workform B: Identifying and Evaluating Activities by Goal and Cluster for each goal.

Who Should Complete Workform C

The person completing this workform should be able to enter, move, and sort data in an Excel worksheet.

Factors to Consider When Completing Workform C

1. Use a separate copy of the workform to consolidate the activities from all clusters for each goal into a single copy of the workform. You will end up with a copy of Workform C for each goal in your strategic plan.

2. You must use an electronic version of this workform. The information on this workform will be used again, and it will be easier to transfer if it is in a machine-readable format.

To Complete Workform C

1. Copy the data from the embedded Excel spreadsheet in Workform B for the first cluster of activities for the goal to a new spreadsheet and save the spreadsheet with the file name "workform_c_goal_x," with "x" being the goal number.

2. Then copy the data from the embedded Excel spreadsheet in Workform B for the second cluster of activities for the goal in the new spreadsheet. Continue until all of the activities for all of the clusters of activities for the goal have been recorded on a single spreadsheet.

3. Delete column B: Other Information.

4. Delete columns D.1 (Audience), D.2 (Results), and D.3 (Reaction).

5. When you have finished items 2 and 3, the spreadsheet should have column A (Activity), column C (Type), and column D.4 (Effectiveness—Total). Change the header in column C: Type to column B: Type and the header in column D.4: Total to column C: Effectiveness Total.

6. Sort the data in the spreadsheet using two sort criteria: ascending order by column C: Effectiveness Total and descending order by column B.1. That will result in the new and current effective activities being listed in order by the total numerical effectiveness ratings, followed by the current ineffective activities (INEFF), and the new ineffective activities (INEFF).

7. Copy the final spreadsheet into the embedded spreadsheet on Workform C or write "Workform C: [goal]" in the header of the spreadsheet.

Factor to Consider When Reviewing Workform C

Are all of the activities for all of the clusters of the goal included on Workform C?

WORKFORM C Consolidating and Sorting Activities by Goal

I. Goal: _____

A. Activity	B. Type		C. Effectiveness Total
	1. Current	2. New	
1.			
2.			
3.			
4.			
5.			
6.			
7.			
8.			
9.			
10.			
11.			
12.			
13.			
14.			

Completed by _____ Date completed _____

Source of data _____ Library _____

Purpose of Workform D

Use this workform to record the priority of current and new activities that were evaluated as effective on Workform B and merged and sorted by goal on Workform C.

Note about the Electronic Version

Use the Microsoft Word (with an embedded Excel worksheet) version of this workform (available at http://e-learnlibraries.mrooms.net) to add rows and expand the size of columns.

Sources of Data for Workform D

1. The data for columns A, B, and C come from the data in columns A, B, and C for the effective activities on the sorted copy of Workform C: Consolidating and Sorting Activities by Goal.

2. The data for column D come from the library's senior managers.

Who Should Complete Workform D

1. The person moving the data from columns A, B, and C on Workform C to this workform should be able to enter, move, and sort data in an Excel worksheet.

2. The priority of each activity (column D) will be determined by the library's senior managers.

Factors to Consider When Completing Workform D

1. Complete a separate copy of Workform D for the current and new effective activities for each goal.

2. The effective activities are not all *equally* effective.

3. The library may not have the resources needed to implement all of the effective activities identified in Step 5.2.

4. Consider the objectives for the goal as you evaluate the effectiveness of each activity.

5. You must use an electronic version of this workform. The information on this workform will be used again, and it will be easier to transfer if it is in a machine-readable format.

To Complete Workform D

1. Line I: Record the goal.

2. Line II: Record the objectives for the goal.

3. Columns A–C: Copy the data in columns A–C for all of the effective activities on Workform C: Consolidating and Sorting Activities by Goal to the corresponding columns on this workform.

4. Column D: Determine the priority of each activity using the following rubric:

   A = Essential: The activity must be implemented to reach the targets in the objectives for the goal.

   B = Desirable: The activity would make significant contributions to meeting the targets in the objectives for the goal.

   C = Supplementary: The activity would have a modest effect on meeting the targets in the objectives for the goal.

Factors to Consider When Reviewing Workform D

The factors to consider when reviewing the priorities are described in detail in Steps 6.1 and 6.2.

Determining the Priority of Effective Activities by Goal

I. Goal: _____

II. Objectives: _____

A. Activity	B. Type		C. Effectiveness Total	D. Priority
	1. Current	2. New		

Completed by _____ Date completed _____

Source of data _____ Library _____

Instructions

WORKFORM E Addressing Current Ineffective Activities That Support Each Goal

Purpose of Workform E

Use this workform to record the actions that will be taken to address the library's current activities that were evaluated as ineffective (INEFF) on Workform B: Identifying and Evaluating Activities by Goal and Cluster and consolidated and sorted by goal on Workform C: Consolidating and Sorting Activities by Goal. Use a separate copy of this workform for each goal in your strategic plan.

Note about the Electronic Version

Use the Microsoft Word (with an embedded Excel worksheet) version of this workform (available at http://e-learnlibraries.mrooms.net) to add rows and expand the size of columns.

Sources of Data for Workform E

1. The data for column A are copied from column A for the *current* ineffective activities on the sorted copy of Workform C: Consolidating and Sorting Activities by Goal.

2. You will not copy the *new* ineffective activities to this workform, and so you will not need to copy the data from columns B.1 and B.2 from Workform C. All of the activities on this workform will be *current* activities.

3. You will not copy the data in column C from Workform C to this workform. All of the current ineffective activities have the same rating of INEFF.

4. The data for columns B.1 and B.2 come from the library's senior managers.

Who Should Complete Workform E

1. The person moving the data from column A on Workform C to column A on this workform should be able to enter, move, and sort data in an Excel worksheet.

2. The action that will be taken to address each ineffective current activity (column B) will be determined by the library's senior managers.

Factors to Consider When Completing Workform E

1. If you don't eliminate or significantly reduce current ineffective activities, you will not have the resources needed to implement effective activities.

2. You must use an electronic version of this workform. The information on this workform will be used again, and it will be easier to transfer if it is in a machine-readable format.

To Complete Workform E

1. Line I: Record the goal.

2. Column A: Copy the data from column A for all of the *current* ineffective activities on Workform C: Consolidating and Sorting Activities by Goal to column A on this workform.

3. Column B.1: This column is completed by the library's senior managers. They will select one of the following eight options for addressing each ineffective activity and record the letter of the option in column B.1:

    A = Eliminate the activity in all units

    B = Eliminate the activity in selected units

    C = Continue the activity with reduced resources in all units

    D = Continue the activity with reduced resources in selected units

    E = Modify the activity to make it effective in all units

    F = Modify the activity to make it effective in selected units

    G = Continue the activity unchanged in all units

    H = Continue the activity unchanged in selected units

4. Column B.2: Use this column for notes about your decisions (units to be affected, type of modification, etc.).

Factors to Consider When Reviewing Workform E

The factors to consider when reviewing the decisions you have made about ineffective activities are described in detail in Step 9.1 and figure 20.

I. Goal: _____

A. Current Ineffective Activity	B. Decision	
	1. Option	2. Notes

Completed by _____ Date completed _____

Source of data _____ Library _____

Instructions

WORKFORM F   Identifying and Addressing Current Activities That Do Not Support Priorities

Purpose of Workform F

Use this workform to record and sort the activities that support service responses that were not selected as priorities during the planning process and to record decisions about how each of those activities will be addressed.

Note about the Electronic Version

Use the Microsoft Word (with an embedded Excel worksheet) version of this workform (available at http://e-learnlibraries.mrooms.net) to add rows and expand the size of columns.

Sources of Data for Workform F

The data for this workform will come from the sticky notes that were produced during the team meetings described in Step 7.2.

Who Should Complete Workform F

1. A small team of two or three members who are appointed by the library director will complete columns A–C.

2. The library's senior managers will complete columns D.1 and D.2.

Factors to Consider When Completing Workform F

1. The order in which you list the activities doesn't matter. When all of the activities have been recorded on the worksheet, the information will be sorted.

2. You must use an electronic version of this workform to record your work. The information will need to be sorted to be used in this workform and later in the process.

To Complete Workform F

1. Column A: Record the activities that support the service responses that were not selected as a priority in this column.

2. Column B: Place a two- or three-letter abbreviation of the service response supported by this activity in this column.

3. Columns C.1–2: Place a check in the appropriate column to indicate whether the activity is proactive or reactive. There is more information on proactive and reactive activities in Step 7.3.

4. Sort the data in columns A, B, C.1 and C.2 in order by column C.1 (Proactive) and then by column C.2 (Reactive). Then sort each of these two groups by column B (Service Response). This will result in all of the proactive activities being listed in alphabetical order of service response, followed by the reactive activities listed in alphabetical order of service response.

5. Column D.1: This column is completed by the library's senior managers. They will select one of the following eight options for addressing each ineffective activity and record the letter of the option in column D.1:

   A = Eliminate the activity in all units

   B = Eliminate the activity in selected units

   C = Continue the activity with reduced resources in all units

   D = Continue the activity with reduced resources in selected units

   E = Modify the activity to make it effective in all units

   F = Modify the activity to make it effective in selected units

   G = Continue the activity unchanged in all units

   H = Continue the activity unchanged in selected units

6. Column D.2: Use this column for notes about your decisions (units to be affected, etc.).

Factors to Consider When Reviewing Workform F

1. Have all of the activities that support service responses that were not selected been listed?

2. The factors to consider when reviewing the information in column D are described in detail in Step 9.2.

A. Activity	B. Service Response	C. Type		D. Decision	
		1. Proactive	2. Reactive	1. Option	2. Notes

Completed by _____

Source of data _____

Date completed _____

Library _____

Instructions

Purpose of Workform G

This workform has two purposes. The Sacred Cows worksheet on the next page will be distributed to staff before they attend the sacred cow meetings described in Step 8.1 so they will know what to expect during the meetings. The Corralling Sacred Cows workform will be used to record the results of the sacred cow meetings in each unit.

Note about the Electronic Version

Use the Microsoft Word (with an embedded Excel worksheet) version of this workform (available at http://e-learnlibraries.mrooms.net) to add rows and expand the size of columns.

Sources of Data for Workform G

1. Individual staff members will receive the Sacred Cow worksheet prior to unit meetings held to identify sacred cows so they will have an opportunity to think about the questions.

2. The data for the workform will come from the meetings held in each unit to identify sacred cows (Step 8.1).

Who Should Complete Workform G

1. The Sacred Cows worksheet on the next page will be distributed to library staff so they will know what questions will be asked during the sacred cow meetings. Staff may choose to make notes on the worksheet if they wish, but the notes they make will be for their personal use. The worksheets will not be collected during the sacred cow meetings.

2. The Corralling Sacred Cows workform will be completed by the facilitator and recorder from each unit meeting held to identify sacred cows.

Factors to Consider When Completing Workform G

1. The facilitator and recorder from each unit should record all of the sacred cows identified during all of the unit meetings on a single copy of the Corralling Sacred Cows workform.

2. If the unit manager did not facilitate the sacred cow meetings, she should review the completed Corralling Sacred Cows workform before it is submitted to her supervisor for review.

To Complete Workform G

1. Line I: Record the unit name.

2. Column A: Record a unique code to identify each unit in this column. You will need this information when the lists of sacred cows are merged at the end of Step 8.2.

3. Column B: Provide a brief but clear description of the sacred cow in this column.

4. Column C: Use the following list to indicate the type of sacred cow. These three terms are defined in Step 8.2:

   Policy

   Practice

   Procedure

5. Column D: If the staff recommended specific actions to address a sacred cow, those recommendations should be noted here. The unit manager may also suggest ways to address one or more sacred cows in this column.

Factors to Consider When Reviewing Workform G

1. Are the descriptions of the sacred cows clear and easy to understand?

2. Are the recommended actions clear and easy to understand?

SACRED COWS

Practices that have been immune from scrutiny or criticism, often for no good reason, are called *sacred cows*. Many library sacred cows have been firmly entrenched for decades, although new ones are added regularly. These practices continue because no one has asked "why?" Take a few minutes to think about the work that you and your colleagues do every day.

1. Have you ever wondered why you or your colleagues do certain things?

_____

_____

_____

_____

_____

_____

_____

_____

2. Have you ever thought there must be a better way to accomplish some of the things that you do?

_____

_____

_____

_____

_____

_____

_____

_____

(cont.)

WORKFORM G **Corralling Sacred Cows—Unit Information** (cont.)

I. Library Unit: _____

A. Unit Code	B. Sacred Cow (from the staff meetings)	C. Type of Sacred Cow	D. Recommended Action(s)

Completed by _____   Date completed _____

Source of data _____   Library _____

Instructions

Purpose of Workform H

Use this workform to consolidate all of the sacred cows from all of the copies of Workform G: Corralling Sacred Cows—Unit Information onto a single workform.

Note about the Electronic Version

Use the Microsoft Word (with an embedded Excel worksheet) version of this workform (available at http://e-learnlibraries.mrooms.net) to add rows and expand the size of columns.

Sources of Data for Workform H

The data in this workform come from the completed copies of Workform G: Corralling Sacred Cows—Unit Information.

Who Should Complete Workform H

1. The person completing this workform should be able to enter, move, and sort data in an Excel spreadsheet.

2. One or two people appointed by the library director will review the sacred cows from all of the units and merge those that are the same.

Factors to Consider When Completing Workform H

1. Use a single copy of the workform to consolidate the sacred cows from all the units in the library.

2. Be careful to record in column A the unique codes from all of the units in which a sacred cow was mentioned.

3. Be sure to record all of the suggested recommended actions for each sacred cow in column D.

4. Only merge sacred cows that are very similar. Be careful not to lose the details the senior managers will need to make decisions about how to address the sacred cows. Nothing should be deleted.

5. You must use an electronic version of this workform. The information on this workform will be used again, and it will be easier to transfer if it is in a machine-readable format.

To Complete Workform H

1. Copy the data from the embedded Excel spreadsheet in Workform G for the sacred cows from one unit to a new spreadsheet and save the spreadsheet with the file name "workform_h_sacred_cows."

2. Then copy the data from the embedded Excel spreadsheet in Workform G from a second unit to the new spreadsheet. Continue to add the data from each unit until all the sacred cows from all of the units have been recorded on the new spreadsheet.

3. Sort the data in the spreadsheet in order by column C: Type of Sacred Cow. That will result in all of the sacred cows relating to policies being listed first, followed by all of the sacred cows that are practices and all of the sacred cows that are procedures.

4. Columns A, B, and C: Review and merge sacred cows that are very similar. As you do so, be sure that all the unit codes for all of the units in which the sacred cow was mentioned are recorded in column A and all of the suggested solutions for the sacred cow are recorded in column D.

5. Copy the final spreadsheet into the embedded spreadsheet on Workform H or write "Workform H: Consolidating and Sorting Sacred Cows" in the header of the spreadsheet.

Factor to Consider When Reviewing Workform H

Are all of the sacred cows clear and easy to understand?

WORKFORM H Consolidating and Sorting Sacred Cows

A. Unit Codes	B. Sacred Cow	C. Type of Sacred Cow	D. Recommended Action(s)

Completed by _____ Date completed _____

Source of data _____ Library _____

Instructions

Purpose of Workform I

Use a separate copy of this workform to record the decisions made by the senior managers about each of the three types of sacred cows: policy sacred cows, practice sacred cows, and procedural sacred cows.

Note about the Electronic Version

Use the Microsoft Word (with an embedded Excel worksheet) version of this workform (available at http://e-learnlibraries.mrooms.net) to add rows and expand the size of columns.

Sources of Data for Workform I

The data for this workform come from the completed Workform H: Consolidating and Sorting Sacred Cows.

Who Should Complete Workform I

1. The person moving the data from Workform H to this workform should be able to enter, move, and sort data in an Excel worksheet.

2. The senior managers will record their decisions about each sacred cow in columns D.1 and D.2.

Factors to Consider When Completing Workform I

1. Use a separate copy of this workform for each of the three types of sacred cows: policy, practice, and procedure.

2. Be sure to copy all of the data for each sacred cow from Workform H to this workform accurately.

3. You must use an electronic version of this workform. The information on this workform will be used again, and it will be easier to transfer if it is in a machine-readable format.

To Complete Workform I

1. Line I: Record the type of sacred cow listed on this copy of the workform.

2. Columns A and B: Copy columns A and B from Workform H for all of the sacred cows of the type being recorded on this workform into these two columns.

3. Column C: Copy column D from Workform H for all of the sacred cows of the type being recorded on this workform into this column. Be sure that the recommendations in the column match the correct sacred cows in column B.

4. Column D.1: This column is completed by the library's senior managers. They will select one of the following eight options for addressing each sacred cow and will record the letter of the option in column D.1:

   A = Eliminate the activity in all units

   B = Eliminate the activity in selected units

   C = Continue the activity with reduced resources in all units

   D = Continue the activity with reduced resources in selected units

   E = Modify the activity to make it effective in all units

   F = Modify the activity to make it effective in selected units

   G = Continue the activity unchanged in all units

   H = Continue the activity unchanged in selected units

5. Column D.2: Use this column for notes about your decisions (units to be affected, etc.).

Factors to Consider When Reviewing Workform I

The factors to consider when reviewing sacred cows are described in Step 9.3.

WORKFORM I **Addressing Sacred Cows**

I. Type of Sacred Cow: _____

A. Unit Codes	B. Sacred Cow	C. Recommended Action(s)	D. Decision	
			1. Option	2. Notes

Completed by _____   Date completed _____

Source of data _____   Library _____

WORKFORM J Eliminating Activities Performed by Staff in a Single Classification—System Information by Unit

Purpose of Workform J

Use this workform to record the staff, collection, facility, and technology resources that will be made available for reallocation if an activity that is always performed by staff in the same classification is eliminated. You will also use this workform to record information about any resources that might be required if the activity is eliminated.

Note about the Electronic Version

Use the Microsoft Word (with an embedded Excel worksheet) version of this workform (available at http://e-learnlibraries.mrooms.net) to add rows and expand the size of columns.

Sources of Data for Workform J

1. The information about the activity to be eliminated (line I) come from the completed copies of Workform E: Addressing Current Ineffective Activities That Support Each Goal, Workform F: Identifying and Addressing Current Activities That Do Not Support Priorities, and Workform I: Addressing Sacred Cows.

2. The "time to complete a single instance" data on line II.C are determined by sampling. The process is explained in detail in Step 10.1.

3. The "number of instances each year" data in column II.D.2 are obtained from existing data (integrated library system, etc.) or gathered through sampling. The process is explained in detail in Step 10.1.

4. The information about the other resources in section III is collected from the unit managers.

Who Should Complete Workform J

1. The workform will be completed by a data coordinator appointed by the library director.

2. The data coordinator may ask other staff to assist with sampling.

3. The unit managers will provide information about unit collection, facility, and technology resources.

Factors to Consider When Completing Workform J

1. Record data for all units in which the activity to be eliminated is performed on a single copy of the workform.

2. Only use this workform for activities performed by staff in the same classification and which are being eliminated. If the activity is going to be modified, use Workform K: Reducing or Streamlining Activities Performed by Staff in a Single Classification—System Information by Unit.

3. Only use this workform for activities that are always performed by staff of the same classification. If steps of the activity are performed by staff with different classifications, use Workform L: Eliminating Activities Performed by More Than One Classification of Staff—Unit Information or Workform M: Reducing or Streamlining Activities Performed by More Than One Classification of Staff—Unit Information.

4. You do not need data that are absolutely statistically valid. Instead, you need to use sampling to develop reasonably close estimates of the time that is required for each instance of the activity that is being eliminated.

5. Use an electronic copy of this workform. The Excel spreadsheet in the workform includes the formulas to determine the annual time to be reallocated.

To Complete Workform J

1. Line I: Record the activity that is being eliminated.

2. Staff Resources

   a. Line II.A: Record the classification of staff who perform the activity.

   b. Line II.B.1: Record the starting point for the activity (see Step 10.1 for more information about starting points).

   c. Line II.B.2: Record the ending point for the activity (see Step 10.1 for more information about ending points).

   d. Line II.C: Record the average time it takes to complete a single instance of the activity.

   e. Column II.D.1: List the library units in which this activity is performed.

(cont.)

WORKFORM J | **Eliminating Activities Performed by Staff in a Single Classification—System Information by Unit** (cont.)

f. Column II.D.2: Record the number of times an instance of the activity is performed in a year in each unit.

g. Column II.D.3: Record the average time in minutes it takes to perform one instance of the activity from line II.C.

h. Column II.D.4: If you use the electronic version of Workform J, the information in this column will be calculated automatically. If you have not used the electronic version of the workform, multiply the Number of Instances Each Year (column II.D.3) times the Time per Instance in minutes (column II.D.2) times the Time per Instance in minutes (column II.D.3) to determine the total number of minutes each year. Then divide the number of minutes by 60 to determine the number of hours that will be available for reallocation.

3. Other Resource Implications

a. Column III.A.1: List the library units in which this activity is performed.

b. Column III.A.2: Briefly describe the collection resources that would be available for reallocation if the activity were eliminated, if any.

c. Column III.A.3: Briefly describe the additional collection resources that would be required if the activity were eliminated, if any.

d. Column III.B.1: List the library units in which this activity is performed.

e. Column III.B.2: Briefly describe the facility resources that would be available for reallocation if the activity were eliminated, if any.

f. Column III.B.3: Briefly describe the additional facility resources that would be required if the activity were eliminated, if any.

g. Column III.C.1: List the library units in which this activity is performed.

h. Column III.C.2: Briefly describe the technology resources that would be available for reallocation if the activity were eliminated, if any.

i. Column III.C.3: Briefly describe the additional technology resources that would be required if the activity were eliminated, if any.

Factors to Consider When Reviewing Workform J

1. Is the information on the workform reasonable?

2. Are there unexpectedly significant differences in the resources allocated to this activity in different units?

WORKFORM J Eliminating Activities Performed by Staff in a Single Classification—System Information by Unit

I.   Activity Being Eliminated: _____

II. Staff Resources

   A. What is the classification of the staff who complete this activity? _____

   B. What are the starting and ending points of each instance of this activity to be eliminated?

   1. Starting point of an instance of the activity: _____

   2. Ending point of an instance of the activity: _____

   C. How long does it take to complete a single instance of the activity? _____

   D. Calculate the staff time that will be available for reallocation if the activity is eliminated.

1. Unit	2. Number of Instances Each Year	3. Time per Instance (from II.C above)	4. Annual Time Saved (in hours)

III. Other Resource Implications

   A. Identify the effect that eliminating the activity will have on collection resources, if any.

1. Unit	2. Collection Resources Available for Reallocation	3. Additional Collection Resources Required

(cont.)

WORKFORM J **Eliminating Activities Performed by Staff in a Single Classification—System Information by Unit** (cont.)

B. Identify the effect that eliminating the activity will have on facility resources, if any.

1. Unit	2. Facility Resources Available for Reallocation	3. Additional Facility Resources Required

C. Identify the effect that eliminating activity will have on technology resources, if any.

1.Unit	2. Technology Resources Available for Reallocation	3. Additional Technology Resources Required

Completed by _____

Source of data _____

Date completed _____

Library _____

WORKFORM K **Reducing or Streamlining Activities Performed by Staff in a Single Classification—System Information by Unit**

Purpose of Workform K

Use this workform to record the staff, collection, facility, and technology resources that will be made available for reallocation if an activity that is always performed by staff in the same classification is modified. You will also use this workform to record information about any resources that might be required if the activity is modified.

Note about the Electronic Version

Use the Microsoft Word (with an embedded Excel worksheet) version of this workform (available at http://e-learnlibraries.mrooms.net) to add rows and expand the size of columns.

Sources of Data for Workform K

1. The description of the activities that will be modified (line I) will come from Workform E: Addressing Current Ineffective Activities That Support Each Goal, Workform F: Identifying and Addressing Current Activities That Do Not Support Priorities, and Workform I: Addressing Sacred Cows.

2. The "time saved" data in column II.B.2 are determined by sampling. The process is explained in detail in Step 10.1.

3. The "number of instances each year" data in column II.D.2 are obtained from existing data (integrated library systems, etc.) or gathered through sampling. The process is explained in detail in Step 10.1.

4. The information about the other resources in section III is collected from the unit managers.

Who Should Complete Workform K

1. The workform will be completed by a data coordinator appointed by the library director.

2. The data coordinator may ask other staff to assist with sampling.

3. The unit managers will provide information about unit collection, facility, and technology resources.

Factors to Consider When Completing Workform K

1. Record data for all units in which the activity to be modified is performed on a single copy of the workform.

2. Only use this workform for activities performed by staff in the same classification and which are being reduced or streamlined. If the activity is going to be eliminated, use Workform J: Eliminating Activities Performed by Staff in a Single Classification—System Information by Unit.

3. Only use this workform for activities that are always performed by staff of the same classification. If steps of the activity are performed by staff with different classifications, use Workform L: Eliminating Activities Performed by More Than One Classification of Staff—Unit Information or Workform M: Reducing or Streamlining Activities Performed by More Than One Classification of Staff—Unit Information.

4. Only record the steps that are being reduced or streamlined in column II.B.1.

5. You do not need data that are absolutely statistically valid. Instead, you need to use sampling to develop reasonably close estimates of the time that is required for each instance of the steps within the activity that are being changed.

6. Use an electronic copy of this workform. The Excel spreadsheet in the workform includes the formulas to determine the annual time to be reallocated.

To Complete Workform K

1. Line I: Briefly describe how the activity will be modified.

2. Staff Resources

   a. Line II.A: Record the classification of staff who perform the activity.

   b. Column II.B.1: Describe the steps within the activity that are being changed.

   c. Column II.B.2: Record the average time that will be saved in each instance of a step that will be changed.

   d. Line II.C: Add the average time saved in each step in column II.B.2 and record the total here.

(cont.)

Instructions

e. Column III.D.1: List the library units in which this activity is performed.

f. Column III.D.2: Record the number of times an instance of the activity is performed in a year in each unit.

g. Column III.D.3: Record the total time for all steps that will be changed from line II.C.

h. Column II.D.4: If you use the electronic version of Workform K, the information in this column will be calculated automatically. If you have not used the electronic version of the workform, multiply the Number of Instances Each Year (column II.D.2) by the Time per Instance in minutes (column II.D.3) to determine the total number of minutes each year. Then divide the number of minutes by 60 to determine the number of hours that will be available for reallocation.

3. Other Resource Implications

a. Column III.A.1: List the library units in which this activity is performed, if any.

b. Column III.A.2: Briefly describe the collection resources that would be available for reallocation if the activity were modified, if any.

c. Column III.A.3: Briefly describe the additional collection resources that would be required if the activity were modified, if any.

d. Column III.B.1: List the library units in which this activity is performed.

e. Column III.B.2: Briefly describe the facility resources that would be available for reallocation if the activity were modified, if any.

f. Column III.B.3: Briefly describe the additional facility resources that would be required if the activity were modified, if any.

g. Column III.C.1: List the library units in which this activity is performed.

h. Column III.C.2: Briefly describe the technology resources that would be available for reallocation if the activity were modified, if any.

i. Column III.C.3: Briefly describe the additional technology resources that would be required if the activity were modified, if any.

Factors to Consider When Reviewing Workform K

1. Have all of the steps that are being changed been listed in column II.B.1?

2. Is the information on the workform reasonable?

3. Are there unexpectedly significant differences in the resources allocated to this activity in different units?

WORKFORM K Reducing or Streamlining Activities Performed by Staff in a Single Classification—System Information by Unit

I. Activity Being Modified: _____

II. Staff Resources

   A. What is the classification of staff who complete this activity? _____

   B. Calculate the time required to complete one instance of each of the steps to be reduced or streamlined and the total time that will be saved.

1. Step That Will Be Changed	2. Time Saved as a Result of the Change

   C. Total time saved for all steps (total of column II.B.2): _____

   D. Calculate the time that will be available for reallocation if the activity is modified.

1. Unit	2. Number of Instances Each Year	3. Time per Instance (from II.C)	4. Annual Time Saved (in hours)

(cont.)

Reducing or Streamlining Activities Performed by Staff in a Single Classification—System Information by Unit (cont.)

III. Other Resource Implications

A. Identify the effect that modifying the activity will have on collection resources, if any.

1. Unit	2. Collection Resources Available for Reallocation	3. Additional Collection Resources Required

B. Identify the effect that modifying the activity will have on facility resources, if any.

1. Unit	2. Facility Resources Available for Reallocation	3. Additional Facility Resources Required

C. Identify the effect that modifying the activity will have on technology resources, if any.

1. Unit	2. Technology Resources Available for Reallocation	3. Additional Technology Resources Required

Completed by _____

Source of data _____

Date completed _____

Library _____

WORKFORM L Eliminating Activities Performed by More Than One Classification of Staff—Unit Information

Purpose of Workform L

Use this workform to record staff, collection, facility, and technology resources that will be made available if an activity that is performed by more than one classification of staff is being eliminated. You will also record information about any resources that might be required if the activity is eliminated on this workform.

Note about the Electronic Version

Use the Microsoft Word (with an embedded Excel worksheet) version of this workform (available at http://e-learnlibraries.mrooms.net) to add rows and expand the size of columns.

Sources of Data for Workform L

1. The description of the activity that will be eliminated (line II) will come from Workform E: Addressing Current Ineffective Activities That Support Each Goal, Workform F: Identifying and Addressing Current Activities That Do Not Support Priorities, and Workform I: Addressing Sacred Cows.

2. The Starting Point (column III.A.2) and Ending Point (column III.A.3) will be determined by the data coordinator working with one or more unit managers.

3. Time Saved (column III.A.5) is determined by sampling. The process is explained in detail in Step 10.1.

4. Number of Instances Each Year (column III.B.2) is obtained from existing data (integrated library systems, etc.) or gathered through sampling. The process is explained in detail in Step 10.1.

5. The information about the other resources in section IV is available from the unit managers.

Who Should Complete Workform L

1. Before the workform is sent to the unit managers, the data coordinator will record Activity Being Eliminated (line II), Step(s) That Will Be Eliminated (column III.A.1), Starting Point (column III.A.2), Ending Point (column III.A.3), and Time Saved (column III.A.5).

2. If Number of Instances Each Year (column III.B.2) is known, the data coordinator will also complete that column and Annual Time Saved (column III.B.4). If not, those columns will be completed by the unit managers.

3. The unit managers in which the activity is performed will complete the parts of the workform not completed by the data coordinator. (See figure 28.)

Factors to Consider When Completing Workform L

1. Record data for each unit in which the activity is performed on a separate copy of this workform.

2. Only use this workform for activities performed by staff in different classifications that are being eliminated. If the activity is going to be modified, use Workform M: Reducing or Streamlining Activities Performed by More Than One Classification of Staff—Unit Information.

3. Only use this workform for activities that are performed by staff in different classifications. If the activity is performed by staff in the same classification, use Workform J: Eliminating Activities Performed by Staff in a Single Classification—System Information by Unit or Workform K: Reducing or Streamlining Activities Performed by Staff in a Single Classification—System Information by Unit.

4. The instructions for this workform are based on the assumption that managers in each unit have divided the responsibilities for performing this activity into the same steps. If that is not the case, unit managers will have to complete all of the columns in the table in III.A. There is more information about this in Step 10.1.

5. Some activities require staff from several units to perform one or more steps. If an activity you are eliminating requires staff from several units to work together, record the names of all of the units involved in completing the activity on line I (Unit).

6. You do not need data that are absolutely statistically valid. Instead, you need to use sampling to develop reasonably close estimates for the time to be saved in each step of the activity.

7. Use an electronic copy of this workform. The Excel spreadsheet in the workform includes the formulas to determine the annual time to be reallocated.

(cont.)

Instructions

WORKFORM L   **Eliminating Activities Performed by More Than One**
Classification of Staff—Unit Information (cont.)

To Complete Workform L

1. Line I: Record the unit.

2. Line II: Describe the activity that is being eliminated.

3. Staff Resources

a. Column III.A.1: Record the steps that are being eliminated (if the activity is being eliminated, all of the steps within the activity will be eliminated).

b. Column III.A.2: Record the starting point for each step (see Step 10.1 for more information about starting points).

c. Column III.A.3: Record the ending point for the step (see Step 10.1 for more information about ending points).

d. Column III.A.4: Record the classification of the staff who perform the step.

e. Column III.A.5: Record the average time that will be saved by eliminating the step.

f. Column III.B.1: Record the classification of the staff who perform the steps in column III.A.1 in the order they are listed in column III.A.1.

g. Column III.B.2: Record the number of times an instance of the step is performed in a year. In almost all cases, the data in this column will be the same in all of the rows because each step will be performed every time the activity being eliminated is performed.

h. Column III.B.3: Record the time that will be saved by eliminating the step from column III.A.5.

i. Column III.B.4: If you use the electronic version of Workform L, the information in this column will be calculated automatically. If you have not used the electronic version of the workform, multiply Number of Instances Each Year (column III.B.2) by Time per Instance in minutes (column III.B.3) to determine the total number of minutes each year. Then divide the number of minutes by 60 to determine the number of hours that will be available for reallocation.

4. Other Resource Implications

a. Column IV.A.2: Briefly describe the resources that would be made available if the activity were modified, if any.

b. Column IV.A.3: Briefly describe the additional resources that would be required if the activity were modified, if any.

Factors to Consider When Reviewing Workform L

1. Have all of the steps that are being eliminated been listed in column III.A.1?

2. Is the information on the workform reasonable?

3. Are there unexpectedly significant differences in the resources allocated to this activity in different units?

WORKFORM L Eliminating Activities Performed by More Than One Classification of Staff—Unit Information

I.   Unit: _____

II. Activity Being Eliminated: _____

III. Staff Resources

A. Calculate the time required to complete one instance of each of the steps to be eliminated.

1. Step That Will Be Eliminated	2. Starting Point	3. Ending Point	4. Classification of Staff Who Perform Step	5. Time Saved per Instance

B. Calculate the time that will be saved by staff in each classification if the activity is eliminated.

1. Classification of Staff	2. Number of Instance Each Year	3. Time per Instance (from III.A.5)	4. Annual Time Saved (in hours)

IV. Other Resource Implications

A. Describe the effect that eliminating the activity will have on these resources.

1. Unit	2. Available for Reallocation	3. Additional Resources Required
a. Collection		
b. Facility		
c. Technology		

Completed by _____   Date completed _____

Source of data _____   Library _____

Instructions

WORKFORM M Reducing or Streamlining Activities Performed by More Than One Classification of Staff—Unit Information

Purpose of Workform M

Use this workform to record staff, collection, facility, and technology resources that will be made available if an activity that is performed by more than one classification of staff is modified. You will also record information about any resources that might be required if the activity is modified on this workform.

Note about the Electronic Version

Use the Microsoft Word (with an embedded Excel worksheet) version of this workform (available at http://e-learnlibraries.mrooms.net) to add rows and expand the size of columns.

Sources of Data for Workform M

1. The description of the activity that will be modified (line II) will come from Workform E: Addressing Current Ineffective Activities That Support Each Goal, Workform F: Identifying and Addressing Current Activities That Do Not Support Priorities, and Workform I: Addressing Sacred Cows.

2. Starting Point (column III.A.2) and Ending Point (column III.A.3) will be determined by the data coordinator working with one or more unit managers.

3. Time Saved (column III.A.5) is determined by sampling. The process is explained in detail in Step 10.1.

4. Number of Instances Each Year (column III.B.2) is obtained from existing data (integrated library system, etc.) or gathered through sampling. The process is explained in detail in Step 10.1.

5. The information about the other resources in section IV is available from the unit managers.

Who Should Complete Workform M

1. Before the workform is sent to the unit managers, the data coordinator will record Activity Being Modified (line II), Step(s) That Will Be Changed (column III.A.1), Starting Point (column III.A.2), Ending Point (column III.A.3), and Time Saved (column III.A.5).

2. If Number of Instances Each Year (column III.B.2) is known, the data coordinator will also complete that column and Annual Time Saved (column III.B.4). If not, those columns will be completed by the unit managers.

3. The unit managers in which the activity is performed will complete the parts of the workform not completed by the data coordinator. (See figure 29.)

Factors to Consider When Completing Workform M

1. Record data for each unit in which the activity is performed on a separate copy of this workform.

2. Only use this workform for activities performed by staff in different classifications that are being modified. If the activity is going to be eliminated, use Workform L: Eliminating Activities Performed by More Than One Classification of Staff—Unit Information.

3. Only use this workform for activities that are performed by staff in different classifications. If the activity is performed by staff in the same classification use Workform J: Eliminating Activities Performed by Staff in a Single Classification—System Information by Unit or Workform K: Reducing or Streamlining Activities Performed by Staff in a Single Classification—System Information by Unit.

4. The instructions for this workform are based on the assumption that managers in each unit have divided the responsibilities for performing this activity into the same steps. If that is not the case, unit managers will have to complete all of the columns in the table in III.A. There is more information about this in Step 10.1.

5. Some activities require staff from several units to perform one or more steps. If an activity you are modifying requires staff from several units to work together, record the names of all of the units involved in completing the activity on line I (Unit).

6. Only record the steps that are being reduced or streamlined in III.A.1.

7. You do not need data that are absolutely statistically valid. Instead, you need to use sampling to develop reasonably close estimates for the time to be saved in each step of the activity.

8. Use an electronic copy of this workform. The Excel spreadsheet in the workform includes the formulas to determine the annual time to be reallocated.

To Complete Workform M

1. Line I: Record the unit.

2. Line II: Briefly describe how the activity will be modified.

(cont.)

Reducing or Streamlining Activities Performed by More Than One Classification of Staff—Unit Information (cont.)

Instructions

3. Staff Resources

a. Column III.A.1: Record the steps that are being changed or eliminated (if the activity is being modified, some steps may be changed and others may be eliminated entirely).

b. Column III.A.2: Record the starting point for each step that will be changed or eliminated (see Step 10.1 for more information about starting points).

c. Column III.A.3: Record the ending point for each step that will be changed or eliminated (see Step 10.1 for more information about ending points).

d. Column III.A.4: Record the classification of the staff who perform the step.

e. Column III.A.5: Record the average time that will be saved by changing or eliminating the step.

f. Column III.B.1: Record the classification of the staff who perform the steps in column III.A.1 in the order they are listed in column III.A.1.

g. Column III.B.2: Record the number of times an instance of the step is performed in a year. In almost all cases, the data in this column will be the same in all of the rows because each step will be performed every time the activity being changed or eliminated is performed.

h. Column III.B.3: Record the time that will be saved by changing or eliminating the step from column III.A.5.

i. Column III.B.4: If you use the electronic version of Workform M, the information in this column will be calculated automatically. If you have

not used the electronic version of the workform, multiply Number of Instances Each Year (column III.B.2) by Time per Instance in minutes (column III.B.3) to determine the total number of minutes each year. Then divide the number of minutes by 60 to determine the number of hours that will be available for reallocation.

4. Other Resource Implications

a. Column IV.A.2: Briefly describe the resources that would be made available if the activity were modified, if any.

b. Column IV.A.3: Briefly describe the additional resources that would be required if the activity were modified, if any.

Factors to Consider When Reviewing Workform M

1. Have all of the steps that are being changed or eliminated been listed in column III.A.1?

2. If some of the steps are performed by staff in different classifications at different times, has that been noted?

3. Is the information on the workform reasonable?

4. Are there unexpectedly significant differences in the resources allocated to this activity in different units?

WORKFORM M **Reducing or Streamlining Activities Performed by More Than One Classification of Staff—Unit Information**

I. Unit: _____

II. Activity Being Modified: _____

III. Staff Resources

A. Calculate the time required to complete one instance of each of the steps to be changed.

1. Step That Will Be Changed	2. Starting Point	3. Ending Point	4. Classification of Staff Who Perform Step	5. Time Saved per Instance

B. Calculate the time that will be saved by staff in each classification if the activity is changed.

1. Classification of Staff	2. Number of Instances Each Year	3. Time per Instance (from III.A.5)	4. Annual Time Saved (in hours)

IV. Other Resource Implications

A. Describe the effect that modifying the activity will have on these resources.

1. Unit	2. Available for Reallocation	3. Additional Resources Required
a. Collection		
b. Facility		
c. Technology		

Completed by _____ Date completed _____

Source of data _____ Library _____

Instructions

WORKFORM N Estimating Resources Available for Reallocation—Unit Summary

Purpose of Workform N

Use this workform to summarize the resources that will be available for reallocation in each unit as a result of eliminating or modifying activities and the additional resources that will be required because the activities were eliminated or modified.

Note about the Electronic Version

Use the Microsoft Word (with an embedded Excel worksheet) version of this workform (available at http://e-learnlibraries.mrooms.net) to add rows and expand the size of columns.

Sources of Data for Workform N

The data for this workform come from Workform J: Eliminating Activities Performed by Staff in a Single Classification—System Information by Unit, Workform K: Reducing or Streamlining Activities Performed by Staff in a Single Classification—System Information by Unit, Workform L: Eliminating Activities Performed by More Than One Classification of Staff—Unit Information, and Workform M: Reducing or Streamlining Activities Performed by More Than One Classification of Staff—Unit Information.

Who Should Complete Workform N

This workform should be completed by the manager of each unit in which activities will be eliminated or modified and should be reviewed by the unit manager's supervisor.

Factors to Consider When Completing Workform N

1. This workform will serve as a cover to a packet of all of each unit's copies of Workforms J, K, L, and M. The information recorded on this workform needs to be an accurate summary of Workforms J, K, L, and M but does not need to be a detailed copy of each of those workforms.

2. Use an electronic copy of this workform. That will allow you to record as much information as needed in each column.

To Complete Workform N

1. Line I: Record the unit name.

2. Column II.A: Record each of the classifications of staff who perform activities that will be reduced or eliminated in your unit in this column.

3. Column II.B: Add up all of the time that staff in each classification will have available for reallocation and record it in this column.

4. Column II.C: Number each of the copies of Workforms J, K, L, and M that include information about activities performed in the unit and record those numbers in this column to link the summary data on Workform N with the detailed information on the activity workforms. For example, if the first row in column II.A relates to the paraprofessional time that will be made available as a result of eliminating or modifying several activities, write the numbers of the copies of Workforms J, K, L, and M that provide the details about those activities in column II.C.

5. Column III.B: Briefly summarize all of the resources that would be available in your unit if all of the activities listed on Workforms J, K, L, and M were eliminated, reduced, or streamlined.

6. Column III.C: Refer to the copies of the workforms with detailed information (see #4 above).

7. Column IV.B: Briefly summarize all of the additional resources that would be required if all of the activities listed on Workforms J, K, L, and M were eliminated, reduced, or streamlined.

8. Column IV.C: Refer to the copies of the workforms with detailed information (see #4 above).

Factors to Consider When Reviewing Workform N

1. Has all of the information about the unit from all of the copies of Workforms J, K, L, and M been included on this workform?

2. Are there questions about any of the data elements on Workforms J, K, L, and M that need to be clarified?

WORKFORM N **Estimating Resources Available for Reallocation—Unit Summary**

I. Unit: _____

II. Summarize the staff resources that are available for reallocation as a result of eliminating, reducing, or streamlining activities.

A. Classification	B. Total Hours Available for Reallocation per Year	C. Notes

III. Summarize the other resources that will be made available for reallocation as a result of eliminating, reducing, or streamlining activities.

A. Resource	B. Describe	C. Notes
Collection		
Facility		
Technology		

IV. Summarize the other resources that will be required as a result of eliminating, reducing, or streamlining activities.

A. Resource	B. Describe	C. Notes
Collection		
Facility		
Technology		

Completed by _____ Date completed _____

Source of data _____ Library _____

WORKFORM O   Estimating Resources Required to Implement a New or Expanded Activity—Unit Information

Purpose of Workform O

Use this workform to summarize the resources that will be required in each unit to implement a new activity or to substantially expand an existing activity.

Note about the Electronic Version

Use the Microsoft Word (with an embedded Excel worksheet) version of this workform (available at http://e-learnlibraries.mrooms.net) to add rows and expand the size of columns.

Sources of Data for Workform O

The data for this workform come from the "critical resources" sections of the service responses selected as priorities in the library, from Workform N: Estimating Resources Available for Reallocation—Unit Summary, and from resource allocation estimates made by staff working with the data coordinator (Step 11.1). If necessary, workforms from other Results titles (see appendix) can be used to collect the data to determine the resources that will be required to implement a new activity.

Who Should Complete Workform O

1. The data in line I (Unit), line II (Activity), and column II.A (Resources Required to Implement the Activity in the Unit) will be recorded by the data coordinator.

2. Column II.B (Resources Available through Reallocation in the Unit) and column II.C (Additional Resources Required and Suggested Source) will be completed by the unit managers and their supervisors.

Factors to Consider When Completing Workform O

1. There are a finite amount of resources available. If the activity cannot be implemented by reallocating resources within the unit, there are only two choices: take resources from other units, or modify or eliminate additional ineffective, inefficient, or nonpriority activities in the unit in order to make the needed resources available.

2. Use an electronic copy of this workform. That will allow you to record as much information as needed in each column.

To Complete Workform O

1. Line I: Record the unit name.

2. Line II: Describe the activity. Include enough information to make the scope of the activity in the unit clear. Include information on expected number of instances, and so on.

3. Column II.A: Record the resources that will be required in the unit to perform the activity as described in line II. Note that the resources required to implement the activity might be different in each unit in which it will be performed, depending on the expected number of instances.

4. Column II.B: Record the resources available for reallocation *within the unit* to implement the activity.

5. Column II.C: Record the additional resources that will be required and suggest a source for those resources.

Factors to Consider When Reviewing Workform O

1. Does the information in column II.A (Resources Required to Implement the Activity in the Unit) seem realistic?

2. Does the information in column II.B (Resources Available through Reallocation in the Unit) seem realistic?

3. Have you totaled all of the resources required for all of the new activities that will be implemented in your unit and compared that total with the total resources available for reallocation?

4. Can you realistically expect to get the additional resources you recorded in column II.C from the source you suggested?

WORKFORM O **Estimating Resources Required to Implement a New or Expanded Activity—Unit Information**

I. Unit: _____

II. Activity: _____

	A. Resources Required to Implement the Activity in the Unit	B. Resources Available through Reallocation in the Unit	C. Additional Resources Required and Suggested Source
1. Staff Resources			
a. Hours			
1) Manager			
2) Librarian			
3) Paraprofessional			
4) Clerical			
5) Page			
6) Maintenance			
7) Other			
b. Knowledge, Skills, and Abilities			
2. Collection Resources			
a. Print Materials			
b. Media			
c. Electronic Resources			

(cont.)

3. Facility Resources		
a. Furniture and Equipment		
b. Square Footage		
c. Shelving		
d. Physical Plant (electrical, lighting, etc.)		
e. Access, Spatial Relationships, Signage		
4. Technology Resources		
a. Servers		
b. Workstations and Other Equipment (printers, etc.)		
c. Software		
d. Bandwidth		

Completed by _____ Date completed _____

Source of data _____ Library _____

Instructions

WORKFORM P **Estimating Resources Required for New or Expanded Activities—Unit Summary**

Purpose of Workform P

Use this workform to summarize the resources that will be required to implement the essential new or substantially expanded activities in each unit.

Note about the Electronic Version

Use the Microsoft Word (with an embedded Excel worksheet) version of this workform (available at http://e-learnlibraries.mrooms.net) to add rows and expand the size of columns.

Sources of Data for Workform P

The data on this workform come from all of the copies of Workform O: Estimating Resources Required to Implement a New or Expanded Activity—Unit Information completed by each unit.

Who Should Complete Workform P

This workform should be completed by the manager of each unit in which activities will be eliminated or modified and should be reviewed by the unit manager's supervisor.

Factors to Consider When Completing Workform P

1. This workform will serve as a cover to a packet of all of each unit's copies of Workform O. The information recorded on this workform needs to be an accurate summary of all of the copies of Workform O but does not need to be a detailed copy of each of those workforms.

2. Use an electronic copy of this workform. That will allow you to record as much information as needed in each column.

To Complete Workform P

1. Line I: Record the unit name.

2. Column II.A: Record each of the classifications of staff who will perform new essential activities in the unit.

3. Column II.B: Add up all of the time required for staff in each classification and record it in this column.

4. Column II.C: Number each of the copies of Workform O that include information about new essential activities that will be implemented in the unit and record those numbers in this column to link the summary data on Workform P with the detailed information on the activity workforms. For example, if the first row in column II.A relates to the paraprofessional time that will be needed for several new activities, write the numbers of the copies of Workform O that provide the details about those activities in column II.C.

5. Column III.A: List the formats of collection resources that will be required for all of the new activities.

6. Column III.B: Add up all of the collection resources that will be required for each format and record the totals in this column.

7. Column III.C: Refer to the copies of the workforms with detailed information (see #4 above).

8. Column IV.A: List the types of facility resources that will be required for all of the new activities (for example, square feet, furnishings, etc.).

9. Column IV.B: Add up all of the resources that will be required for each type of facility resource and record the totals in this column.

10. Column IV.C: Refer to the copies of the workforms with detailed information (see #4 above).

11. Column V.A: List the technology resources that will be required for all of the new activities.

12. Column V.B: Add up all of the resources that will be required for each type of technology and record the totals in this column.

13. Column V.C: Refer to the copies of the workforms with detailed information (see #4 above).

Factors to Consider When Reviewing Workform P

1. Has all of the information about the unit from all of the copies of Workform O been included on this workform?

2. Are there questions about any of the data elements on Workform P that need to be clarified?

I. Unit: _____

II. Summarize the staff resources that will be required to implement the new or expanded essential activities in your unit.

A. Classification	B. Total Hours Required per Year	C. Notes

III. Summarize the collection resources that will be required to implement the new or expanded essential activities in your unit.

A. Format	B. Total Required Each Year	C. Notes

IV. Summarize the facility resources that will be required to implement the new or expanded essential activities in your unit.

A. Resource	B. Amount Required	C. Notes

V. Summarize the technology resources that will be required to implement the new or expanded essential activities in your unit.

A. Resource	B. Amount Required	C. Notes

Completed by _____ Date completed _____

Source of data _____ Library _____

221

Instructions

WORKFORM Q **Summarizing Unit Resources**

Purpose of Workform Q

Use this workform to compare the resources required to implement new activities and the resources available through reallocation.

Note about the Electronic Version

Use the Microsoft Word (with an embedded Excel worksheet) version of this workform (available at http://e-learnlibraries.mrooms.net) to add rows and expand the size of columns.

Sources of Data for Workform Q

The data on this workform come from each unit's copies of Workform N: Estimating Resources Available for Reallocation—Unit Summary and Workform P: Estimating Resources Required for New or Expanded Activities—Unit Summary.

Who Should Complete Workform Q

This workform should be completed by the manager of each unit in which activities will be eliminated or modified and should be reviewed by the unit manager's supervisor.

Factors to Consider When Completing Workform Q

1. This workform will serve as a cover to a packet of all of the unit's copies of Workforms N and P.

2. Use an electronic copy of this workform. That will allow you to record as much information as needed in each column.

To Complete Workform Q

1. Line I: Record the unit name.

2. Column II.A: Record each of the classifications of staff who will perform new essential activities in the unit or who have time available because an activity has been eliminated or reduced.

3. Column II.B: Total all of the time that will be required to perform new activities for staff in each classification and record it in this column.

4. Column II.C: Total all of the time that will be made available because activities are being eliminated or reduced for staff in each classification and record it in this column.

5. Column II.D: Record the difference between the totals in columns II.B and II.C. If there is a difference it will either be a surplus of X hours or a shortfall of X hours. In some instances, the times in columns II.B and II.C may match.

6. Column II.E: Use this column to make notes about any of the data that may need additional explanations.

7. Column III.A: List any significant surpluses in this column.

8. Column III.B: List any significant shortfalls in this column.

9. Column III.C: Use this column to make notes about any of the data that may need additional explanations.

Factors to Consider When Reviewing Workform Q

1. Have you accurately totaled all of the information about the unit from all of the copies of Workforms N and P?

2. Are there significant surpluses or shortfalls that you cannot explain?

3. Do you have the data you need to discuss the information on this workform with your supervisor?

4. Do you have recommendations for addressing any shortfalls in resources?

5. Do you have recommendations for allocating any surplus resources?

WORKFORM Q Summarizing Unit Resources

I. Unit: _____

II. Staff Summary

A. Classification	B. Total Hours Required per Year for All New Activities	C. Total Hours Available per Year from Reallocation	D. Difference (+ or –)	E. Notes

III. Summary of Other Resources

	A. Significant Surplus	B. Significant Shortfall	C. Notes
1. Collection			
2. Facility			
3. Technology			

Completed by _____ Date completed _____

Source of data _____ Library _____

WORKFORM R Planning to Implement New or Expanded Activities—System Information

Purpose of Workform R

Use this workform to record the final decisions about the new or substantially expanded activities that will be implemented during this planning cycle.

Note about the Electronic Version

Use the Microsoft Word (with an embedded Excel worksheet) version of this workform (available at http://e-learnlibraries.mrooms.net) to add rows and expand the size of columns.

Sources of Data for Workform R

The data on this workform come from Workform D: Determining the Priority of Effective Activities by Goal, from the unit copies of Workform N: Estimating Resources Available for Reallocation—Unit Summary and Workform P: Estimating Resources Required for New or Expanded Activities—Unit Summary, and from the decisions made by the library's senior managers.

Who Should Complete Workform R

1. Column A should be completed by a staff member appointed by the library director before the senior managers meet.

2. Columns B–E should be completed by the library's senior managers.

Factor to Consider When Completing Workform R

Use an electronic copy of this workform. That will allow you to record as much information as needed in each column.

To Complete Workform R

1. Column A: Record the essential activities from Workform D in this column.

2. Column B: Record the units in which each activity will be implemented in this column.

3. Column C: Record the names or positions of the person or people who will be responsible for initiating or coordinating the activity. In some instances this may be a specific staff member. In others it may be a more generic designation such as "branch managers" or "youth services librarians."

4. Column D: Record the date by which the activity will be implemented. In many libraries, managers will decide to stagger the implementation dates (see Step 12.1 for more information).

5. Column E: Record any notes about the activity in this column. Notes could include a brief description of why the implementation date was selected, a suggestion for partnering with a community organization to provide the activity, and so on.

Factors to Consider When Reviewing Workform R

1. Have you been able to allocate the resources needed to implement all of the activities that you decided were "essential" on Workform D?

2. If you were not able to reallocate the resources needed to implement all of the essential activities, have you reconsidered the activities that were determined to be ineffective, inefficient, or to support service responses that were not priorities in order to find the needed resources?

3. Are there additional resources available that could be reallocated to implement some of the activities you decided were "desirable" on Workform D?

A. Activity	B. Units in Which the Activity Will Be Offered	C. Person Responsible for Initiating or Coordinating the Activity	D. Date the Activity Will Begin	E. Notes

Completed by _____ Date completed _____

Source of data _____ Library _____

Instructions

WORKFORM S Planning to Eliminate, Reduce, or Streamline Activities—System Information

Purpose of Workform S

Use this workform to record the final decisions about the ineffective, inefficient, and nonpriority activities that will be eliminated or modified during this planning cycle.

Note about the Electronic Version

Use the Microsoft Word (with an embedded Excel worksheet) version of this workform (available at http://e-learnlibraries.mrooms.net) to add rows and expand the size of columns.

Sources of Data for Workform S

The data on this workform come from Workform E: Addressing Current Ineffective Activities That Support Each Goal, Workform F: Identifying and Addressing Current Activities That Do Not Support Priorities, Workform I: Addressing Sacred Cows, and from the decisions made by the library's senior managers.

Who Should Complete Workform S

1. Column A should be completed by a staff member appointed by the library director before the senior managers meet.

2. Columns B–F will be completed by the library's senior managers.

Factor to Consider When Completing Workform S

Use an electronic copy of this workform. That will allow you to record as much information as needed in each column.

To Complete Workform S

1. Column A: Record the activities to be eliminated or modified from Workforms E, F, and I in this column. If the activity is being modified, describe the planned changes.

2. Column B: Record the units in which the activity will be eliminated or modified in this column.

3. Column C: Record the names or positions of the person or people who will be responsible for eliminating or modifying the activity. In some instances this may be a specific staff member. In others it may be a more generic designation such as "branch managers" or "youth services librarians."

4. Column D: Record the date by which the changes in the activity will begin. In many libraries, managers will decide to stagger the dates that changes will be made (see Step 12.1 for more information).

5. Column E: Record the date by which the changes in the activity will be completed.

6. Column F: Record any notes about the activity in this column. Notes could include a brief description of why the beginning or completion dates were selected, potential issues to be resolved, and so on.

Factors to Consider When Reviewing Workform S

1. Were you able to allocate the resources needed to implement all of the activities that you decided were "essential" on Workform D?

2. If you were not able to reallocate the resources needed to implement all of the essential activities, have you reconsidered the activities that were determined to be ineffective, inefficient, or to support service responses that were not priorities in order to find the needed resources?

3. Are there additional resources available that could be reallocated to implement some of the activities you decided were "desirable" on Workform D?

WORKFORM S Planning to Eliminate, Reduce, or Streamline Activities—System Information

A. Activity	B. Units in Which the Activity Will Be Eliminated, Reduced, or Streamlined	C. Person Responsible for Initiating or Coordinating the Change	D. Date the Change Will Begin	E. Date of Completion	F. Notes

Completed by _____ Date completed _____

Source of data _____ Library _____

Index

identified in adjustment period, 163–164, 166
and reallocation of resources, 142
responses to, 96, 97
supporting the library's goals, 97
and Workform E, 69f, 97, 121–123, 149, 151, 190–191
inefficient activities, 88–95
not supporting priorities, 98–102
ongoing response to, 96
and reallocation of resources, 142
See also sacred cows
innovation as leadership skill, 10
intellectual freedom and service priorities, 132
interlibrary loan, use of, 132
Internet and identification of potential activities, 33
intranets
and communications plan, 18, 20, 21
in identification of activities that support nonpriority service responses, 86–87
in identification of sacred cows, 95

J

"just in case" and "just in time" collection development, 132

K

knowledge in staff, definition, 113f

L

large libraries, communication patterns in, 17–18
large libraries with no branches, current activities in, 29, 30
libraries, other, and identification of potential activities, 33, 48
library, definition, xvi, 30
library board
basic library activities expected by, 100–101
communications with, 21, 142, 158
and criteria for evaluation, 53, 75
definition, xvi
monthly report form, 160
and policy sacred cows, 103
library director
characteristics of, 10–11, 21
and determining evaluation criteria, 58
as facilitator of meetings, 30
investment in process, 142
meetings with staff, 114, 129

library management team, definition, xvi. *See also* managers; senior management team
library services as series of interlinking activities, 25
library systems, identifying current activities in, 29, 30
library visits and identification of potential activities, 33
library website (example), streamlining activities, 78
line-item budgets and support for status quo, 2
listening for staff feelings, 7–8
local view of library, 44–45, 47

M

managers
commitment to change, 7–9, 21
definition, xvi
development of, 14–16
in goals and objectives review, 27
identification of activities supporting nonpriority service responses, 81–82
identification of sacred cows, 92–93
and implementation process, 48
lack of management training of, 3, 15
responsibilities of, 170
responsibility for data collection, 156
See also senior management team; unit managers
marketing of library services
effectiveness of, 79
reports to target audiences, 161
materials budget
and delays in meeting targets, 162
revision of to support goals, 130–132
See also budget
measurement of services vs. evaluation of services, 146
media formats, changing needs for, 6
meetings
as communication, 18, 114
to determine evaluation criteria, 58–60
ground rules for, 61–62
identification of current activities, 29–33
identification of potential activities, 34–38
identification of sacred cows, 90–92
merging duplicative activities, 42–44
middle managers. *See* managers
midsized libraries, communication patterns in, 17

minutes from meetings as communication, 18
monitoring implementation, 153–166
adjustments to plan, 161–166
collecting data, 153–161
monthly reports, need for, 157–161, 170

N

networks as resource, definition, 113f
new activities
estimation of resources, 135–137, 140–142
insufficient for meeting targets, 164–165, 166
setting priorities for, 71
staff training for, 162
and underserved target audiences, 45–46
and Workform O, 115, 137–138, 139f, 217–219
and Workform P, 115, 138–139, 140f, 220–221
See also potential activities
nonpriority service responses, activities supporting. *See* activities supporting nonpriority service responses

O

objectives for collection-based measures, 130–131
online discussion groups and identification of potential activities, 33
opportunities and setting priorities, 72
organization of activities. *See* categorization of activities
organizational competencies
and integration of change into ongoing operations, 168
and overcoming resistance, 8–9

P

partnerships and adjusting activities, 100
planning project coordinator and identifying current activities, 30
policy and procedures manuals
as communication, 18
and sacred cows, 95
policy sacred cows, 94–95, 103, 105
policy statement, definition, 93
political implications of eliminating activities, 101–102
poster sessions and identification of potential activities, 34

You may also be interested in

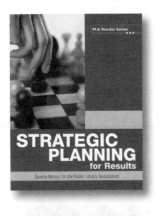

Strategic Planning for Results: Sandra Nelson, senior editor of the PLA Results Series, focuses on the essential steps in a results-driven, strategic planning process that libraries can complete over the course of four months, regardless of organizational structure or size. Reflecting on the current planning environment for public libraries, Nelson makes the case for strategic rather than long-term planning and includes a wealth of information about understanding and managing the change process.

Creating Policies for Results: If your staff makes decisions on the fly and policies are nonexistent, outdated, or cloaked in mystery, your library may be experiencing policy chaos. The answer is to create current, customized policies geared to your library, and it's easier than ever with this step-by-step guide. Covering governance and organizational structure, management policies, and services relating to customers, circulation, information, and groups, this comprehensive how-to addresses each major library area.

Managing for Results: Using this planning guide, librarians will be able to better prioritize and assign resources to achieve the best results for their library. This resource requires librarians to take a proactive approach to marshaling and managing all of the library's resources effectively and focuses on the four most critical resources each library needs to best utilize to achieve its mission: staff, collection development, technology, and the library facility.

Managing Facilities for Results: Carving out new service areas within existing space, forgoing massive additions or expensive new buildings, offers a cost-effective solution for budget-conscious libraries. With examples ranging from small to large public libraries, the process outlined here is equally valuable for school, special, and academic librarians who are faced with space repurposing challenges. This guide will help you create a blueprint that prioritizes services and creates the space for them within your existing facility.

Check out these and other great titles at www.alastore.ala.org!